Groundwork of Theology

John Stacey

London EPWORTH PRESS

SBN 7162 0289 1

Enquiries should be addressed to
The Methodist Publishing House
Wellington Road
Wimbledon
London SW19 8EU

Printed in Great Britain by
The Garden City Press Limited
Letchworth, Hertfordshire SG6 1JS

Acknowledgements

T H E following publishers have kindly given permission for quotations, in excess of one hundred words, from the works named.

Abingdon Press: John Knox, *The Death of Christ*
Adam and Charles Black: Dom Gregory Dix, *The Shape of the Liturgy*
Mitchell Beazley: H. A. Williams, *True Resurrection*
Cambridge University Press: John Knox, *The Humanity and Divinity of Christ*
T. and T. Clark: John Baker, 'The Essence of Christianity', *Expository Times* LXXXVII.2
Collins: C. S. Lewis, *Mere Christianity*
Darton, Longman and Todd: Simon Tugwell, *New Heaven? New Earth?*
J. M. Dent and Sons: Constantine Fitzgibbon, *Selected Letters of Dylan Thomas*
Victor Gollancz Ltd: Victor Gollancz, *My Dear Timothy*
James Nisbet: W. Norman Pittenger, *The World Incarnate*; Reinhold Niebuhr, *The Nature and Destiny of Man*; F. W. Dillistone, *The Christian Understanding of Atonement*; C. H. Dodd, *The Parables of the Kingdom*
Oxford University Press: William D. Maxwell, *An Outline of Christian Worship*
Penguin Books: Peter Berger, *Rumour of Angels*; Alistair Kee, *The Way of Transcendence*
SCM Press: Paul Tillich, *The Shaking of the Foundations*; Jürgen Moltmann, *Theology of Hope*; John V. Taylor, *The Go-Between God* and *Enough is Enough*; John A. T. Robinson, *The Human Face of God*; John Macquarrie, *Principles of Christian Theology*

5

Tidings, The United Methodist Board of Discipleship, Nashville, Tennessee: Dow Kirkpatrick (Ed.), *The Holy Spirit*
Quotations from the Bible, unless otherwise stated, are from the *Revised Standard Version*, by permission of Thomas Nelson and Sons

Contents

Abbreviations

MSB   *The Methodist Service Book*
MHB   *The Methodist Hymn Book*

Preface

I T is said among scholars that the day of writing systematic theologies covering the whole range of Christian doctrines is over, and I can well believe it. For those beginning the study of theology, however, it would still seem to be the best method; hence this book. *Groundwork of Theology* has been written for Methodist local preachers on trial studying for the Connexional Examination in Christian Doctrine, though if others find it useful that will be gratifying.

In Part I Christian theology is set against the background of religion and theology in general and in relation to living the life of faith, hope and love. In Part II the various doctrines contained within such a theology are treated according to a threefold pattern. First, each chapter begins with statements from what are, for Methodists, foundation documents, so that preachers may know the tradition within which they stand. These documents include quotations from the sermons of John Wesley and the hymns of Charles, though they are not sources in the same precise sense as the historic creeds. *The Thirty-Nine Articles* are included because Methodists find their way back to the 'fundamental principles of the Protestant Reformation' not through Calvinism or Lutherism, but through the Church of England. There follows, secondly, an account of the way in which the doctrine concerned is rooted in the Bible and has been traditionally understood in the Church. Thirdly, attention will be drawn, in each chapter, to some contemporary insights which may make the doctrine the more able to be believed and preached in the twentieth century.

The book has been set out in ten chapters for the con-

11

venience of those taking the correspondence course for local preachers on trial, and questions for their use (or for discussion) are in the study scheme. Chapter 7 is shorter than the rest to avoid duplicating material that is more conveniently treated later. The passages in smaller type, other than the *indented* identical quotations, are not essential for a preliminary understanding of the subject and can be omitted on a first reading by those to whom theology is unfamiliar. Such passages should be included in a subsequent reading, for they are examinable.

In preparing *Groundwork of Theology* as a textbook sanctioned by the Methodist Conference I have worked with the Local Preachers' Studies Board under the chairmanship of Sister Margaret Siebold and particularly with the Christian Doctrine panel under the chairmanship of Rev. Kenneth Ford. Rev. Dr Denis Inman, a member of that panel, and Rev. Roy Crew, a correspondence course tutor, have made many valuable suggestions for improvement; so too has Rev. John Munsey Turner. The manuscript had been read by Rev. Rupert E. Davies, Rev. A. Raymond George and Rev. Dr A. Skevington Wood, by my two colleagues on the Editorial Sub-committee of the Methodist Publishing House, Professor Morna Hooker and Rev. Graham Slater, and by my brother Rev. Dr W. David Stacey; all have made comments that have considerably improved the book and I am greatly in their debt. They are not to blame for the shortcomings that persist nor are they to be held responsible for the opinions expressed. I am also grateful for the support of Rev. Christopher Bacon, General Secretary of the Division of Ministries, for the co-operation and kindness of Mr Albert Jakeway, General Manager of the Methodist Publishing House, for the assistance of my secretary, Miss Mary Briant and for the toil of Mr Sidney Herbert who read the proofs.

Westminster 1977   JOHN STACEY

Part 1

Chapter 1

Religion and Theology

1. RELIGION

A. The approach to religion

I T is possible to know a good deal about potholing without ever having been in a cave. You can study the subject scientifically, learning about cave formation by the action of running water on soft, limestone rock; you can become knowledgeable about swallets, stalactites and stalagmites, chimneys, drops and ruckles, for there is a considerable literature available; you can talk to potholers, listen to their descriptions of the world underground and try to appreciate the fascination it has for them; you can even go to Yorkshire and peer down the frightening drop of Gaping Gill or Alum Pot or to the Mendips and see the potholers in their 'gear' squeezing through the tight entrance of Swildon's Hole. All this will give you a knowledge and understanding of the matter much beyond the average without your ever having had direct experience of the darkness closing in on you and the icy water cutting through your clothes. From your study and observation you could give a fair description of the subject.

This is the way in which, at the start of this book, religion will be approached. It will be described as it has existed, and still exists, in the world. Religion is an old and widespread phenomenon in the experience of man and it will be written about descriptively, just as it has appeared upon the human

13

scene. In order to describe religion in this general sense effectively the large question of commitment to a particular form of it because that is believed to be the truth will, for the moment, be left open.

This method may be something of a shock to Christians who open their first book on theology and expect to find immediately an exposition of the Gospel and arguments for its truth. They can be reassured: what they are looking for will later appear. The value of doing things this way at the start is that to do so provides a broad view of things as they actually have been and are in the matter of religion. The stage is thus set for what is to follow. Against such a general back-cloth Christianity will be considered, and should be valued all the more as a result.

This approach can be argued against on three grounds.

(i) It can be contended that participation in and commitment to some form of religion are necessary to describe and understand it (only potholers can describe and understand potholing). Justice can only be done to religion if it is handled by the people who, in one form of it, believe its doctrines, share in its rituals and have some experience of its god or gods. Now it is certainly true that an appreciative and understanding approach to the subject of study is essential. A book on potholing by someone who considered potholers to be irresponsible nuisances, a danger to themselves and to those who have to rescue them when they are in trouble, is not likely to be a sympathetic and fair account. One could go further and say that it is necessary in appreciating a religion to 'get into its skin'; in studying Judaism, for example, 'to be a Jew for a day'. What is not possible in the approach of this chapter is to pass judgement on whether what the particular religion asserts corresponds with reality.

(ii) The second objection is that as this book is intended primarily, though not exclusively, for Christian preachers, readers will already be heavily committed to religion (in one of its forms), and thus a neutral and descriptive approach is impossible. To a religion, yes, but the scene to be surveyed is much wider than that. It is in the second and following chapters, when the subject is the Christian religion and its theology (theology will be defined later), that participation and commitment will be seen to be indispensable. To return to the illustration, that will be the parallel to putting on the boots, the heavy clothing and the hat with the light and entering the dark but exciting underground world of the potholer. But for the present religion is to be thought of as a phenomenon in the life of man and clearly this includes forms of it to which the Christian preacher would not subscribe. He must, therefore, during the description, do his best to be neutral, objective and sympathetic.

(iii) There is a third, and more radical objection to what we are suggesting. It can be put as follows: 'By all means go ahead and describe religion, and include Christianity with the rest, but don't imagine that in doing this you are talking about the Word of God and the Gospel of Grace. That is something entirely different from, and indeed in opposition to, all religion.' This probably sounds confusing to the preacher beginning theology, for he, not surprisingly, regards his concern with the Gospel as a concern with religion. Such confusion can be partly dissipated by realizing what those who talk in this way have in mind when they use the word 'religion'. The greatest of them is Karl Barth and in the section of his *Church Dogmatics* entitled 'The Revelation of God as the Abolition of Religion' he distinguishes between the Gospel, God's revelation of himself in Christ, in which the initiative is entirely God's and to which man can contribute nothing at all, and religion which is man's attempt to search for meaning and security in life, to find God for himself and to justify himself to God by his works. On this showing religion and the Christian Gospel are enemies. Religion, said Barth, is unbelief.

Later in this book we shall be concerned with the Word of God and the Gospel of Grace, and their primacy for the Christian will be recognized. All that can be asserted here is that, in addition, Christianity does in fact exist as a religion, possessing the features now to be described. Whether, as such, it is in implacable opposition to the Gospel is a matter that can better be decided at the end of this book than at its beginning.

B. Features of religion

(1) Community

It is the unwritten rule in cricket and golf clubs (and doubtless in other places) that one may talk about anything and everything except politics and religion. This is partly due to the controversial nature of these subjects and partly to the feeling that both politics and religion are private affairs that most people wish to keep to themselves. Religion particularly is intensely personal: what transpires between a man and his Maker; 'what a man does with his own solitariness', as A. N. Whitehead has put it. As such it is not a seemly subject for affable conversation at the nineteenth hole.

This view, though intelligible to the modern Western world, and exemplified in hermits and mystics of many religions, is

15

nevertheless quite alien to the broad sweep of religion going back as it does to man's earliest days on earth. For man's basic, primeval dread is the dread of solitariness, of being cut off from his fellow men at the moments of his extremity, not least when he confronts his god and when he dies. The solace for this dread is in the community to which man belongs, for there he is not alone. Religion is thus communal from the start. The other 'features of religion' subsequently described in this section are concerned with men, not separately, but together.

The clan or tribe (the latter was an expansion of the former) was the community in which man found and expressed his religion. But to talk of 'finding' and 'expressing' in this way, as if the matter were basically and originally personal, is altogether too modern and too Western. Man *existed* in his clan or tribe and religion was inseparable from that corporate existence.

One example frequently given from the Old Testament to illustrate the existence of the corporate personality of the tribe is that of Achan in Joshua 7. The sin of this unfortunate man appears to have been that when the tribe was under obligation to do one thing (destroy everything and everybody in Jericho) he did another (purloined something for himself). For this assertion of individualism Achan was stoned to death. And if, as seems probable but not certain, his family were killed with him, that makes the point doubly clear. No man was, indeed, an island.

This community religion is clearly seen in what is called 'totemism', in which a class of objects or animals is thought to have a kinship and solidarity with a tribe. (Cub Scouts in the Panther Patrol is a juvenile imitation.) The clan or tribe bears the totem's name, believes itself to be descended from the totem and refuses to kill or eat the totem on that account. Often inter-marriage between members of a tribe under the one totem was forbidden for that would be virtually to marry one's own blood relation. There is not much scope for individual religion here.

The bond that holds people together in such communities is both deep and wide. The sleepy Basuto girl actually blames her own drowsiness on one of her relatives who is having a nap in a corner. Indeed when the community is the extended family, and the one blood flows in everybody's veins, relationships could not be closer. A man must raise up children by his dead brother's wife and blood revenge is a sacred duty; murder of one's brother is not fratricide but suicide. In family, clan and tribe the community was virtually equated with existence and to be expelled from the community was to be as good as dead.

In this context religion, like everything else, was communal. Nothing was known, as John Wesley said about the Bible, of solitary religion. It would appear from even a hasty glance at the phenomenon of religion since time began that the community element is of the nature of religion itself. To suppose that what has been described is all very primitive and that we can trace a steady progress from it to higher, individualistic forms of religion is a vast over-simplification and misses the true significance of the community for religion. Communities change, of course, in their size and in their purpose. Within the natural community of tribe or (later) nation there can develop a more specific and intense religious community: the secret societies of Africa, the mystery-religion communities of the Hellenistic world, the Christian Church. What does not change is the fact that in the large majority of its manifestations religion has more to do with man with his fellows than with man on his own.

(2) Myth

In modern, conversational English the word 'myth' carries roughly the same meaning as the word 'lie'. If you say, 'The idea that I am any good at studying for examinations is a complete myth', the meaning is that you are no good at all at studying for examinations. The word 'lie' could be substituted for the word 'myth' and the meaning of the sentence would remain the same. The result of this identity of meaning is that anything described as a myth is immediately taken to be a falsehood.

From the point of view of the study of religion, nothing could be more unfortunate. For myths are commonly found in religious communities and, as we shall see, whatever else

17

they may be, they are certainly not lies. It is therefore essential that the student clear his mind of the modern English usage and be prepared to accept that if a scholar in this field refers to a familiar story as a myth he is most certainly not dismissing it as a pack of lies.

A myth is not a lie, it is a story. In the first instance men reflect on the conditions of human life, and particularly on the contradictions that exist in the natural order, in society and in themselves. They struggle to explain their experiences, but soon find that they cannot do so simply in terms of themselves and the world around them. So they resort to the supernatural. They are not, however, able to think in abstract terms so the struggle results in a story—the myth. Here are men's reflections on their own existence, their explanations of their experiences in terms of the supposed origins of those experiences and the part played by the supernatural, the god or gods, who as likely as not behave just as men behave. Thus in Genesis 11:1–9 the origin of the diversity of the language of mankind is described in the story of the tower of Babel, and a significant part in the action is played by 'the Lord'. Genesis 3:1–19 is a further example. Here is a story told by human beings who have to sweat with hard work, bear their children in pain and, in the end, die, recounting the origin of these experiences and relating them to the overriding activity of 'the Lord God'.

Such myths vary in quality, some giving profounder insights into man's situation and the nature of the supernatural than others. It is often contended that the myths of the Old Testament, particularly in their disclosure of the nature of the supernatural, are superior to those recorded in other Middle Eastern literature. Hence the category 'revelation' is frequently used of them.

When modern people with their scientific approach to history probe into the thought-world of ancient people they ask all the wrong questions, i.e. those that seem important to them and not those that were important to the ancients themselves. The questions that will inevitably be asked of a myth by twentieth century people are 'did it actually happen?'; is it real history?'; 'is the story true?'. What we have to understand is that in appreciating the truth of a myth what matters is that the

18

stories mediate profound truth about man's situation in the world, the origin of that situation and, above all, its relation to the supernatural power or powers. This is what gives a myth its value, and a very considerable one it is. To say 'It is only a myth' is a highly inappropriate remark in the study of religion. A more fitting comment would be 'It's a myth, so it's true'! And true, not because it is history in our sense, for it is probably not, but because it discloses in a penetrating and timeless way man's relation to the world and to the supernatural. Is it not, after all, of more significance to be aware of man's experience of and judgement on human language and the commanding position given to 'the Lord' than it is to know whether or not there was an actual tower of brick and bitumen in the land of Shinar?[1] The myth which makes no pretension at all to relate something that actually happened, settles the matter. A theme often recurring in African mythology is that once the sky was nearer the earth, so that the god or gods were close to man, but that 'things had gone wrong' and the distance had been increased as a result; hardly history, but profoundly true.

Ritual as a feature of religion belongs to the next section, but it must be said now that the home of the myth is in ritual. It was at worship that the stories were told. But much more is involved than an ancient version of 'story-time' in Sunday school. In the ritual the events described in the myth are recounted or celebrated and in the recounting and celebration are believed to happen all over again. The past is thus brought into the present and the power of the original event or events is available in the celebration. In the Old Testament the Exodus and the Passover, taken together, are an example, though because of the centrality of Yahweh, living and active, the matter has to be expressed a little differently: that in the representation of the events the deity confronts the worshippers in the present (the Passover) just as he did in the past (the Exodus). If such notions seem strange, reflect for a moment on the phenomenon of a Christian congregation at a midnight

[1] Some scholars argue that archaeological evidence gives support to a historical view.

19

communion on Christmas Eve, celebrating the birth of their Lord, and singing:

> O Holy Child of Bethlehem,
> Descend to us, we pray;
> Cast out our sin, and enter in;
> *Be born in us today.*

Here the recounting and celebration of the story (in this case one with historical foundations) enables the redemptive event to happen again, thought not in the precise physical and originating sense. But the past is undoubtedly brought into the present and the power of Jesus is believed to be as available as it was in Palestine. It is understandable that the myths were told and celebrated at the worship, for that was the time and place when the gods were honoured, and myths were so often about their affairs.

Some myths are myths of the future and not of the past: the myth of the Celestial City, for example. In such cases it is the future that is brought into the present and the power of the future event is experienced in the present celebration: 'Glory begun below' as the Christian hymn has it.

In the light of what has been said about myth one can understand why in his study of Christian origins the New Testament scholar, Rudolf Bultmann,[2] used the word 'demythologizing'. Simply to recount the myths of one age and culture to the people of another, especially one like ours given to scientific and abstract thought, and expect them to grasp immediately the truth of what was being said and celebrated is asking altogether too much. The myth needs interpreting, or transposing,[3] a formidable work for both scholars and preachers. But at least we can start with the right questions: not 'Did it actually happen?', but 'What did they mean by this?' and, at least for the preacher, 'What does it mean now?'

---

[2] Bultmann used the word 'myth' in a very broad sense: to include an entire view of life and the universe.

[3] This word is deliberately chosen, for a number of modern scholars contend that one should approach mythology as one approaches music, with imagination not literalism, ready to admit that there can be many variations on a theme, none without value.

(3) Ritual

Ritual is frequently regarded by modern people as a matter for individual preference. One man likes his religion plain and unadorned, another likes it embellished with colour, movement and ceremonial. It is a matter of personal choice. And though people hold strongly, and sometimes bigotedly, to their own position, very few indeed would argue that, once the basic sacraments have been celebrated, the performance of further ritual is anything but the subject of private inclination. It is not therefore part of the essential nature of the religion. 'One can be a Christian without going through all that performance' is a colloquial way of expressing it.

In relation to religion as it is being described in this chapter, religion 'in its broad sweep', such an approach to ritual would be quite inaccurate. For generally in religion ritual is the means of getting things done. Because of the word spoken and the action performed in the ritual, *something happens*. And that something is not an inconsequential triviality, it is concerned with man's entire relationship with the god or gods and his continued existence in the world. Nothing therefore could be more essential than the ritual.

The point can be illustrated from the sacrificial rituals that have been, and are, at the centre of so much religion. The phenomenon of sacrifice is indeed almost universal. In the Inca empire thousands of human beings were slaughtered on the altar of the Sun God. The Ainu, primitive inhabitants of Japan, captured a young bear, had it suckled, reared, pampered and spoilt by a woman, then killed it, mourned it and ate it. The Romans sacrificed to the hearth (Vesta) by throwing small gifts into the fire which was for them the essence of divine life. In the Old Testament many pages are devoted to the details of the ritual of sacrifice. These four references must do duty for all the rest.

Scholars differ about the precise way in which sacrifice worked. Some interpret it as a gift to the gods in order to win favour or to avoid reprisals. And this is no minor matter, for in an agricultural society unless the god can be persuaded to make the crops grow there will be famine and death. A Hindu ritual expresses this approach very succinctly: 'Here is

21

the butter; where are thy gifts?' Other scholars hasten to point out that there is much more to this than cajolery. They argue that the giving of a gift creates a bond, for the giver always gives something of himself with the gift, and that bond enables the power of the god to flow into the life of the giver. Giver and receiver share in the gift and therefore in each other. So the stream of life continues to flow. Others stress the communal meal that so frequently accompanies the sacrifice. At many such meals the eating of the sacrificial animal is thought to be an eating of the god himself, so ensuring that the power of life inherent in the god is mediated to the people. There is the additional advantage that this creates and sustains the unity of the people. Those who eat the same god and share the same life are one people.

Still others link sacrifice with the recounting and celebration of a myth, particularly myths that recount the origin of things. For example, there is the myth of Hainuwele in which that goddess was murdered at the creation and out of her hacked-up body came the plants on which men lived. In the sacrificial ritual the goddess assumes the form of a pig and that pig is slaughtered. The murder of the goddess is re-enacted and, as in the first instance, plants will be the result and men can continue to eat.

Other, later sacrifices, made on a much larger scale, concerned the expiation of ('making atonement for') sin and guilt. This can be interpreted either as men having forgotten the rules by which the world was run, and needing to have their awareness restored, or as an offence against a holy god. In either case the sacrifice repaired the damage.

Whatever the nature of the sacrificial ritual and of the explanation that is reckoned to lie behind it, at least it is clear, even from such a brief account as this, that the ritual of sacrifice was concerned with central matters, not peripheral ones. How can man please the gods? How can life go on? How can the crops grow? How can wrong be righted? These were the questions that sacrificial ritual answered.

Though the practice of sacrifice establishes the point that ritual is no optional extra for religion, other rituals confirm it. Religions that have sacramental meals regard those ritual

22

occasions as of importance because there the 'Lord' (Serapis, Attis or, with historical justification, Jesus) and the believer are brought together. In this context the 'Lord' speaks and acts and man can only submit. This is why dressing up is usually associated with ritual. It is not meant to demonstrate the importance or the academic achievement of the officiant. Quite the reverse. It is meant to conceal his individuality, to stress his anonymity so that the active role of the god can be unimpeded. The proper successors of the primitive costumes and masks are the vestments that make no distinction between one officiant and the next. Under these conditions the way is open for the gods to participate in the rituals of men. This is central to religion as it has appeared in human experience.

For the fascinating details of ritual acts the reader must turn to larger works on the study of religion: the place of the dance (when among the Mexican Indians the harvest is being brought in someone remains at home and dances all day long for a good harvest; he is *achieving it* by his dance); the place of drama, in which the myth was re-enacted as we should act a play; the place of the procession that gets the whole thing moving and extends the divine activity over the area covered by the ritual march; the place of festivals and their importance for the ordering of human life, greatly enhanced when what people were celebrating was held to be an event in history like the exodus of the Jews from Egypt; the place of the sacred locality (caverns, springs, mountains) or building (temples, mosques, synagogues, churches) so closely associated with the appearance of the god and his action in ritual; the place of incantation and prayer in ritual and the remarkable effects they have produced; the place of praise ('Great is Artemis of the Ephesians!'); the place of symbols, which are not simply a reminder with which we could dispense if our imaginations and memories were better, but an actual participation of the sacred in the ritual life of man. Unless ritual is taken seriously, and not regarded as an appendage of little significance, the phenomenon of religion is not likely to be fully understood.

(4) Gods
The word has to be in the plural even though a Christian

23

reader may recoil from it. For him, there is only one God, 'the God and Father of our Lord Jesus Christ', as he would put it, and all other so-called gods simply do not exist. But we are now trying to *describe* religion as it has appeared in the life of man and to do that with any show of accuracy the word must go into the plural.

The three features of religion so far described imply an acceptance of the reality of gods. Communities are bound up with gods, myths are stories involving gods and rituals are focused upon gods. Gods have to be reckoned with.

Modern people, creatures of a scientific age, are evolutionists by instinct. We see everything in terms of development. We appreciate that the transistor radio developed from the crystal set, that Gothic cathedrals evolved from mud huts, that cavemen turned eventually into Greek philosophers and Oxford dons. When therefore we survey the religious scene, and particularly the place of gods in it, we immediately begin to look for development. We expect to see something very crude at the beginning and something very refined at the end. We look at first for primitive spirits and at last for 'the God and Father of our Lord Jesus Christ'.

This was exactly how the students of religion in the last century approached the subject. They were the first people to study scientifically the 'broad sweep' of religion and they too were 'evolutionists by instinct'. And they made the gods fit the theory. One[4] claimed that man began with atheism and developed through nature worship and idolatry to belief in one God (now entitled to a capital letter). Another[5] traced a development from personal spirits active in the trees and stones and mountains through gods who behaved much like human beings (Thor, Mercury, Aphrodite and the rest) to the great skygod who again can have the title 'God'. If only it were as simple as that students of religion could give three cheers for the evolutionists, for they would have written a plain history of the gods. But alas it is not so. The gods are clearly unwilling to be categorized in this way.

The evidence for asserting this is that another student[6] of

[4] John Lubbock (1834–1913).   [5] Edward Burnett Tylor (1832–1917).
[6] Andrew Lang (1844–1912).

religion immediately came forward to argue the opposite view, i.e. that among very primitive peoples there existed belief in a great creator-god. Different functions were attributed to him by different peoples—he lived in heaven, he dispensed rain and sunshine, he behaved in a fatherly fashion, he gave laws, he judged men and women at their death—but he was always the great high god (we might very well say 'God'). Other writers probed this thesis more deeply, some arguing that once he had created the world the high god retired to his home in the sky, not to be disturbed, so to speak, and others arguing that he could be worshipped, prayed to and given offerings. But on this view lesser gods were believed in not before, but after, the great high god.

The evolutionist view compels us to recognize the existence of the low gods. Before we even have their names we notice that stones and trees and mountains are thought to be recipients and vehicles of the mysterious power of life itself and when we have the names of such gods we find them associated with those stones and trees and mountains. Other objects in the natural world were venerated, to use no stronger word. This Babylonian hymn to the moon does not sound unfamiliar to the reader of the Psalms:

O Lord! Who is like you? Who is equal to you?
Great hero! Who is like you? Who is equal to you?
Lord Nannar! Who is like you? Who is equal to you?
When you lift up your eyes, who can flee?
When you draw near, who can escape?[7]

In Heliopolis huge temples were built in honour of the sun. Animals, too, came to be regarded as sacred and were worshipped. There have been mother-gods (Demeter the corn-mother in Greece) and saviour-gods (Osiris in Egypt) and king-gods (Pharaohs in Egypt) and then whole companies of gods in pantheons—as in India, Scandinavia, Rome and Greece —where life with its eating, drinking, making love and fighting

[7] H. Zimmern, *Babylonische Hymner und Gebete* II, 1911, 6. Translated (in a 'thou' form) by G. van der Leeuw (*Religion in Essence and Manifestation* (George Allen and Unwin 1938), p. 66.

25

was never dull. But already this paragraph is becoming too much of a catalogue. What is religion without its gods?

The students of religion who opposed the evolutionists have placed us in their debt by bringing to our notice the extent of 'high-god' religion, though some critics would contest the evidence. Others are not happy with the notion of 'degeneration': one god making way for many, and the many very much inferior to the one. Others point out, with justification, that we have no explanation as to why primitive people should have a god who seems not to be primitive.

(5) Sacred texts

In the Methodist Church in which I was brought up the evening service on Sunday was prefaced by a home-made ritual. Two minutes before 6.30 p.m. the door leading to the vestry was opened and the caretaker appeared, wearing a verger's black gown. He carried in his outstretched arms the large pulpit Bible and with all the dignity he could muster he climbed the pulpit steps and deposited the sacred book on the desk. He switched on the reading light over the book, glanced down to see the size of the congregation and then retreated to the vestry. The motives behind the institution of the 'caretaker' ritual were doubtless mixed and probably confused, but one of them was to impress upon the congregation the importance for the Christian community of their sacred text, the Bible. The evening service that followed would itself give significance to the 'caretaker' ritual, for there would be two readings from the Bible and a sermon which, if it did not expound a text from one of them direct, would have the Bible as its primary source of truth. In different ways and in varying degrees all Christian churches share this view of the Bible. It is the holy book.

Other religions treat their sacred texts in the same fashion and give them the same, or a more pronounced, veneration. When the Chinese Buddhist *Tipitaka*—extending to more than 5,000 volumes—is arranged in rotating cases in the temple, just to turn the case so that one may read is regarded as an action making salvation that much easier. There is to this day a bearded gentleman in a synagogue in Nablus who guards an ancient copy of the Samaritan Pentateuch with his life. Orthodox Muslims believe that the Koran is uncreated and eternal.

An explanation must go back to early times. The written word was preceded by, and bore a close relation to, the spoken word. The power attributed by early people to the latter was considerable. It had the power to create: 'God *said*, Let there be light: and there was light' (Gen. 1:3). It had the power to destroy: some primitive peoples called the hunting knife 'the sharpness at the thigh' because to mention the actual word might rob the knife of its cutting, killing power. It had the power to bless: the reason why Rebekah and Jacob were prepared to cheat the old man Isaac for his blessing (Gen. 27) was not that they were bothered about a few pious words but because they believed that the words spoken—'May God give you ... plenty of grain and wine. Let people serve you, and nations bow down to you'—carried with them the power to bring about what was spoken. It had the power to curse: the gypsy from whom you have refused to buy clothes pegs is not just calling you nasty names; she is speaking the words that will themselves bring you bad luck and an untimely end. Some primitive tribes believed that the spoken word existed even before the god and was in fact the means of his creation.

Why then was the spoken word, charged with such power, ever written down to form a sacred text? One assumption is that it was to preserve for posterity the sacred words of religion: the myths, the stories, the prayers, the praises, the blessings, the cursings. What is written down can never be forgotten. But in early times this was not likely to be the case, for people were entirely satisfied with the system of oral tradition. The answer probably is in magic. To write something down was to imprison the vitality of the words; the written words enabled writer and reader to control the power at work. The point is that the written words are there in front of you and nothing happens. You can relax. But once the words are read aloud they become spoken words again, exercising that power which always belongs to them.

Once the sacred text came into existence it began to be used in the practice of the religion. It is used as an oracle to obtain

27

guidance in complex circumstances and insoluble problems (the Romans opened the Sybilline books only in times of crisis), as a charm to be buried with the dead (as in ancient Egypt), as a means of effecting blessings or curses (read Numbers 5:23-8 where the accused woman actually had to drink the words of the sacred text) and as a claim to the divine origin of the religion (the *Book of Mormon* written on plates of gold and hidden in a hill by an angel). Furthermore, the sacred text has been held to contain the essence of a religion. What it truly is can be be found in its scriptures. Finally the holy book assumes a place in the liturgical and institutional life of the religious community. There is no clearer illustration of this than the veneration of the Torah in the Jewish synagogue and the effect of the contents of the Torah on Jewish life.

The fact that the sacred text has been made to assume these roles has not made critical enquiry into holy books any easier. If a sacred text is your oracle, your companion in the grave or a gift from an angel of God, you are not going to take very kindly to modern scholars sharpening their wits upon it. You will forbid them if you can, discourage them if you cannot forbid them, and if they persist you will take no notice of what they say. This process, illustrated so clearly in the case of the *Koran* and the *Book of Mormon*, is as understandable psychologically as it is disastrous intellectually. It is entirely understandable that if the holy book is thought to contain the essence of a religion and has become the most significant factor in that religion's liturgical and institutional life, the scholar who arrives upon the scene—as he must inevitably do today—with his penetrating questions about textual accuracy, authorship, historical context and the rest is not the most welcome of men. A religion is put immediately upon the defensive. But this has to be faced if the sacred text is still to be credible. Otherwise one may well be found shutting out the god (no capital 'G' for the moment) of truth from his own dominions. In any case there is no need for alarm, for the different ways of approaching sacred texts may in the end prove to be not contradictory but complementary. The scholar, the priest and the preacher may find themselves to be friends.

This brings us to the question of interpretation, for inevitably once the words have been written down the question will subsequently be asked, 'What do these words mean?' This question can be subdivided: *What did these words mean to those who wrote them? What do these words mean for us now?*

(i) Ancient texts have an integrity that has to be respected. Nothing is easier, and nothing is more disrespectful than to assume that what *we* mean by the words in the book is what the writer or writers meant. When the Huddersfield Town Hall resounds to the singing of 'Unto us a child is born', is the meaning in the minds of the audience the same as was in the mind of the prophet Isaiah? Is the 'you shall not covet' of the tenth commandment (Exodus 20:17) concerned with the inward motive that we understand coveting to be? Exegesis is the attempt to find out what the words meant for those who wrote them and is the first duty of anyone who sets himself to study an ancient text. Christian preachers are not exempt from this discipline. Nor is there release in the fact that sometimes the enquiry has to go unrewarded.

(ii) When one turns to the question 'What do these words mean for us now?' the question of interpretation arises in a very acute form. It was G. K. Chesterton who said that a Mormon reads the Bible and finds polygamy; a Christian Scientist reads it and finds that we have no arms and legs. It is the same with every holy book—seek its meaning for today's readers and you have almost as many meanings as there are seekers. At this point attention has to be paid to the *rules of interpretation*, the discipline of hermeneutics, as it is called. This frankly recognizes the distance that separates the text from modern readers and acknowledges that those who wrote and those who now interpret do not share the same world of thought. It then seeks to find the criteria for justifiable interpretations of the text: for example, the recognition that much of the material in the Gospels was written to be *preached* and should be interpreted on that assumption. Into the complexity of this exercise it is impossible to enter now. We can leave the subject with the apposite quotation from

29

Leonard Hodgson, covering both the integrity of the text itself and its interpretation for today:

What must the truth have been and be if men who thought and spoke as they did put it like that?[8]

This is what interpretation is all about. This is the question to ask of every holy book.

(6) Religious experience
This particular feature of religion does not afford quite the same direct access to its secrets as some of those already treated. Communities are made up of real people who can be talked to when they are alive and read about when they are dead. Myths are there to be told and retold, Ritual takes place and can be seen. Sacred texts can be studied. But an experience is, of its very nature, inward and subjective and so more elusive. This makes the descriptive task all the more important, for (the person or persons who have actually gone through the experience apart) the description is virtually all that the rest of us have.

Of course any results that issue from an alleged experience must be examined. If Cyril says he has had the experience of falling in love with Mabel, and is still in love with Mabel, observable results will follow. His behaviour towards her may be seen to be more tender and devoted: they may hold hands in the cinema. This is evidence that the experience of falling in love has in fact occurred in the life of Cyril—and perhaps Mabel—just as in religious experience different behaviour patterns and a new sense of purpose are evidence that something has indeed happened to the person or persons concerned.

But of the actual experience itself there is only the description, and that must inevitably be put together from the assertions made about it by the subject. Cyril says that he is in love with Mabel and might be persuaded to divulge the nature of the experience: physical attraction, affection, devotion and so forth. A fair description of what it means to be in love might well be the result. Whether Cyril actually *is* in love

[8] *For Faith and Freedom* (S.C.M. 1968), Vol II, pp. 15–16.

with Mabel (assuming that such a state is capable of definition) is not for the observer to judge. His task is only to describe. This distinction is rather more clear in the case of religious experience. If a person makes the assertion—to use the illustration of a Christian—'I was confronted by the Lord Jesus Christ' or 'I was possessed by the Holy Spirit', then what the neutral observer can do and what he cannot do are plain enough. He can extract from the person an account of *what it was like* to be 'confronted by the Lord Jesus Christ' or to be 'possessed by the Holy Spirit', just as Cyril could reveal *what it was like* to fall in love and to be in love with Mabel. The observer may be told of an experience of adoration, of penitence, of vocation, of ecstasy and he will probably find no great difficulty in establishing that it was indeed an experience of that sort. What the observer must not do is to accept at the same time and by the same criteria the assertion about the object of the experience. To say that a man experiences ecstasy is one thing. To say that the ecstasy was the result of being possessed by the Holy Spirit is quite another. The descriptive task includes only the first. The second, a matter of theological interpretation, must be considered later. Having made this distinction, it will be useful to look at two examples of religious experience.

(i) The first is the experience of *the numinous*. This word, coined by Rudolf Otto in his famous book, published in 1917, *The Idea of the Holy*, is an attempt to express the experience of both terrifying dread and fascinating appeal that occurs when man is confronted by what he believes to be the supernatural, the Wholly Other (to use Otto's expression). The great mysterious unknown can both terrify and fascinate us. Not infrequently it is through nature that this experience of super-nature comes: walking by the sea at night, finding oneself alone on a moor or in a forest, contemplating (as Wordsworth did in *The Prelude*) a huge, black mountain crag. It has indeed been argued that religion can be deduced from man's response to the daybreak. Sometimes the experience is more direct, for example when, as the Bible records, Jacob falls asleep in the desolate hills of central Palestine he dreams of the supernatural (Gen. 28:12–15) and when he wakes up he

31

is afraid and says 'How awesome is this place! This is none other than the house of God and this is the gate of heaven' (Gen. 28:17). A similar experience is also found in other faiths—in the terrifying quality of the Hindu experience of the god Vishnu in the *Bhagavad-Gita*:

> I behold Thee bearing diadem, mace and disc, massed in radiance, on all sides glistening, hardly discernible, shining round about as gleaming fire and sun, immeasurable. . . .
> For as I behold Thee touching the heavens, glittering, many-hued, with yawning mouth, with wide eyes agleam, my inward soul trembles and I find not constancy nor peace, O Vishnu.[9]

That there is a religious experience of the numinous seems impossible to deny. The claim that what, or rather who, is being experienced is the god Yahweh or the god Vishnu is one that cannot at present be either substantiated or denied. Atheists have doubtless been frightened by crags.

(ii) A second experience, around which much argument rages, is that of *religious conversion*. That some people do experience a turning about at a deep level of the personality is impossible to refute. One book that in modern times has investigated the Christian—and predominantly Protestant—phenomena is William James's[10] *The Varieties of Religious Experience*. One of his examples, typical of many, is the case of S. H. Hadley, a New York drunkard. He found his way to a mission hall and as the account[11] puts it:

> When the invitation was given, I knelt down with a crowd of drunkards. Jerry made the first prayer. Then Mrs M'Auley prayed fervently for us. Oh, what a conflict was going on for my poor soul! A blessed whisper said, 'Come'; the devil said, 'Be careful'. I halted but a moment, and then, with a breaking heart, I said, 'Dear Jesus, can you help me?' Never with mortal tongue can I describe that moment. Although up to that moment my soul had been filled with indescribable gloom, I felt the glorious brightness of the noonday sun shine into my heart. I felt I was

9 *Bhagavad-Gita*, ch. XI, quoted in Otto *The Idea of the Holy* (English trans., O.U.P. 1923), p. 192.
10 1842–1910.
11 William James, *The Varieties of Religious Experience* (Longmans, Green and Co. 1920), pp. 202–3. (Also Fontana 1960.)

· ·

a free man. Oh, the precious feeling of safety, of freedom, of resting on Jesus! I felt that Christ with all his brightness and power had come into my life; that, indeed old things had passed away and all things had become new.

The phenomenon of conversion experience is by no means confined to Christianity. The dramatic change in the New York mission hall could be paralleled by 'the opening of the heavenly eye' in a Hindu temple. In *Religion in Essence and Manifestation*[12] G. van der Leeuw refers to the conversion of Lucius, as described in the works of Apuleius. Lucius, after a chequered career (to put it mildly), is made repentant and contrite and in a complete turn about dedicates himself to the service of the goddess Isis. But, as so often in Christian accounts, the initiative is said by the convert to be taken and the dominating role is said to be played by the god or goddess. She (in this case) 'by her providence brings to new birth'. By the action of what Christians would call 'sovereign grace' Lucius enjoys an experience of being born again.

The same point must be made here as was made about the experience of the numinous, that ascribing the conversion experience to the activity of the Holy Spirit or the goddess Isis is a claim to truth that must be examined on other grounds than those that aim only to describe the experience itself. Such an examination is both a fascinating and a controversial procedure. William James's view that conversion is due to divine activity in the unconscious mind has been attacked as a dangerous 'psychologizing of faith. Though if an experience can be satisfactorily explained psychologically that does not of itself rule out the action of God or gods in the experience. But this is to drift into the realm of explanation and here the aim is less ambitious: simply to assert that the religious experience of conversion does occur and can be described.

Three other points need briefly to be made:

(i) It would be a mistake to dismiss religious experience as mere feeling. One can imagine the protestations of our mythical (!) Cyril

[12] Pp. 530–1.

if he were told that what he was calling love was in fact only an effervescent emotion. He would doubtless refer to the involvement of his will, his mind, his body, to illustrate the totality of his love. The same is true of all religious experience that deserves to be taken seriously. The whole person is involved.

(ii) Religious experience, though related to all the other features of religion, has particularly close relations with gods and with ritual. Neither can now be taken beyond the descriptive stage but clearly the presence of God (if it be he) or Isis (if it be she) in a religious experience is of considerable importance. By its truth or error a religion will stand or fall. And the way in which the experience is expressed in ritual contributes to and then helps to perpetuate the experience itself. The Roman soldier who was initiated into the mysteries of Mithra stood in the *taurobolium*, a pit over which a bull was held, and received a ritual bath once the animal had been slashed with a sword. The soldier then referred to himself as *renatus in aeternum*, reborn in eternity. The experience and the ritual fed upon each other.

(iii) The origin of most religious communities lies in the religious experience of the 'first fathers'. Such originative experiences tend to be both more comprehensive and more profound than those that follow them, hence the constant appeal to return to the 'first fine careless rapture' with which it all began. And, even if a return is not called for, the originative experience is reckoned to be the touchstone by which all subsequent experience is measured. More than that, the first experience—mediated now by sacred texts—seems to possess the power to broaden and deepen that which comes after it. Islam, Judaism and Christianity have each proved this to be true.

(7) Values and ethics

Take the case of a national newspaper; it can be analysed as follows. On the one hand there is the general policy of the paper, its right-wing, or its left-wing, stance, and on the other there is the 'nuts and bolts' operation, the translation of that general policy, right-wing or left, into the writing and publishing of particular news items, leading articles, features and so forth. A similar such broad division exists between values and ethics as a joint feature of religion.

(i) *Values* correspond to the general policy. Just as the general policy of a newspaper is its basic stance to the life around it, so the values of a religion are those that determine its basic stance to man's life in the world. Now if man were simply an animal there would be no need to spend any time on this at all. He would just be as God made him, so to speak, and would adjust to the world about him in the unreflective way that animals do. But precisely because man is not just an animal he finds himself over against the world, reflecting upon himself as distinct from it, and therefore having to come to terms with it. This indeed can, and frequently does, take the form of an alienation from, a hostility between, man and the world.

In order to cope with this situation, man must have values by which to live, criteria by which to assess his situation, guide-lines to direct his path through the world; and it is these things that religion claims to provide. It gives him his 'general policy', his basic stance. So, for example, Buddhism advocates a peaceful, kindly disposition as the basic stance of life and many of its stories teach the truth that hatred cannot end hatred; only by love will hatred be overcome. The Buddha is reckoned to have said:

> He has abused me, beaten me, worsted me, robbed me; those who dwell upon such thoughts never lose their hate.
> He has abused me, beaten me, worsted me, robbed me; those who dwell not upon such thoughts are freed of hate.[13]

(ii) But just as the general policy of a newspaper has to be translated into the 'nuts and bolts' of news items, leading articles and features, so the values taught by a religion have to be translated into the 'nuts and bolts' of *ethics*, of practical behaviour.

Buddhism expresses its basic values in a fair quantity of advice in the realm of ethics. *The Dhammapada* includes plenty:

> To all life is dear. Judge then by yourself, and forbear to slay or to cause slaughter.
> Speak the truth, be not angry, give of your poverty to the suppliant. To be hospitable and courteous, this is to be glad and to make an end of sorrow.[14]

[13] *The Dhammapada*, see S. E. Frost, *The Sacred Writings of the World's Great Religions* (Blakiston 1947), p. 145.
[14] Pp. 147, 149, 150 in a 'thou' version.

Sometimes the ethical practices of a religion seem to us not to be matters of ethics (i.e. morality) at all, but rather matters of procedure, of custom, of habit—which, incidentally, is what the word 'ethics' means by derivation. This distinction would, however, be repudiated by the followers of the religion concerned. Such practices are the ones we meet most quickly in even the most superficial acquaintance with a religion. One has only to fly *El Al* to encounter *kosher* food. All that most of us know about the religion of the Sikhs is that because they wear turbans they cannot, and will not, wear motor-cycle crash helmets or bus conductors' caps. Indeed, so well known are the ethical practices (of whatever kind) of religions that people can mistake the part for the whole. 'You don't have to go to church to be a Christian' is a familiar example from the English scene.

2. THEOLOGY

In some quarters theology is a dirty word. Speaking in a Christian context, when a young person offers for the ordained ministry and leaves the native heath for a theological college, there are some who view the departure with misgiving, if not alarm. For, they suppose, the theology that is the purpose of such a college to dispense will first erode and then destroy the simple faith of its students. They will leave home believing everything but they will return each vacation doubting more and more. This, it is thought, is highly regrettable, and it is all the fault of theology.

Others regard the subject as guaranteed to cause confusion. Anything written or spoken about religion that is clearly and intelligibly expressed cannot possibly be theology; anything full of muddled thinking and obscure language almost certainly is. Theology, it is supposed, perversely makes difficult that which is basically easy; it confuses people of simple faith.

Sometimes theology is thought to be synonymous with irrelevance. In a speech in the important debate about Clause 4 of the Labour Party constitution, Harold Wilson described those parts of the constitution that were not relevant to the daily strains and stresses of politics as 'the theology of it'.

The theoretical, the nebulous, the academic and the remote are lumped together and labelled 'theology'.

Criticisms and misunderstandings like this demand a definition of the subject, and to say what theology is may expose what it is not.

Definition of theology

The word 'theology' has its origin in two words in the Greek language, one meaning 'god' and the other 'words'. Thus theology is 'words about a god', 'god-talk' as we might now describe it. Since the second word of the two, *logos*, meant not simply the spoken word but also the meaning that lay behind it, we can have as the starting point for our definition 'speaking and thinking about a god'. The theologian (*theologos*) of classical Greece was 'one who treats of the gods'.[15] This has to be widened to include, for example, matters like the nature of man, salvation, the Church (in Christianity) which are, so to speak, an extension of 'god-talk'. Even further widening is required by religions that have no god, for as one scholar[16] has light-heartedly remarked, if we keep to the strict literal meaning of the word, Buddhists would have to do, not theology, but Buddhology.

Sometimes this 'speaking and thinking about a god' is referred to as *the science* of theology. In so far as there are similarities in method between theology and the natural sciences (physics, chemistry, biology, zoology and the rest)—the use of imagination and critical reason, taking a risk and working on the assumption that a hypothesis is true—it may be useful to call theology a science. But because theology must deal with the supernatural as well as the natural it is probably better not to press this particular claim. The 'queen of the sciences' must find another throne to sit on.

It is necessary to move on from a rough and ready definition to one that spells it out more fully. Here is the definition with which John Macquarrie opens his notable book, *Principles of Christian Theology*:[17]

[15] *The Shorter Oxford English Dictionary* (O.U.P. 1973).
[16] Ninian Smart, *The Phenomenon of Religion* (Macmillan 1973), p. 12.
[17] S.C.M. 1966, p. 1.

Theology may be defined as the study which, through participation in and reflection upon a religious faith, seeks to express the content of this faith in the clearest and most coherent language available.

The advantage of this definition is that it includes the three basic elements of theology as it addresses itself to a religion: participation, reflection and expression or, to use another set of words, commitment, thinking and communication. All three are necessary for the making of a theology, and they can be taken in turn.

(1) Participation
The first section of this chapter described religion, leaving open the question of commitment to a particular form of it. But once the theological task begins, as it does in the succeeding chapters, then this neutralist attitude will have to go. For theology is not content merely to describe a religion. It makes the claim that the religion it is studying is in fact *true*; truth-claims are its business. It is this that introduces elements of importance and excitement into the study of theology. For *it matters* whether all that is claimed for a religion is in fact true (if Jehovah's Witnesses are right we had better join them quickly), and the descriptive study does not gamble on the truth as theology must. (It is certain that Christians believe in heaven, but who *knows*?) Two things follow from this state of affairs.

(i) Every religious community will have its own theology. There is Christian theology, Hindu theology, Islamic theology, and so on, and each is concerned to establish and assert the truth of its particular religion. No dialogue, however charitable, can conceal this; indeed it should not try. Our concern will be with Christian theology but it would be a large mistake to suppose that other theologies and theologians are not in contention. They are. Our multi-racial society is slowly making us more aware of this than once we were.

(ii) The theologian, whether a professional scholar or a lay person doing his theology in the working world (both are necessary) is a committed person. To use our previous

38

illustration, he is not a writer of books about potholing. He is
a potholer. He participates in the religious faith that he is
studying: he is a committed member of the religious community, he believes its doctrines, he shares in its ritual and he
worships its god. Hence the folly of supposing that theological
colleges exist to destroy faith. It is no use therefore looking to
theologians for unbiased and dispassionate accounts of a
religion. They are enthusiasts. They have axes to grind.

(2) Reflection

In the early part of this chapter reference was made to the
broad sweep of religion going back to man's earliest days on
earth. If we were able to begin at the beginning we should
have to look very hard for anything that could be called
'reflection'. Primitive religion had myths and ritual but no
great intellectual content and consequently no doctrine.[18]
(This word, from the Latin verb 'to teach', has virtually the
same meaning as 'theology' though 'that which is taught' does
perhaps carry an emphasis upon the traditional.) The nearest
approach to it was when, at their initiation into the tribe,
boys or young men were told about the existence and nature of
the tribal gods.

But as man's evolving life gave a more prominent place to
the activity of the mind, reflection took its place as part of the
theological task. The theologian has to *think* about his religion.
Theology is a discipline of the mind. Many thousands of words
have been written and many arguments waged over the place
that reason should occupy in religion, but no one denies it has
some place, not even the extremist who has to find a reason for
abrogating reason. The arguments are about its proper place.
Can reason think its own way through to truth? Can it shape
an entire theology on its own? Or should its chief task be to
organize in a coherent fashion the various features of religion?
Should it confine itself to explaining aspects of religion that
are otherwise obscure? How critical can it be of the rest of

[18] It is hard to say at what stage primitive religion passes into something more advanced. Although the Pentateuch contains early myths it
would obviously be incorrect to say that it has no intellectual content and
no doctrine.

religion—religious experience, for example—without over-stepping the mark? When and where does reason have to submit to something else? These questions have been debated for centuries, and the debate continues. Their very existence is a testimony to the stubborn fact that men insist on thinking about their religion. The life of the religious community. the myths, the ritual, the gods, the sacred books—all are open to the enquiring, reflecting mind. And out of the enquiry and the reflection theology emerges.

(3) Expression

To speak of expressing 'the content of this faith in the clearest and most coherent language available' brings us straight away to a subject of some complexity, but of considerable import-ance for religion—language.

The power attributed to the spoken word from the earliest times has ensured its importance. In the myth of Osiris the lamentations, the spoken words of grief, of the two goddesses Isis and Nephthys, actually had the power to raise the dead god to life, a matter of some moment. We no longer expect such dramatic effects from our words, but we do expect *some* effects. We look to words, spoken or written, to explain our beliefs, to share our experiences, to persuade people of the truth as we see it, to urge people to action, to be the vehicle of our worship, even to answer questions in theology examina-tions! Hence the importance of language.

As for its complexity: this is not a reference to the existence of difficult words (immutability, existentialism, and the rest) or to obscure sentences that have to be read three or four times before the meaning can be grasped, but to the existence of different *kinds* of languages: not Chinese, Hindustani, Gaelic and so forth, but different ways of using words, whether in English or any other tongue. It is fashionable to call these 'language games'. What is meant is that, though the words used are the same words, the ways in which they are used and the meaning given to them are very different. For example, the statement 'Christmas comes but once a year' means one thing to manufacturers of diaries, another to postmen and yet another to preachers preparing their sermons.

So too the various disciplines of study have their own 'language games' to play. The statement 'John Wesley's home at Epworth was haunted by a poltergeist' would have an interest both for the historian and the psychical research student. To one it speaks of a possible series of events and an investigation to see if it can be established that those events actually took place. To the other it speaks of phenomena, bumpings up and down the stairs, doors opening and closing without a human touch, and evidence to be gathered about the precise nature and significance of the phenomena. The framework within which these two disciplines work is obviously different, though the basic statement is the same for both. To put it another way, the words are the same but they are playing different games with them. In similar fashion, both science and religion would have something to say about the words with which the Bible opens: 'In the beginning God created the heavens and the earth' (Gen.1 : 1). One would be concerned with exactly how the creation came about, the other with who did it, and why. They would therefore be looking for different meanings in the same set of words.

Every language game is played according to its own rules, and to play one game with the rules of another is like determining chess moves by throwing a dice. Chess and snakes and ladders do not mix in this way. The language of geometry is exact, subject to mathematical proof and almost entirely impersonal. If we are taught the theorem of Pythagoras, that in a right-angled triangle the square on the hypotenuse equals the sum of the squares on the other two sides, we know exactly what is meant, it can be demonstrated (Q.E.D.),[19] and our personal feelings towards Pythagoras are neither here nor there. But the language of religion veers in the opposite direction. To make the statement 'God loves people' is not exact because neither God nor people, nor for that matter love, can be defined as precisely as a right-angled triangle. The statement cannot be proved by steps in an argument ending with the magic letters Q.E.D., and it is intensely personal. It is difficult to imagine which is the greater disaster— to play the geometry language game with the rules of the

19 *Quod erat demonstrandum,* 'That which was to be proved'.

41

religious one (Pythagoras was a great fellow so we can trust him to produce a good theorem; we can't prove it but we will believe it) or to play the religious game with the rules of the geometry one (we must know exactly what we mean by God and be able to prove what we say about him).

This does not mean that words cannot be borrowed from one language by another (as when the Freemasons refer to God as the Great Architect of the Universe) or be translated from one language into another (as when the lover says 'I adore you'). But it does mean that religion, like other disciplines, has its own game to play according to its own rules. It has been a reluctance to concede this, an attempt to argue that the rules of the science game were the only *real* rules, that has made for tension between science and religion. What can one do with a rugby man who insists that golfers, cricketers, wrestlers and netball players should all scrum down?

But we must be clear about our own rules. And there are two that preachers more than most have to recognize:

(i) We wish to use a rational language that can be understood by people prepared to make the effort to understand it. Some language is not like that—the language of sexual experience, for example. Words used in private by two lovers are often unintelligible to anyone but themselves. We have to strive not for a secret language but for a public one. This accounts for many of the stances that are taken in religion today from the dropping of Latin in the Mass to the insistence that charismatic experiences, however liberating, should never be allowed to stifle rational enquiry.

(ii) Religious language has very often to be symbolic in character and to proceed by way of analogy. Thus if a religious man asserts 'God is love' he is not speaking literally, i.e. God = love (we cannot tie God down by our definitions: he is much more than ever we can say) but symbolically, for in using the word 'love' he is making earthly love symbolize the love of God. We use the analogies of Father or Shepherd for God and we speak of acting, sending, judging, speaking, and so forth, using by analogy verbs that describe human activities. It would of course be extraordinarily useful if we knew the

42

language of heaven and could speak of God as he really, totally, is, but at present we do not and we have to make do with our own.

Once religious language has been seen in this way there is no great problem about theological language. The language of theology is simply a specialist form of the language of religion, arising from that thinking, that use of reason, that reflection which are part of the definition of theology. To quote Macquarrie's words again, 'theological language seeks to express the content of a religious faith' and the major part of this book will be an examination of that content. Moreover, the expression must be 'in the clearest and most coherent language available'. (Hence the criticism that theology confuses merely indicates what poor theologians most of us are.) This is necessary for communication—a passage from one state of comprehension to another—to take place. And communication is essential because theology is preaching; theologians, as has been said, have axes to grind.

Theology and culture

Here we use the word 'culture' not to mean refinement (visits to symphony concerts and art exhibitions are 'culture' in this sense) but to refer to a whole civilization in its entire life. So we may speak of the ancient Chinese culture, the Roman culture, the culture of the modern Western world. Just as each culture has its own way of doing its science, its art, its history, so it has its own way of doing its theology. And its way is not necessarily our way. This can readily be seen in disciplines other than our own. We would not expect ancients who thought the sun went round the earth to feel at home at Jodrell Bank nor Norman architects to enthuse about the Hilton hotel. But there is a tendency, for reasons that will emerge as this book proceeds, for theology to drop its anchor while other ships sail on. Though this may give substance to the criticism that theology is irrelevant, it may prove to be in some ways defensible. But the dangers are obvious. To speak in the thought forms and languages of a culture other than our own, to retell ancient Hebrew stories, to repeat the

43

theological formulae of the fourth century or to sing the hymns of the eighteenth, is to take a risk, the risk of being incomprehensible to the people of our own culture. So theology has to be a flexible discipline, ready to think and speak as an integral part of a culture that thinks and speaks in its own way. Does this mean then that theology must reject the past? It means nothing of the kind, for if that were done in the case of a religion rooted in history (like Christianity, unlike Hinduism) that religion would have to shut up shop. But it does mean that looking to a past culture must always be balanced by looking to the present one and, furthermore, seeing the present one not simply as the recipient of past wisdom but as a contributor to a religion's developing theology.

Theology as disclosure

People who write novels, compose music, paint pictures, often spend hours and hours working away at outlines, possibilities, lines of approach, only to reject one after another. It is a frustrating business and can bring some to the point of giving up. It seems as if the plot, the theme, the composition, will never come. Then suddenly it does. As we say colloquially, 'it clicks'. Whatever it is to be—book, music, picture—a disclosure has been made, the author, composer, painter has 'seen it' and from that moment nothing can stop him.

Religion has its moments like that. Sometimes it is a very big moment as when in a first (often called 'primordial') revelation the nature of reality is seen as never before and a new religion and its theology begin. Gotama the Buddha receiving enlightenment under the Bodhi Tree in sixth-century India and Jesus of Nazareth living, dying and (as Christians believe) rising from the dead in first-century Palestine are two examples of this. In these and similar cases there is a large disclosure, and in the light of it things 'click' for religious people and for theologians for hundreds of years afterwards. Who or what is being disclosed is a question for future consideration, but the phenomenon of the big disclosure is present in most religions and is the first source of their theology.

But there are little disclosures as well, though they are not

44

normally described as 'revelation'. They vary from those that result in new religious movements (the 'warmed heart' of John Wesley, the claim of Joseph Smith, founder of Mormonism, to have been visited by an angel) to those that come to most religious people at some—usually unexpected—times in their lives. Avoiding the technical religious language so often used on these occasions, things then 'click' into place, and life in general, and our lives in particular, make sense. In however modest a fashion, we are at the receiving end of a disclosure. And it is precisely this element of 'given-ness' that, as we reflect upon it, comes through into our theology.

Chapter 2

Christian Theology

C. K. B A R R E T T once said to the Methodist Conference[1] 'I can teach anything I am myself capable of learning and apprehending; but I can preach only what I believe.' This states succinctly the difference between the first and second chapters of this book. The first chapter looked at religion and theology as phenomena that occur. To use Barrett's words, it was a question of learning, apprehending and teaching. Believing and preaching did not come into it at all. But they do now. For, as has been said, theologians have axes to grind, and this is the process that must continue in the following pages. It will not be possible simply to say that Christian theology asserts this, that or the other thing; the claim made by Christian theologians that what they assert is the truth will have to be examined. In doing this readers will inevitably be forced to make up their own minds, to believe or to disbelieve. This is an essential requirement for a preacher, as Barrett's words imply.

How then, briefly, do Christian theologians see their religion as expressing the 'features'[2] of chapter 1?

(1) Community
They will argue that the Christian Church is the community of the Chosen People of God, the new Israel in succession to

[1] Ministerial Session, Newcastle upon Tyne, 27th June 1973. Published in *Epworth Review*, Vol. 1, No. 1, January 1974.
[2] Some Christian theologians would not wish to have Christianity limited (as they would say) by these features. Others, no less committed, are convinced that Christianity loses nothing by being described in this way.

the old, the very Body of Christ. 'But you are a chosen race, a royal priesthood, a holy nation, God's own people', as the New Testament puts it (1 Peter 2:9a). This is an area of controversy and contention, for if the Church is the Chosen People of God it is difficult to see how Jews or Muslims can be, a state of affairs they are inclined to resist.

(2) Myth

In chapter 1 a myth was defined as a story and, to avoid misunderstandings of the word 'myth', 'story' is used here, in relation to Christianity. Christian theology asserts that the Christian story is true. The Christian claim is a double one: first, that the story of Jesus Christ is true historically. It happened. This is, of course, an advance on the primitive, unhistorical myths of chapter 1. The claim is made in different degrees, some biblical scholars arguing for much more historicity than others, but it is central to Christianity in the sense that, if it were demonstrated beyond dispute that Jesus Christ never lived at all, that would be the end of the Christian religion. But the Christian story is *also* true mythologically: 'it discloses in a penetrating and timeless way man's relation to the world and to the supernatural'.[3] The story here is that in Jesus Christ the great, eternal God himself actually lived a human life, by the death of Jesus on the Cross he redeemed men from their sin, and by his raising Jesus from the dead, death, and all other hostile forces with it, have been conquered. In this story is man's total salvation, brought about for him by God himself in the person of Jesus: 'God was in Christ reconciling the world to himself' (2 Cor. 5:19a). Anything less than this may be more attractive, more reasonable, more credible, more acceptable to other religions, but it would not be traditional Christianity. The story of the Incarnation of the Son of God is not expendable.

(3) Ritual

As for ritual, the Christian claim is that something does indeed happen in Christian worship. Although this is an area in which Christians are themselves divided, none would contend

3 See p. 19.

that Christian worship consists of *mere* words and *mere* actions. Roman Catholic, Orthodox and Protestant would all say that in the praises, the prayers and the preaching there is a dialogue between the natural and the supernatural; God speaks to man and man speaks to God. It is in the eucharist[4] that this is focused. Here in celebration the story of salvation is recounted and represented and through the sacred signs of bread and wine (though there is much disagreement on *how* it happens) God in Christ comes to his people again.

(4) Gods

In this chapter God can most certainly be given a capital 'G', for the assertion here is that the Christian God is the one, true God, and the only God. Christians did not have to fight for this, for the battle was won by the Hebrews centuries before. The Old Testament Yahweh became 'the God and Father of our Lord Jesus Christ'. Later in this book close attention will be paid to the doctrine of God, so for the moment we can be content with having the Christian claim summed up in the opening words of the Nicene Creed:[5]

> We believe in one God,
> the Father, the Almighty,
> maker of heaven and earth,
> of all that is, seen and unseen.

(5 and 6) Sacred texts and religious experience

With the next two features of religion, sacred texts and religious experience, a double claim is made by Christian theology. For not only is it contended that the Bible fulfils the role of a sacred text and that the experience of Christians is authentic religious experience, but when it is asked, as it is later in this chapter, 'On what authority can all these Christian claims be substantiated?' two of the answers will be appeals to the Bible and to Christian religious experience. This is a

---

[4] This term is used simply because it is the normal one in works of theology and liturgy to signify what elsewhere is variously called the Mass, the Holy Communion, the Lord's Supper, the Breaking of Bread.

[5] The creed commonly called 'Nicene' is an adaptation, probably made in the fourth century, of the creed of the Church of Jerusalem.

curious position in which to be and perhaps the best way to avoid the tedium of dealing with the same subjects twice is simply to record here that the Christian theologian does indeed make large claims for the Bible and Christian experience, and register that the precise nature of those claims will emerge when the authorities that lie behind the Christian claims are considered.

(7) Values and ethics
Immediately the question is asked: 'What are the values put forward by Christian theologians as being the specifically Christian ones?' we meet a distinction between Christianity and other religions that we shall find to be a crucial one. Christian theology insists that the values that are determinative for Christians are expressed and consummated in a *person,* Jesus Christ. He provides in himself the values by which Christians should live, the criteria by which they should assess every situation and the guidelines to direct their paths through the world: compassion, single-mindedness, self-sacrifice are examples. This expression of values in a person, though not entirely foreign to Buddhism in the person of the Buddha, nor to Islam in the person of Muhammad, is in Christianity given a central position because of the unique claims made for Jesus Christ (they will be examined later).

Christian theology, when it turns from the general question of values to the more precise one of ethics, is sometimes called Christian moral theology or simply Christian ethics. Rules of behaviour for Christians to observe as the proper expression of their religion have never been wanting. Indeed the 'science' of casuistry exists to work out with minute exactness what is right and what is wrong in every conceivable circumstance. On this basis it is always possible to know in every situation what is the Christian thing to do. Those Christians, mostly Protestants, who are not happy with the intricacies of casuistry, have their own substitutes: acting from Christian principles, for example. Both attempt to say what Christian behaviour should be. Sometimes such behaviour will be the same, at least in outward expression, as the behaviour of people who are not Christians, sometimes it will not. This is incidental to the claim of Christian theology that the Christian religion should not only tell people whom they should worship and what they should believe, but also how they should behave.

On what grounds?

If a man stands up at Speakers' Corner in Hyde Park and announces, for example, that spiritualism can put people in touch with the dead, those in the crowd who are prepared to take him seriously will ask: 'How do you know?' The question may not be put too politely, but it gets to the heart of the matter. In areas where the truth is not self-evident this is the question that must always be put. So the Christian theologian, making the claims listed so far in this chapter, can expect to be asked: 'How do you know?' This introduces what is known in more conventional terms as the question of religious authority and the sources of theology.

The answers of the Christian theologian must now be spelt out, and the 'Christian' before 'theologian' or 'theology' can be dropped, for no other kind will be under discussion.

First, then, the Christian account of what was described in chapter 1 under 'Theology as disclosure'.

A. REVELATION

Consider how heroes are often discovered. A very ordinary man, retiring, unassuming, slightly nervous perhaps, disliking pain and trouble as we all do, gives no indication whatever in the humdrum round of life that he is of the stuff of which heroes are made. But in the sudden crisis, the emergency situation of exploding bomb or painful death or house on fire, he is the one who produces the most remarkable bravery. And the comment of those who know him well? 'We did not know he had it in him. It was a revelation.'

Revelation is not something that can be 'cooked up' from human reason or human experience; it cannot be manufactured; it cannot always be anticipated. On the contrary, like the bravery of the nobody it is something that is *shown* to be the case, something that up to that point was not known, but is now disclosed. Indeed the expression 'disclosure situation' has been used[6] to refer to those situations in which revelation takes place.

It must not be thought that revelation is something mechanical or contrived, either on the side of the revealer or the person to whom the revelation is made. One must have suspicions, to put it no more strongly, about, for example, a revelation written out in full in a golden volume buried in a hill, the supposed origin of the *Book of Mormon.* Much closer to reality are the occasions, known to most of us, described by Ian Ramsey in the following words:

> The Christian claim is obviously centred on 'disclosure' situations where the penny drops, the light dawns; where there breaks in on us a situation characteristically different from its immediate predecessors.[7]

One of the examples Ramsey himself gives[8] is of David and Nathan in 2 Samuel 12:1-7. He points out that David, after hearing the story of the rich man stealing the poor man's solitary lamb, gave (in verses 5 and 6) the kind of objective judgement that might be delivered in a law court. Then comes Nathan the prophet and confronts David with the dramatic, penetrating words 'You are the man'. As Ramsey says, 'The penny drops; there is indeed a disclosure'. This for David was revelation. He learned something (about himself) that he did not know before and the revelation, the disclosure, came to him from outside. It was given.

This is the characteristic of revelation. It is found in the most ordinary of human experiences: when with a slap on the thigh we exclaim 'Got it'; when we walk in the solitude of the hills and some insight into the meaning of a personal relationship 'comes' to us. It is found in the revelatory experience of the religious man, as described by John Macquarrie:[9]

> A mood of meditation or preoccupation; the sudden in-breaking of the holy presence, often symbolized in terms of the shining

6 Notably by Ian T. Ramsey in *Religious Language* (S.C.M. 1957).
7 P. 153.　　8 P. 113.
9 *Principles of Christian Theology*, p. 7.

of a light; a mood of self-abasement (sometimes terror, sometimes consciousness of sin, sometimes even doubt of the reality of the experience) in face of the holy; a more definite disclosure of the holy, perhaps the disclosure of a name or of a purpose or a truth of some kind (this element may be called the 'content' of the revelation); the sense of being called or commissioned by the holy to a definite task or way of life.

The theologian of course uses the name 'God' for 'the holy'. God is the source of revelation. It is God who discloses, not only the truth about this or that but also something of his own nature. The classic biblical example of this is in Exodus, Chapter 3. In Exodus 3:14 the revealing of the name of God ('I am who I am' or 'I will be what I will be') is not the disclosure of a personal proper name, an exalted example of 'Good morning, I'm Charles Jenkins: call me Charles' (though that in its own way is a revelation). It is a disclosure of God's *nature* and the Hebrew words that have been so variously translated are meant to signify that this is a revelation of the one to whom the total commitment of the religious man is due. But there is no over-exposure. Indeed the paradox of revelation is that what is revealed is itself mysterious, making God more mysterious (though not of course more concealed) than he was before the revelation took place. Thus in no sense did Moses have God in his pocket. But after the burning bush he did know where his commitment lay.

The accounts of the Resurrection appearances of Jesus in the New Testament are not dissimilar. The stories tell of Jesus, now risen from the dead, appearing and disappearing on the Emmaus Road (Luke 24:13–35), passing through closed doors to meet his followers (John 20: 19–23), distributing bread and fish for breakfast (John 21:9–14). These stories describe 'disclosure situations'. They were revelations of Jesus, risen from the dead. 'I have seen the Lord', said Mary Magdalene, speaking for them all. But this did not clear the matter up. Jesus was now more mysterious than ever. Who exactly was he and what precisely was he doing? These questions were to be pursued by his followers for centuries. The one thing, however, that the disclosure did was to make it devastatingly clear that the claim of Jesus upon their allegiance was a total one. This

CHRISTIAN THEOLOGY

is the disconcerting thing about religious revelation. It tells you, from outside, what you have to do with your life.

A previous generation of theologians made much of a distinction between general revelation, given to all men through the medium of the natural world, and special revelation, given through the actions of God in the history of Israel and supremely in the life, death and resurrection of Jesus Christ. As it is the same God active in all forms of revelation, this seems to be a somewhat artificial distinction. But the use of the word 'special' indicates that proper attention must now be given to the traditional ways in which Christians have en-countered, or rather, been encountered by, revelation.

(1) Jesus Christ

Though the space in this chapter will be given to Scripture and tradition as the means of revelation (Jesus Christ is the subject of chapter 5), strictly speaking *the* revelation for Christians is Jesus Christ (John 14:9). Scripture and tradition come into this category in so far as they are witnesses to him.

(2) Scripture

When in 1932 the Wesleyan Methodist Church, the United Methodist Church and the Primitive Methodist Church united to form the Methodist Church, in order to provide some theological cement for the new structure the *Deed of Union* laid down what are known as 'doctrinal standards'. These were not, to be sure, a list of doctrinal propositions that have to be believed on pain of excommunication, but *standards* against which all theology purporting to be Methodist has to be tested. The doctrinal standards of the Deed of Union include these two sentences:

> The Doctrines of the Evangelical Faith which Methodism has held from the beginning and still holds are based upon the Divine revelation recorded in the Holy Scriptures. The Methodist Church acknowledges this revelation as the supreme rule of faith and practice.

53

There is some significance in the word 'recorded'. We speak loosely of Scripture *being* revelation but, to speak precisely, it is not. It is the *record*[10] of revelation, the account of the way in which God has disclosed himself and his purposes to the two communities (the Deed of Union puts 'Scripture' into the plural), first the Jewish, then the Christian. Reference was previously made[11] to the first or primordial revelation, that is to say to those disclosures that start a religion off. The religion must return to them again and again, both to renew its faith and life and to test whether what is subsequently claimed to be revelation is in harmony with the primordial disclosures. For the Jews this revelation is contained in the Old Testament, and particularly in the first five books, the Pentateuch. Here, acting in history, through Abraham, Isaac, Jacob, Moses and their successors, God reveals both himself and his purpose to bring his chosen people Israel to their true destiny as the bearers of salvation for all mankind. For the Christians there is both a sharing in the revelation of the Old Testament and the arrival of fresh disclosures in the New. These disclosures centre in the person of Jesus Christ. As has been said, he *is* the Christian revelation. The New Testament bears witness to him; it is the unique means by which the revelation is communicated to each generation afresh; it contains the words that mediate the Word.

Such a process cannot be achieved by cold print. The Bible is not like a British Rail timetable where rows and rows of figures simply give information, and that is the end of the matter. On the contrary, the Bible is concerned with a whole community's experience of the God who reveals himself in Jesus Christ, and the individual's sharing in that experience. This includes the people who wrote the Bible. No doubt there was an assiduous clerk in British Rail who compiled the timetable and ensured that all the trains for Bristol did not leave Paddington at the same time, but it can hardly be said that his personality leaps at you out of the rows of figures. But Hosea, Jeremiah, the writer of the Fourth Gospel, Paul, do

[10] Some Christians prefer to say that it is the *means* of revelation, as on p. 52.
[11] See p. 44.

54

exactly that. They are real people mediating, within the community of faith, a real revelation. Then, at the end of the process, there is the reader who, within the community of faith (Judaism or the Church), is able to share in the revelation himself.

It is important to realize that having an access to and sharing in the primordial revelation of the Christian community in this way is not threatened by the work of modern Biblical scholarship. Morna Hooker recounts[12] how she was walking with a friend (a Professor of Divinity in fact) through the entrance of King's College, London, and high above their heads, on the parapet, were workmen with pickaxes, hacking away at the cement at the base of the coping stones *on which they were standing*. With dry humour the professor said, 'Don't those men remind you of New Testament scholars?' He did not mean it, but others would. The scholars who come to the Bible and find there alternative readings for the same text, passages quite impossible to translate, contradictory accounts of the same event, confusion and ignorance about authorship, widely differing theologies and so forth, are judged by some to be wreckers, knocking away the stones on which they, and the whole company of believers, stand.

This impression is understandable. The mystique that has gathered around the book with the black covers and the red edges, its place in the worship and devotion of the Church, the psychological need for an unchanging, infallible authority ready to hand, the conservatism that seems native to religion, these conspire to set up a resistance to Biblical scholarship and its findings. But it is the kiss of death. Of course the wilder excesses of scholarly adventurers should be rejected. Those who contend, as apparently some still do, that Jesus never lived or that, if he did, we can know nothing about him, and that we can never be sure that anything was in fact written by Paul, should not make us lose much sleep (though the reason for rejecting their work is not that it militates against the notion of infallibility but that it is bad scholarship). Granted that, why is resistance to Biblical scholarship the kiss of death? There are at least two reasons.

[12] *Epworth Review*, Vol. 3, No. 1, January 1976, p. 49.

(i) One is, to take up a phrase used before, the danger that we shall be found excluding the Lord of truth from his own dominions. The Lord of Scripture is also the Lord of historical, literary and theological truth and to oppose the search for the latter on the grounds of loyalty to the former is to imply a schizophrenic God. But God is not so divided and his truth is indivisible. To ask such questions as: 'Is the historical evidence for the raising of Lazarus from the dead as strong as that for the feeding of the five thousand?', 'Did Jesus actually say "Go therefore and make disciples of all nations, baptizing them in the name of the Father and of the Son and of the Holy Spirit", or is this the conviction and practice of the first Christians "read back" on to the lips of Jesus?', 'Did Paul write Ephesians or did somebody else?', is to engage in the search for truth and therefore to be in the Lord's service. Provided the quest is a disinterested one, that is to say, that the mind has not been made up about the answer before the question has been asked, there is nothing to fear from it.

(ii) Biblical scholarship, disciplined and responsible as it normally is, makes participation in the original, primordial revelation not more difficult, but easier. For example, the search for the most accurate text (textual criticism), work on the literary sources of the Gospels (source criticism), the study of the shape the Gospel material took before it was written down (form criticism), the examination of the purpose of the evangelists in writing their Gospels in the way they did (redaction criticism), lead us to a deeper appreciation of the way in which the first Christians experienced the primordial revelation and therefore to a deeper appreciation of Jesus who is himself that revelation.

Three other matters which underline what has already been written must now be stated explicitly, though briefly:

(i) *The inspiration of the Bible.* Christians believe the Bible to be an inspired book. The figure here is that of 'in-breathing' and it refers to the activity of the Holy Spirit in the process of writing and compiling the Bible. A distinction has to be made between the actual writing and the source of what was written. If inspiration is seen in the light of this distinction there is no problem about the writing and editing of the books of the Bible by many different people nor their being part of a particular culture. And to regard God the Holy Spirit as the *source* rather than the writer explains the unity of purpose in the Bible.

(ii) *The authority of the Bible.* Christians submit to the authority of the Bible. But an important distinction must be made here too. The submission is not to *a book*, however revered. It is to the truth that the book contains or, to use religious language, to the mind and will of God that the book reveals. Christians do not bow down to paper and ink any more than they do to wood and stone. Bibliolatry is simply a form of idolatry. What gives the Bible its authority is the extent to which it mediates the truth and reveals the Lord of truth.

(iii) *The Bible as the word of God.* Christ is the living Word of God, the perfect expression of all that God is.[13] Scripture, though inspired by the Holy Spirit[14] is not the living Word. It is the written word,[15] which, under the continuing guidance of the Holy Spirit, mediates Christ to believers. Strictly speaking, therefore, the Bible is not the Word (captial 'W') of God. It contains, and witnesses to, that Word.

(3) Tradition

In the 1960s, in the course of preparing the abortive scheme for uniting the Church of England and the Methodist Church, two or three theological 'hot potatoes' were singled out for special treatment. In 1963, 1967 and again in 1968, 'Scripture and Tradition' was one of them. It was found to be divisive, though the divisions did not entirely follow denominational lines. Why is it such a contentious matter?

Before this is pursued it is necessary to be clear about the meaning of the word 'tradition'. It can refer to the way in which truths and practices are passed on down the years, as in the sentences:

In India leg-spin bowling is passed on by tradition.

13 See chapter 5.
14 See p. 56.
15 See pp. 26–30.

The stories about Jesus were preserved by oral tradition. It can also refer to the truths and practices themselves, as in the sentences:

The doctrine of the Trinity is part of tradition.

The Nicene Creed is tradition.

The argument is about the relation to Scripture of the second meaning. Nobody wishes to quarrel about the first. It is therefore in the second sense that the word is used in this section.

It is supposed by many Protestants that where the Bible stops, tradition begins and, since the Bible is venerated as the holy book, that which follows after it is reckoned to be inferior. The last full-stop in the book of Revelation was, on this view, of immense significance. For if, as Protestants have believed and still do believe, the Bible is the revelation of God *par excellence*, inspired by the Holy Spirit, then that which trails behind it is, by contrast, 'man-made'. The traditions of men are not to be compared with the Word of God.

Roman Catholics have not seen it this way at all. They have often been at pains to point out that the Bible itself emerged out of tradition: the oral tradition which determined the form the gospels took. Furthermore, they have argued, it was the Church in its role of guardian of the tradition that decided which books should be included in the New Testament and which should not. And what, said the Roman Catholics, of the Holy Spirit? Did he go out of business once the content of the Bible had been agreed?

The Anglican-Methodist Commission tried, for obvious reasons, and with some success, to see that these positions did not become polarized. They therefore asserted the supremacy of Scripture:

Holy Scripture is and must always be the supreme standard of faith and morals in the Church because it embodies the testimony of chosen witnesses to God's saving action.[16]

And they had this to say about tradition:

Every tradition, whether of teaching, custom or institution, will

16 *Conversations* (C.I.O and Epworth 1963) p. 15.

enrich the Church from age to age ... just in so far as it witnesses to Christ as the deed of God in the world ... [17]

Then came the *rapprochement* :

Scripture and tradition ought not to be put over against one another. Both are gifts and instruments of the Holy Spirit within the Church. Behind both is the Living Word of God, the Word made flesh in Jesus Christ.[18]

All this is well said and reflects the mutual appreciation, and even the partial sharing, of one another's positions by both Roman Catholics and Protestants that has developed in recent years. It leads to comment upon the role of one (tradition) as the interpreter of the other (Scripture). Private interpretations of Scripture are notoriously unreliable and almost anything can be proved or disproved from the Bible by the enthusiast for this cause or that. Pacifists interpret the New Testament in terms of opposing war and non-pacifists in terms of waging it; Jehovah's Witnesses find in the Bible grounds for refusing blood transfusions and British Israelites for believing that the British and the Americans are the ten lost tribes of Israel. The traditions of the Church at least save us from some of the worst excesses. On the other hand, the Roman Catholic view that the Church, and the Church alone, is competent to interpret Scripture can stifle free enquiry and historically has not always performed well. Cannot the Holy Spirit use both?

Tradition can be broken down into three parts.[19]

(i) There is *Catholic*[20] *tradition*, formed by the Fathers and recognized by the universal Church as orthodox. One thinks, for example, of the doctrine of the Trinity, incipient only in the Bible but developed in the Catholic tradition; or of eucharistic worship which has sustained the Church for centuries but was very much a development from the 'breaking bread' (Acts 2:46) of the first Christians; or of the formation of the canon of Scripture already referred to. This is the

[17] P. 17.   [18] P. 17.
[19] These divisions were made by Rupert E. Davies in *Religious Authority in an Age of Doubt* (Epworth 1968), p. 27.
[20] The word 'Catholic' is used in a number of ways. Here it refers to the doctrine believed 'everywhere, always, and by all', and thus has the meaning 'universal'.

tradition expressed in the liturgies and creeds of the universal Church and it is both the witness to and the interpreter of the Bible.

(ii) There are *the separate traditions of the worldwide* communions, Roman, Orthodox and Protestant (often called Confessional traditions). They include the different doctrines of the ordained ministry (the threefold ministry of bishop, priest and deacon, or the single presbyteral ministry such as the Methodist), different approaches to the problem of election and grace (Calvinists for election, Methodists for grace), different views of the eucharist (Mass, Holy Communion, Lord's Supper, Breaking of the Bread, to distinguish them only by name for the moment); and so on. The optimist hopes and believes that these may be brought into the one tradition of the universal Church. The pessimist looks at the religious wars and persecutions of the past and cannot see it happening.

(iii) There are *the traditions of the denominations*, and they must run into thousands. The Methodists have strong doctrinal traditions, stemming from the preaching and writing of the Wesley brothers. The *Deed of Union*, after declaring that the Methodist Church 'rejoices in the inheritance of the Apostolic Faith and loyally accepts the fundamental principles of the historic creeds and of the Protestant Reformation', goes on to say that the 'Doctrines of the Evangelical Faith ... are contained in Wesley's Notes on the New Testament and the first four volumes of his sermons'. Out of these documents emerge the four Methodist doctrinal emphases, often expressed in the following summary form:

All men can be saved (Universal Salvation)
All men can be saved by grace through faith (Justification)
All men can know they are saved (Assurance)
All men can be saved to the uttermost (Perfect Love)

Each of these will be looked at in the course of this theological journey.

Denominational traditions in other matters also distinguish the Methodists: hymn-singing expressive of Christian fellowship; a centralized Connexion with an itinerant ordained ministry; the use of lay people in the conduct of worship and preaching; a more than average concern with the social expression of the Christian faith.

In each branch of tradition—Catholic, Confessional and Denominational—there is the danger of the tradition becoming fossilized. This is of course a threat in many areas of life: a strong tendency to work according to the formula 'as it was in the beginning, is now, and ever shall be'. Reformers and progressives of all kinds have been reduced to frustration and impotence because of it. In religion it is specially dangerous because that need for security and permanence which is in part met by a religious faith fosters a conservative position. That is why presumably, as critics are not slow to point out to us, many of the most desirable social reforms in the history of Western civilization have been resisted by the representatives of the Church: the bishops voted against the removal of the death penalty for stealing sheep. The assertion of chapter 1 is to the point here: that theology 'has to be a flexible discipline, ready to think and speak as an integral part of a culture that thinks and speaks in its own way'. This is particularly the case when theology is handling those traditions to which it looks to substantiate its claims.

B. REASON

We now take up the questions raised on p. 39 about the proper place of reason. This is a factor of considerable significance and the place we are prepared to give it in our theology is likely to have a marked effect on the eventual content of that theology. What then are the functions of reason in this field?

(1) Organizing

No one will quarrel with the contention that one of the functions of reason in theology is to organize the material for those who wish to study or to use it. How this is done depends on the purpose to which the material is to be put. Thus if one is preaching a sermon on the forgiveness of God through Jesus Christ, one would not organize the material in the same way as for an article on one of the theories of the Atonement in a theological journal. But in both cases one has to *think* about the source material and sort it out in the way best suited for the purpose.

(2) Making clear and explaining

This few people would contest. It is the task fulfilled in the writing of theological books. If I stretch out my left hand I

61

can reach the first two on the shelf. One is John Hick's *Evil and the God of Love* first published in 1966. In the opening chapter the author writes 'The problem dealt with in this book is . . . Can the presence of evil in the world be reconciled with the existence of a God who is unlimited both in goodness and in power?' By the time he has reached the last page the reader has had made clear for him the precise nature of the problem and attempts, both past and present, to solve it. The second book is *Ancient Israel, Its Life and Institutions* by Roland de Vaux, first published in English in 1961. The 'blurb' on the dust cover includes a comment from the *New York Times*: 'The imprint of Perede Vaux's outstanding qualifications and achievements appears on every page of this profound, deeply informative and comprehensive *opus magnum*.' In other words, anything and everything to do with Ancient Israel is here explained. These two scholars represent a very large number: men and women who exercise their not inconsiderable reason in the service of theology, making clear and explaining in every branch of that study.

(3) Criticizing

To consider the critical function of reason in theology is to move to more disputed ground. It has already been noticed that when reason begins to probe and question the Bible its attentions are not always welcome and a similar reaction is often forthcoming when reason addresses itself to tradition, be it Catholic doctrine, Confessional tradition, or denominational emphases. Though the large majority of scholars, and a fair number of other Christians, come to terms with this fairly quickly, there have been some bloody battles in this field.

For example, in 1860, a book called *Essays and Reviews*, written by seven Oxford scholars, was published in England. In it Baden Powell (*not* the Chief Scout) offered the complaint in the ponderous language of those days:

Thus it is the common language of orthodox writings and discourses to advise the believer, when objections or difficulties arise, not to attempt to offer a precise answer, or to argue the point, but rather to look at the whole subject as of a kind which ought to be exempt from critical scrutiny and be regarded with a submission of judgement, in the spirit of humility and faith.[21]

He then proceeds to do exactly the opposite on the subject of miracles. Other authors in the book take a similar position and Benjamin Jowett, writing about the Bible, has this to say:

The diffusion of a critical spirit in history and literature is affecting the criticism of the Bible in our own day in a manner not unlike the burst of intellectual life in the fifteenth or sixteenth centuries. Educated persons are beginning to ask, not what Scripture may be made to mean, but what it does.[22]

The intentions of the authors of *Essays and Reviews* were mild enough. They did not mean to cause an explosion. But they did. The book was condemned by both Houses of the Convocation of Canterbury, ten thousand Anglican clergymen signed a petition denouncing it, two of the authors were persecuted and, as Stephen Neill says,[23] 'Christians in England were almost in a state of panic'. Reason was not a welcome guest in this field.

Although the subject of Christian experience will be discussed later, it should be noticed that reason has been at work critically in that area also. For an illustration of this there is the case of what is called projection or projectionism. This is the view, associated with a German philosopher, Ludwig Feuerbach (1804–72), and developed with others, that God is a projection 'out there' of the qualities, the struggles and the desires that exist 'in there', in the mind and heart of man. Hence Christian experience, so-called, is not an experience of God but of oneself:

Religion is the relation of man to his own nature ... but to his nature not recognised as his own but regarded as another nature,

---

[21] 'On the Study of the Evidences of Christianity', *Essays and Reviews*, (London 1860), p. 98.
[22] 'On the Interpretation of Scripture', p. 340.
[23] *The Interpretation of the New Testament* (O.U.P. 1964), p. 32.

separate, nay contradistinguished from his own: herein lies its untruth, its limitation, its contradistinction to reason.... Feeling makes God a man, but for the same reason it makes man a God.... The purely, truly human emotions are religious: but for that reason the religious emotions are purely human.[24]

Some 'projectionists' (like Feuerbach) draw the conclusion that there is no God to be experienced. Others are content to leave open the question as to whether a God on whom man must project his experience does in fact exist.

Christian theologians today have, by and large, reached a position of maturity in these matters. That is to say, they do not over-react any more to the critical exercise of reason in the theological field. It is unlikely that the authors of *Essays and Reviews* would now be prosecuted. Of course there is difference of opinion, some of it sharp, about the *validity* of critical attacks—witness the *Honest to God* controversy of the 1960s. But theologians would not now resist the critical function of reason in the name of an infallible Bible, unalterable doctrines, untouchable traditions or unassailable experience. On the contrary, most of them would see critical reason, not as an enemy, but as an ally, helping modern man to discern the truth.

(4) Leading to the truth

Even more a matter of dispute is the extent to which reason can lead us to the truth. The crucial question here, under the heading 'On what grounds?'[25] is when the theologian is asked 'How do you know?' Can he then legitimately reply 'Because reason leads to that conclusion'? To what extent can man think his way to the truth?

Traditionally, the answer of theologians to these questions lies in the realm of what is called *natural theology*. There are a number of usages of the word 'natural'. Consider:

I know I should not have kissed her, but it was very natural.
Like Wordsworth, I am a great lover of natural beauty.
That wrong should be punished is a natural law.

[24] Ludwig Feuerbach, *The Essence of Christianity* (London 1854), pp. 196, 275.   [25] See p. 50.

Natural theology involves all three of these uses of the word. It reckons to obtain knowledge by the operation of reason:

(i) on man's nature, that which is natural to him;
(ii) on the works of nature—the created world;
(iii) on the moral code practised by men just because they are men.

From data of this kind reason leads to such conclusions as that God exists, that he is the creator of all that is, that man possesses an immortal soul. As this is plainly not enough to satisfy the theological needs of man, the deficit is made up by revelation.

Objections of some weight have been brought against natural theology and the pride of place it gives to reason. It is argued that such a theology is the prerogative of intellectuals—what can the plumber's mate deduce from the natural order of things? Again, the arguments, however reasonable they seem, are not reasonable enough to prove the case. Or else how could any rational man ever deny the existence of God and the immortality of man? But many rational men, an increasing number one would think, do deny them.

To this has to be added the kind of opposition expressed by one of the greatest of twentieth-century theologians—Karl Barth, particularly in his early works. When Barth was invited to give the Gifford Lecture[26] at Aberdeen University in 1935, he replied: 'I am an avowed opponent of all natural theology.'[27] Why? Principally because he saw theology as operating the other way round, not man reaching up to God by his reason, but God reaching down to man by his grace. Reason, like the rest of man's nature, Barth argued, is fallen and unredeemed and therefore incapable of reaching the truth about either God or man. For Barth, what reason cannot do, revelation can, and does.

In deciding the place of reason in the quest for theological

[26] Lectures delivered in the Scottish universities 'for promoting, advancing, teaching, and diffusing the study of natural theology'.
[27] Quoted by John Macquarrie, *Twentieth-Century Religious Thought* (S.C.M. 1963), p. 322.

truth one has to remember that reason is, like all men's faculties, a gift from God, affected by evil but not rendered ineffective by it. This means that it has to be given a proper place, not only in organizing, explaining, clarifying, criticizing, but also in leading at least to the boundaries of truth in theology, and sometimes across them. This demands a free course for reason, a willingness to follow wherever the thinking mind leads. But the findings of reason have to be tested against the other authorities now being considered.

C. RELIGIOUS EXPERIENCE

The last stage in formulating an answer to this question posed to Christian theologians about their knowledge of the truth is concerned with what actually happens to people. *Experience* is one of the sources of theology. There are two ways of speaking about religious experience and confusion will result unless one is clearly distinguished from the other.

(1) The broader view

Some years ago there was a series of religious meetings up and down the country under the title 'Religion and Life Campaign'. The slogan of that campaign, printed on all the publicity material and reiterated by countless clergymen at church hall meetings, was: 'Religion and life are one.' It was an honest attempt to relate the Christian faith to the practicalities of daily living through a process of identification. 'Religion', said one of the speakers at one of those meetings, 'is an attitude of totality.' On this assumption all experience whatsoever is potential religious experience, and the difference between a religious man and a non-religious one is not that they have different experiences but that they interpret the same experiences differently.

If a theologian or a preacher approaches the matter in this way, then he will tackle questions about religious truth in the light of the whole range of human experiences, thus assuming a broader view of religious experience than was taken in chapter 1. The chapter on God[28] will consider how an analysis of normal human experiences (walking on hills, passing judgement on Nazi war criminals, laughing at jokes, keeping a baby quiet at night) can give intimations of a 'beyond in our midst' and so make belief in God easier for some modern people. Again, it is not difficult to see how other normal experiences (picking up a purse in the street and feeling compelled to take it to the police station, how one responds to the questions on the income tax return) have an immediate relation to that other feature of religion which was described under the heading of 'Values and Ethics'. It is then, by reference to the 'features of religion', that the religious man interprets experiences he shares with his fellow human beings. Indeed, that is what makes him religious.

There are two advantages in thinking of religion and religious experience in this broad way:

(i) To use the now familiar phrase, this is not to shut God out from his own dominions. If he is indeed God then he must in some fashion be concerned with, and involved in, the things that go on in the world and among the people who are his creation. And even if the concern and involvement are matters of mystery, they are enough to give a religious dimension to ordinary experience. As it is sometimes put, religion supplies a 'transcendental dimension' to the whole of life.

(ii) The other advantage is more practical. It enables theologians, and particularly preachers, to begin where people are. To be able to talk to and with people about the common happenings of every day is to speak their language at once. It is to handle not—as they might be tempted to put it—old texts, ceremonial mumbo-jumbo, unbelievable stories, incredible doctrines, but things that make up the stuff of their lives, things that, to them, are real. Without going into the questions raised by the experiential method of religious education, the advantages of this are obvious.

Other Christians, however, have their difficulties with this whole approach. If it is easy, they say, to begin where people are, it is also easy to stay where they are. It is often impossible to establish the progression referred to above from

28 Chapter 4.

ordinary, everyday experience to an equally real experience of all the 'features of religion'. Of course one could reply that such ordinary experiences as people have constitute religion for them, but that seems an unsatisfactory answer in the light of all we know religion to be. This leads us to a consideration of a narrower view.

(2) The narrower view

'Narrow' is not here used in an unfavourable sense. Its meaning is as in the sentence 'medieval London was full of narrow streets' and not as in 'some Christians are very narrow in their attitude to the theatre'. It is a matter of distinguishing religious experience from other forms of experience—musical, or sexual, for example—so that justice can be done to it. The narrowness is a question of specialization. This must involve definition. If religious experience is something different from other experience, then what sort of experience is it?

Again, we turn to the 'features of religion' and ask: what is actually experienced in the life of religious communities, in the recounting of the myths, in the practice of the ritual, in the worship of the gods, in the reading of the sacred texts, in the daily practice of religion? In general terms it is what John Macquarrie describes as 'the opening up of the dimension of the holy'[29] and in Christian terms it is the experience of God as he meets with man in Jesus Christ. The experiences of the numinous and of conversion described in the last chapter[30] are examples of it.

The manner of this (Christian) experience varies considerably. Sometimes God meets a person in the intensity of a private struggle: in the decision-making moments of a career, in a fight with suffering, in (less dramatically) the effort not to detest the managing director. Sometimes the encounter is in the intellectual quest, an experience not entirely unknown to the student of theology. Sometimes it is in the apprehension of beauty or in the contemplation engaged in by the quiet man.

[29] *Principles of Christian Theology*, p. 5.
[30] See pp. 31–3.

It is a mistake to suppose that the manner of a Christian experience should always be the same.

Further, it is clear that in situations of such variety *what is actually experienced* is not the same in one case as in another. In his decision-making moments a Christian may have a 'feeling in his bones' that one way is right for him, the other wrong. In his suffering he may have a sense of the closeness of God. In his private battle to avoid detesting the managing director he may experience repentance and forgiveness; and so forth. How then can all these varieties of experience be spoken of as experiences of God, graciously meeting with man in Jesus Christ?

Only, as has already been said, by recognizing that experience in religion does not stand on its own but is all of a piece with the other features. If we belong to the Christian community (itself a repository of many Christian experiences), worship the Christian God, read the Christian Scriptures, try to live the Christian life, then any religious experience we may have will be understood and interpreted in the terms of that community, that God, that book, that life. John Wesley has a sermon on 'The Witness of the Spirit' in which he describes the Christian experience of assurance:

And first, as to the witness to our spirit: the soul as intimately and evidently perceives when it loves, delights, and rejoices in God, as when it loves and delights in anything on earth. And it can no more doubt, whether it loves, delights and rejoices or no, than whether it exists or no.[31]

Then Wesley announces:

How this joint testimony of God's Spirit and our spirit may be clearly and solidly distinguished from the presumption of a natural mind, and from the delusion of the devil, is the next thing to be considered.[32]

His answer is:

[31] Sermon X, *Wesley's Standard Sermons* (Epworth 1921), Vol. 1, p. 210.
[32] P. 211.

... the holy Scriptures abound with marks, whereby the one may be distinguished from the other. They describe, in the plainest manner, the circumstances which go before, which accompany, and which follow, the true, genuine testimony of the Spirit of God with the spirit of the believer.[33]

Wesley is here relating an experience to the revelation and the experience recorded in the Bible. If he had been a Roman Catholic he might very well have related it instead to the ritual, the Mass.

This process of relating is salutary, for it guards against that excessive subjectivity which threatens all religious experiences. Fascist dictators who believe that God is calling them to exterminate their political enemies and mystics who claim to see the Blessed Virgin Mary at the bottom of the bed all need their experiences related to the rest of the Christian religion. Only then can they—and so it is with our own asserted Christian experience—be tolerably sure that they have in fact encountered the Christian God.

A comment can now be made on the relation between these two ways of looking at religious experience. They are similar in that they both refer experience to the rest of the Christian religion for an interpretation and a judgement. In so far as they are different—one narrowing down religious experience more than the other—perhaps that is simply because some Christians are quicker than others to impress the pattern of their religion upon their experience.

To sum up: when the theologian and the preacher attempt to answer the question 'How do you know?'?[34] an appeal will be made to:

Revelation (Christ—the Bible, Tradition)
Reason
Experience

In these our authority lies. Hence they are the sources of theology, and they indicate the criteria that will be used in the rest of this book.

[33] P. 211.   [34] See p. 50.

But first there are two more nettles to grasp: one theology or many? one faith or many?

A. ONE THEOLOGY OR MANY?

The discussions of both religious experience and the Bible have revealed the existence of at least two points of view. On these matters theologians of equal sincerity and competence see things differently. This phenomenon occurs over a wide field. On the basis of the definition of theology on p. 37, what possibility is there that all those committed to the Christian faith who have reflected upon it will agree in all their conclusions? None at all. It would of course make life much easier for preachers and those taking examinations in theology if one could speak of 'the Christian view of the Bible' or 'the Christian view of religious experience' and know that all Christians would understand these subjects in precisely the same way. But plainly it is not so, it never has been so,[35] and it is not likely to become so.

As this book considers systematically the main Christian doctrines, it will be apparent that there are points of disagreement in each of them.

Factors at work

What factors are at work to bring about this state of affairs? The cultural setting of theology[36] has something to do with it. For example, though there is much scholarly argument about the influence of other virgin birth stories on Christianity, it was easier to accept a miraculous virgin birth in, say, the first century or the twelfth than it is in the twentieth. Again, the place given to the Church as the traditional custodian of truth is also of significance—a much larger place in, say, the Middle Ages than now. Other factors are more personal to the theologian and the preacher. Both the operation of his reason and the nature of his experience may bring him to a different conclu-

[35] The New Testament itself contains several theologies (Pauline, Johannine, etc.) rather than one.
[36] See pp. 43-4.

71

sion from that of his colleagues. Furthermore, it is not merely that one man's theology is different from the next man's, but that one man's theology today may well be different from his theology of yesterday and different again from his theology of tomorrow. He could believe in predestination at twenty-five and disbelieve it at fifty-five, or the other way round. There is nothing reprehensible about this, for theology is a dynamic study and if a person's theology is not changing he may already have become a theological fossil.

Each age has its own theological controversy, vital to itself but dull—though by no means unimportant—to its successors. Who can now get excited over the Christology of Paul of Samosata in the third century? Who in 2160 will read avidly the 1960s' debate on whether or not God was dead? It would indeed be hard to find any doctrine in the Christian faith about which theologians of one sort or another had not disagreed. The recital of a common creed does not nullify this judgement, for once one stops to ask 'What does one *mean* by "We believe in the Holy Ghost, the holy Catholic Church, the Communion of Saints", and so on?' the variations begin to emerge.

What then can be done about this state of affairs? Are we to leave good Christian people for ever in a state of bewilderment? There are three possible ways of proceeding:

(1) Compulsion

One is to compel people to believe what they are told they must believe, and in some periods this has been on pain of being excommunicated or even burnt at the stake. It presupposes or involves a number of other matters:

(i) that the Church, and it alone, can make an absolute and clear distinction between truth and falsehood, orthodoxy and heresy;
(ii) that orthodoxy is the way of salvation and heresy the way of damnation, the Church having a sacred duty to save people from damnation;
(iii) that there is a 'secular arm', a State willing and able to

enforce the judgement of the orthodox, authoritative Church, providing the faggots and lighting them.

These contentions are historically significant but theologically irrelevant, for none of them can be sustained today. The theological ferment in all the churches disproves the first, the undoubted existence of the saintly non-orthodox now disproves the second and the inconceivability of the British Army setting fire to the Moderator of the Free Church Federal Council disproves the third.

(2) Freedom

The second possible way to deal with the problem of theological pluriformity or pluralism (to give it its technical name) is precisely the opposite—to let everybody believe exactly what he likes. In May 1975 in the *Epworth Review*, the theological journal of the Methodist Church, this position was ably argued by Henry Rack. He first rejects the way already described and then asserts that 'the old instincts are by no means dead'. There are those who think that the future for Christianity lies in 'a situation of doctrinal unity, of conformity'. But Rack does not see it that way at all:

> I would argue that, on the contrary, the more healthy, the more honest, the more fruitful future lies in doctrinal freedom. . . . It is understandable that at this point there should be those who will ask: what, then, is the distinction between orthodoxy and heresy, between the Christian and the non-Christian? Is it a matter of anyone who wants to be called a Christian being allowed to count as one? anyone who wants to begin, or continue, to be associated with the Church, being allowed to do so? In practical terms I think it does mean exactly this.[37]

This view of Christians would see them as committed, or seeking to commit themselves, to Jesus Christ (though there would be much debate about this) but for the rest to be as open (or as closed) as they would wish.

[37] *Epworth Review*, May 1975, p. 17.

73

(3) 'Our doctrines'

There is a third way that lies between these two, though in point of time it has followed the first but preceded the second. It is the way of setting up standards of doctrine to which some Christians (ordained ministers and lay preachers particularly) are required to conform, but which allow for a measure of flexibility. This is the way used officially by the Methodist Church, so it must be given space.

The doctrinal standards of the Methodist Church are contained in Clause 30 of the *Deed of Union* and as this is a foundation document the first three paragraphs are quoted in full:

30 *Doctrine*. The doctrinal standards of The Methodist Church are as follows:

The Methodist Church claims and cherishes its place in the Holy Catholic Church which is the Body of Christ. It rejoices in the inheritance of the Apostolic Faith and loyally accepts the fundamental principles of the historic creeds and of the Protestant Reformation. It ever remembers that in the Providence of God Methodism was raised up to spread Scriptural Holiness through the land by the proclamation of the Evangelical Faith and declares its unfaltering resolve to be true to its Divinely appointed mission.

The Doctrines of the Evangelical Faith which Methodism has held from the beginning and still holds are based upon the Divine revelation recorded in the Holy Scriptures. The Methodist Church acknowledges this revelation as the supreme rule of faith and practice. These Evangelical Doctrines to which the Preachers of The Methodist Church both Ministers and Laymen are pledged are contained in Wesley's Notes on the New Testament and the first four volumes of his sermons.

The Notes on the New Testament and the 44 Sermons are not intended to impose a system of formal or speculative theology on Methodist Preachers, but to set up standards of preaching and belief which should secure loyalty to the fundamental truths of the Gospel of Redemption and ensure the continued witness of the Church to the realities of the Christian experience of salvation.

The negative reference to the imposition of a system of formal or speculative theology is a rejection of the kind of rigid, compulsory orthodoxy that was noted above. Methodists obviously do not intend to consign to damnation those who do not accept John Wesley's theology to the last jot and tittle. Instead, they have 'standards', and here there is room for manoeuvre. Again the *Deed* refers to 'the fundamental principles of the historic creeds and of the Protestant Reformation'. But what are they? Some are obvious enough: it would be hard to exclude the existence of God or the Incarnation (leaving aside for the moment what we mean by these doctrines). But do they include the Virgin Birth (in the creeds), the Second Advent (also in the creeds) and the doctrine of predestination (a feature of the Reformation)? Reference to loyalty to 'the fundamental truths of the Gospel of Redemption' raises the same kind of question. It would include presumably the work of Christ (again allowing liberty of interpretation) but would it include the Fall of man and original sin? There is flexibility both in what 'principles' and 'truths' are to be included in the 'standards' and in the meaning of 'principles' and 'truths' once they are included.

This is no cause for complaint. Admittedly there is the considerable, sometimes the agonizing difficulty of drawing a boundary line over which a Methodist preacher cannot step without ceasing to be a Methodist preacher[38] (a minister was put out in 1971 for asserting that he did not believe in God). But there are advantages. For one thing, no one can take the dogmatic view that he is right and everybody else is wrong, and that is that. For another, and this must be stressed lest flexibility be mistaken for theological levity, the doctrinal clause does do what presumably its authors intended: it draws attention to the existence of basic, fundamental doctrines in the Christian tradition, loyalty (however interpreted) to which prevents Methodist preachers having one-man-band theologies of their own and calling them both Christian and Methodist. The doctrinal clause makes it clear that our heritage is 'the faith once delivered to the saints'.

Furthermore, in the delicate question of interpreting 'our doctrines' the *Deed of Union* provides some help. In Clause 31

[38] There is a similar boundary line with regard to the basis of membership. It is only those who, as the Deed of Union puts it, 'confess Jesus Christ as Lord and Saviour and accept the obligation to serve Him in the life of the Church and the world' who are welcome as full members of the Church. The Standing Orders make provision for expulsion.

75

it is laid down that 'The Conference shall be the final authority within the Methodist Church with regard to all questions concerning the interpretation of its doctrines'. The Conference is charged with drawing the boundary lines. Now anyone who has sat through many sessions of the Methodist Conference may well wonder whether it is a suitable instrument for interpreting fine points of theology. But what it does is to provide what these doctrinal clauses permit: a forum for theological debate, a platform for this style of theology and that, a fellowship within which we can learn tolerance and charity in theological affairs and find our tensions to be creative. And from time to time the Conference issues statements[39] that carry forward the work of interpretation.

B. OTHER FAITHS

If there is not one theology but many theologies, are the theologies of other faiths included in the many?[40] Does pluralism embrace Islam, Buddhism, Hinduism and the rest?

Scholars have debated this issue for many years, but at other levels it has hardly been an open question. Methodists sing lustily at their overseas missions anniversaries:

> Let the song go round the earth,
> Lands where Islam's sway
> Darkly broods o'er home and hearth,
> Cast their bonds away ...[41]

while Anglicans (and those Methodists who follow the Book of Common Prayer) have been praying every Good Friday for a very long time that God would have mercy upon 'all Jews, Turks, Infidels, and Heretics' and that he would take from them 'all ignorance, hardness of heart, and contempt of Thy Word'. To suggest that the theology of these people for whose liberation and deliverance we have been singing and praying should stand alongside our own would startle many Christians,

---

[39] For example, on baptism and ordination.
[40] See the definition of theology on p. 37.
[41] MHB 806.

not least those missionaries who went out to convert to Christianity as many 'Jews, Turks, Infidels and Heretics' as they possibly could.

The reasons for a change in attitude need no great elaboration. During the later nineteenth century Western scholars of distinction gave themselves to Oriental studies and disclosed to the Western world that there was very much more to non-Christian religions than heathens in their blindness bowing down to wood and stone. Educated people became aware that the treasures of the East included spiritual riches; that the reason Muslims kept to their Islam and Buddhists to their Buddhism was not wilful ignorance and perversity but simply that they were quite sure that they already had all they required. In our own time the situation has been planted on our doorstep through immigration and now everybody except the incurably prejudiced realizes that other faiths mean as much to their adherents as Christianity does to Christians. In a multi-racial society the questions at the head of this section are thrust at us.

What of the answers? At least we have progressed far enough in charity and mutual respect for the possibility of dialogue between theologians of different faiths to be a genuine one. We will talk any day to our opposite numbers. But how shall we talk? There are those who think that dialogue in this situation is essentially an exercise in clarification. For a Christian theologian to talk to a Muslim theologian in this context means that they should both come to a deeper understanding of the other's religion. This is not to be despised, of course, for much prejudice is the result of ignorance and misunderstanding, but is it as far as dialogue can take us? This is the point where Christians, or at least those who have thought about it, approach the matter in different ways.

Christianity unique?

Many Christians contend that, though they seek good relationships with people of other faiths, and wish to share in the dialogue of understanding, beyond this they are not able to go. They find it impossible to compromise on their belief that the truth as they have come to know it in the Christian revelation is the final, the ultimate, the unchangeable truth and no dialogue, however well-intentioned, can ever alter that. If God has revealed his truth to people of other faiths, it is a partial revelation of what is wholly disclosed in Christ. The precise sticking point is indeed the uniqueness of Jesus Christ. If he was God himself in human form, the complete and final revelation, and if God was in him actually effecting salvation for all mankind, how can there be any accommodation to people who deny these things? This point of view has been put by John Baker, writing in the *Expository Times*.[42] After stating the Christian claim that 'in Jesus of Nazareth God had been living a genuine human life', Baker continues:

> As defined in all its classical rigour this is the unique feature of the Christian religion. A God of goodness, a Creator who cares, it shares with Judaism, Islam, and philosophical theism. A man who truly reflects the nature of the divine is no new thing to the Hindu. A divinely inspired prophet, even one miraculously born, is acceptable to Islam. The Spirit of God indwelling men and guiding and strengthening their lives is a religious commonplace. Divine food received in a sacramental meal is Zoroastrian and Melanesian. Ritual washings and initiation rites are found universally. Islam holds fast to judgment, heaven and hell; Judaism to repentance, amendment, and God's merciful pardon; both to eternal life. At every point accommodation is possible save at this one: this unique claim about Jesus, with the metaphysical structure needed to support it, the doctrine of the Holy, Blessed and Undivided Trinity.

This is the traditional view. To depart from it would be, for many Christians, a denial of their faith and of their commitment to Christ.

More to be said?

Those Christians who think that there is still more to be said usually begin to say it by stressing the activity of God in other faiths (this would not be denied by the others). It is interesting

[42] November 1975, Vol. LXXXVII, No. 2, p. 36.

to notice that a predecessor of this present textbook, *Christian Foundations*, by Maldwyn Hughes, first published in 1927, took a step in this direction. Hughes wrote:

> There is wide agreement today that the non-Christian religions cannot be dismissed as 'false' since with much error there are mingled genuine revelations of God.[43]

Whether Hughes then had second thoughts, supposing that he had given away too much,[44] or whether he was taken to task by a more cautious colleague, we do not know, but he added a footnote:

> It should be noted, however, that these (the revelations) are discovered in so far as the light of Christ is cast upon them.

Advocates of the liberal view would certainly stress the activity of God throughout the religions of mankind—it is yet again the question of excluding the Lord of truth from his own dominions. In talking with people of other faiths they would even feel it right to recognize that God could well have revealed to non-Christians things withheld from Christians.

Hughes's footnote can hardly be contested *as far as Christians are concerned*. We must inevitably see and judge other faiths in the light of Christ. This does not necessarily mean, as some Christians assume, that 'seeing things in the light of Christ' reveals them as inferior to their Christian counterparts. The 'peaceful, kindly disposition as the basic stance of life'[45] of Buddhism is superior to the aggression sometimes found among Christians, but we judge it to be so because that is how we see the matter 'in Christ'. We do not, of course, expect non-Christians to proceed in this fashion, hence the italicized phrase above.

As far as non-Christians are concerned, and this is where the advocates of deeper dialogue pursue their cause, they see

43 P. 6.
44 His overall position approximates to that described in the previous section.
45 See p. 35.

79

things the other way round. They look at Christianity, and at Christ, in the light of what lies at the heart of their own faith. As Max Warren puts it:

> If there is, indeed, a common religious consciousness which unites mankind (Warren has just been arguing that there is) then the significance of the true Manhood of Christ becomes of importance in a new way. He really is 'Very Man' and must be expected to appeal as such to all kinds of men who meet him and who do so inescapably against the background of their own religious and cultural heritage. It will be with their own eyes that they will see him.[46]

How does Jesus of Nazareth look to people whose roots are in ancient Indian and Chinese cultures and not in the Hebrew religion, the Greek philosophy and the Roman law that make up ours? This is a question as yet unanswered, and indeed hardly asked, except on the most superficial level of the shouting match. If it is asked:

> Can we face the disconcerting fact that our orthodoxies may appear to such discoverers to be heresies—relative distortions of the Truth? And should that be disconcerting, seeing how impossible it is for finite minds to comprehend the infinite?[47]

Is this selling the Christian faith down the river, as some would contend? Or does it, as Warren hopes, 'afford a way towards discovering a unity *in Christ*?'[47]

Such developments will be bound to influence our Christian stance. So Hans Küng asserts that in the course of missionary dialogue:

> even Christendom within its own field would *not simply* remain in *possession* of the known truth, *but would be in search* of the even greater and so constantly new unknown truth.[48]

There is the possibility of an exciting future in this field.

46 'Religious Pluralism—some theological implications for the Christian', *New Fire*, Vol. iii, No. 23, Summer 1975, p. 308.
47 P. 309.
48 Hans Küng, *On Being a Christian* (Collins 1977) p. 115 (Author's italics).

The theologies of other faiths, then, must stand alongside our own. In what precise sense they do is not easy to define nor to agree about. For our part, we look for what God has revealed in them, prepared to be surprised. And certainly we want the people of other faiths to look long and hard at the heart of Christian theology: that God was in Christ, reconciling the world to himself.

Chapter 3

Theology and Living

M A R T I N L U T H E R once wrote 'Not reading or speculating make a man a theologian, but living, dying and being damned'.[1] There could not be a better text for this chapter. At this point John Macquarrie's definition of theology[2] is slightly inadequate. It is arguable that 'participation in . . . a religious faith' can include 'living, dying and being damned', but it will not immediately seem to do so to many people. The relation of theology to living needs to be more fully explored and expressed.

If Martin Luther is right, a person makes his theology *as he lives* (we can include dying and being damned in this for the sake of convenience!) As Colin Morris is reported to have said in a sermon: 'You do not think yourself into a new way of living. You live yourself into a new way of thinking.' One more source of theology to add to the list is the daily life of mortal man. Christians should be able to say about their theology what is said (with less justification) about the *News of the World*: 'All human life is there'.

That some 'reading or speculating' is necessary in theology, even Martin Luther would have to admit, for he did his fair share of both. We are, after all, concerned with a study. But if the 'reading or speculating' takes over and the 'living, dying and being damned' never come into it at all, then the theology that results will be a rarefied breed, likely to justify the 'Harold Wilson' view of the subject referred to earlier.[3] The following

[1] Quoted in E. Gordon Rupp, *The Word and the Words* (Baptist Lay Preachers Association), pp. 8–9.
[2] See pp. 37–8.   [3] See p. 36.

82

may not give enough encouragement to preachers studying theology from a book, but it makes the present point:

> The Church needs practical theologians who spend all their time bringing the Gospel to bear on matters like medical ethics and industrial relations, and, even more, bringing the Gospel to individual people in individual situations. It also needs theoreticians who relate all the practical theologies of the moment to the great Christian traditions and work out a massive, consistent theological system that comprehends them all. Which function can you and I fulfil? The question will not take most of us long to answer. Theology of the second kind is quite vital to the life of a Church, but it calls for very special gifts. Fortunately a relatively small number of systematic theologians can maintain the theological vitality of a large Christian body. At no time has Methodism boasted more than a handful of theoreticians of this kind, and few of us will imagine ourselves included in their number. We are the practical theologians, and that, surely, gives us the point at which we begin.[4]

Granted, then, that our kind of theology is intimately related to daily life, just how is it related? Where do we begin, with the daily life or with the systematic theology? Not surprisingly there is more than one answer to these questions.

(1) Beginning where we are

There is no lack of people today who are sure that priority must be given to the actual situations of daily life. These situations are, in their view, the ground of theology. Practical, amateur theologians like you and me begin with them, and in them we have to ask and attempt to answer such questions as: 'What is right and what is wrong for me here?', 'What does "being a Christian" now, demand of me?', 'What value must I put on my fellow man in this situation and why?', 'Am I accountable for what I now do?', 'Is there any power outside myself affecting this situation?', 'Is this actual situation caught

---

[4] W. David Stacey, 'The Gospel and Theology' in *The Preacher's Handbook* No. 2, New Series, *About the Gospel* (Local Preachers' Department of the Methodist Church 1971), pp. 12–13.

up in some large pattern which has an end?'. It is when committed Christians reflect on these matters that their theology begins to take shape.

Some of the emerging theologies of our own time illustrate this very clearly. Black theology, the theology of revolution, the theology of development, the theology of liberation, stem directly from the injustices and deprivations experienced in modern social systems. Alistair Kee has this to say about Black theology:

> Black theology arises from the experience of black Christians in America, especially as they were caught up in the political sequence which began with the civil rights movement of the late 1950s and the early 1960s. . . .
> For those who are aware of the assimilation of Christianity and Western (white) culture and who wish to find some way of distancing the one from the other, the most exciting thing about black theology is that it springs from another cultural setting altogether. But in so far as the experience of the black community is one of oppression, injustice, suffering and powerlessness then there is the possibility that this experience may lead to a truer appreciation of the gospel than is possible for those who live in a society that is affluent and exercises power in the world at large.[5]

Black theology arises out of the real life situation of black people. Take away the life situation of the blacks and there is nothing left to distinguish this theology from any other. This is theology from living, not to mention dying and being damned.

It is possible to support this style of making a theology simply on grounds of educational method. 'Beginning where people are' is reckoned to be sound teaching, technique, in theology as in other subjects. The 'experimental method', as it is called, of religious education works on this basis. Thumb through a modern Sunday school teachers' guide book and you will find that more often than not lessons begin with questions or discussions about what actually happens to young

---

[5] 'Black Theology' in *A Reader in Political Theology* (S.C.M. 1974), pp. 113, 117.

people ('Write down an incident during the past when you know you should have said you were sorry') or with records or play-readings or home-spun stories sung or written in the language of the children and within the range of their day-to-day experience. From such beginnings the teacher is able—so supporters of this method would argue—to progress to the explanation and advocacy of religious truth as yet neither understood nor experienced by the children. Theology is an enterprise that would profit from similar treatment, so one must begin where people are.

But there is a profounder argument than the one about method. The content of the faith that theology seeks to express involves, as subsequent chapters will show, the truth and reality of God, of Jesus Christ, of the Holy Spirit, of salvation and so forth. Theology is concerned with what is true and what is real. Some theologians are content to leave the matter there. Others relate the meaning of words like 'true' and 'real' to human experience, i.e. the situations, the events, the experiences that make up people's daily lives. If our authentic existence (as it is sometimes called) consists of that which is truth and reality for us (it is *true* that for me nature is both beautiful and cruel; the generosity of my father is a *reality* in my life) then it has to be incorporated into our theology. And the sooner the better. So let us start with what we have. Advocates of this view would think that it is better to begin with forgiving, reconciling relationships actually experienced between people in contention than with the theories of the Atonement, with experiences of being resurrected from living deaths in one's own existence than with the empty tomb, with the oppression of black men by white men in Southern Africa and the U.S.A. than with the Epistle to the Galatians.

(2) Beginning at the other end

So far there has been no plastering of theological labels all over these pages. 'Radical', 'conservative', 'existential', and so forth have been avoided, chiefly because this enables arguments to be considered on their merits and not to be subjected to prejudice because of the label they carry. This will generally continue to be done but there are points where to identify a position as belonging to a particular theological school may help the student of the subject the more easily to find his way around. This is perhaps one of those points. If theology has to have a right wing and a left, then the position we have just outlined tends to the left and the one to which we now turn tends to the right.

The holders of this view contend that the proper movement is not from experience to revelation (to use the headings from chapter 2) but the other way round. However practical a Christian may aspire to be in his theology, he must start with God's disclosure of himself in Christ and then proceed to his experience. The order is from theology to living. And this is true whether the experience is either all experience whatsoever (the 'broader view' of pp. 66–8 or 'religious' experience (the 'narrower view' of pp. 68–70).

(i) The narrower view
Some Methodist theologians have carried a torch for Christian experience. Henry Bett, for example, wrote:

> Methodism, without altogether realizing what it was doing, shifted the ultimate authority in religion to the last place and the right place—to religious experience.... It is not too much to claim that in the primacy accorded to religious experience Methodism carried forward the work of the Reformation to its legitimate and logical conclusion.[6]

As a reaction against the cold formality of much eighteenth century religion this emphasis upon the religion of the heart is understandable, but the advocates of the view now being considered would point out that religious experience does not take place in a vacuum. There must be *something* to be experienced. By all means, they say, let experience confirm the truth of the Christian revelation, but let us not mistake the confirmation for that which it is confirming. John Wesley did not make this mistake. Consequently other Methodist scholars put the matter rather differently from Henry Bett:

6 *The Spirit of Methodism* (Epworth 1937), pp. 93–4, 102.

He [John Wesley] based his theology on the Bible and 'experience', but far more on the Bible than on experience.[7]

It is not difficult to substantiate this position from Wesley's works. The primacy of the revelation in Scripture runs through all his sermons, *followed* by the invitation to a confirmatory experience. One example will suffice. In the sermon, 'The way to the Kingdom', as he expounds Mark 1 : 15 he says:

> *The gospel* (that is, good tidings, good news for guilty, helpless sinners) in the largest sense of the word, means, the whole revelation made to men by Jesus Christ; and sometimes the whole account of what our Lord did and suffered while He tabernacled among men. The substance of all is, 'Jesus Christ came into the world to save sinners'.[8]

Wesley exhorts his hearers to believe this, and the Kingdom of God will be theirs. *Then* they will possess 'righteousness, and peace, and joy in the Holy Ghost', i.e. Christian experience.

(ii) The broader view
If this view of what constitutes religious experience is taken it is argued that the movement should still be in the same direction, from revelation to experience, from theology to living. The word that is greatly used in this connection is the word 'apply'. The Christian revelation, the Gospel has to be *applied* to the situations of daily life. Thus a social worker who is a humanist (or indeed a Christian holding the left-wing view already described) will regard his work as its own justification. He is there to help people in need just because they are people in need. But a Christian of this persuasion will be a social worker because that is for him the application of the Gospel: that God loves all men, that Christ died for them on the Cross, that Christians are called to love and serve others for Christ's sake and so forth. This is the traditional way of looking at the Christian life in the world. That is not, however,

7 Rupert E. Davies, *Methodism* (Epworth 1976), p. 82.
8 *Wesley's Standard Sermons*, ed. Edward H. Sugden (Epworth 1935), Vol. 1, p. 159.

to consign it to the past, for many modern Christians are convinced that this is the right way for them to proceed.

Where then does one begin?

Does one start from living and move towards theology or the other way round? And is it irresponsible to suggest that in the last resort it does not greatly matter, provided that the end result is the same and that living and theology are brought into a close and permanent relationship? Among other things, our religious tradition (especially the denominational one), our friends, our psychology and often the apparently trivial accidents of life determine whether we start from A or B. And some of us succeed in starting from both! But the starting point does not greatly matter so long as the journey is made.

The reader, then, can follow his own bent in the ensuing discussion of theology and living in the three areas of faith, hope and love. They are chosen because together they express the basic stance of the committed Christian.

A. FAITH

It is necessary first to notice that the word 'faith' is used in two different ways. Consider these sentences:

I put my faith in herbal medicines
I have faith in God

and compare them with:

John Henry Newman embraced the Roman Catholic faith
Praise God for the faith once delivered to the saints.

The first instances are concerned with *the faith by which* something is believed or trusted and in the second instances with *the faith that is* believed or in which people put their trust. The Christian religion has both usages, for our faith without *the* faith is simply a preoccupation with religious feelings and *the* faith without *our* faith is a set doctrines that can be described without being believed—the stance adopted in chapter 1. It is necessary in all talk about faith that this

88

distinction be borne in mind. This section is concerned with the faith by which something is believed. *The* faith is the overall subject of subsequent chapters.

(1) Faith in the Bible

It would be most useful to the writers and readers of theological books if it were possible to go to *the* (for Christians) theological book and find there a simple and clear account of such a fundamental matter as faith. But the Bible is a library spanning two thousand years of history, not an introductory guide to the study of theology. Profound truth is there, but it does not usually lie on the surface. Such is the case with faith.

In the Old Testament

It is something of a shock to discover that concordances of the Bible have virtually nothing to offer on faith in the Old Testament. The word occurs only twice in the Authorised Version and less than ten times in most other versions. Hence the question: if the Old Testament uses the word so sparingly, what has it to say in this field?

Certainly there are over a hundred instances in the Old Testament of the Hebrew word commonly translated 'trust'. 'Trust' can be placed in fortified walls (Deut. 28:52) or in a bow (Ps. 43:6) or in a person (Judges 9:26, where the word 'confidence' is used); or in God (2 Kings 18:5; 19:10).

There is another Hebrew word, used in this area of meaning, that is the despair of translators. Our *Amen* (much stronger than 'so be it') is derived from it. It refers to that which is unshakeable and dependable, a house (1 Sam. 2:35) or a kingdom (2 Sam. 7:16), and means, furthermore, that the person who recognizes dependability in a thing or a person takes some of that dependability into his own character (Hab. 2:4). So the unshakeability of the rock makes those who shelter in it unshakeable too (Ps. 62:2, 6–7). The rock is a metaphor for God. In the Old Testament he is the one who, in all his actions, is unshakeable and dependable, and these

89

qualities 'rub off' on those who, like Abraham, trust him and
do his will.

In the New Testament

The New Testament inherits from the Old the faith-evoking,
rock-like existence and power of God and then faces the
question as to whether that existence and power are now made
evident in the life of Jesus. The answer is a resounding yes.
It is the 'yes' of faith, given when Jews recognize Jesus as
Messiah and Gentiles call him Lord. The matter is divisive
(Matt. 10:34), one of life and death (John 6:53-4). Either you
see the Rock in Christ, are seized by it and respond in faith,
or you do not see it, fail to be seized by it and are lost in
unbelief.

This was the confrontation that occurred when people met
Jesus in the flesh. Some responded to him in faith, others did not.
The importance of miracles in this connection is considerable.
There is debate about whether miracles evoke faith (John 2:11,
23; 4:48) or whether they are a response to faith already present
(Matt. 8:13; 9:28; Mark 5:34), but this is to introduce the
kind of analysis that comes naturally to Western minds but
not to Hebrew ones. Faith in Jesus was bound up with the
miracles of Jesus. Where there was no faith there were no
miracles (Mark 6:5). The analysis goes no further than that.

A large part of the New Testament, however, is concerned
with the period after the life of Jesus and here the choice is
offered in the proclamation, the preaching, about Jesus. This
essential activity ('And how are they to hear without a
preacher?'—Rom. 10:14), passionately done, asserts that the
unshakeable, dependable God acted in raising Jesus from the
dead (Rom. 10:9). Those who then believe that he did are
the people of faith, confessing Jesus as Lord, and they are the
saved. It is all so obvious to Paul that the problems are caused
by the people who do not and will not respond in faith.

The same pattern is found in the Gospel according to John.
The noun 'faith' does not occur at all in this gospel, but the
verb 'to have faith', 'to believe' (there is no need to distinguish
between those two for the moment) is on every page. It is

again the response to Jesus, knowing who he is (the 'I am' sayings, 6:51; 10:9–14; 11:25; 14:6) and that God is acting in him and through him (14:10); it is believing in him (14:1,12; 17:20). Not to respond by believing, by having faith, is sin (16:9), but the results of faith for the believer are incalculably good (3:16; 5:24; 6:35; 11:26, etc.).

This pattern is not dissimilar from the Old Testament one. It begins with the acceptance of the unshakeable reality of God, whose activity is now focused in Jesus and proclaimed as such by Christian preachers. Some people, though not all, are seized by the message and confess that it is true; they believe, they have faith—not only *that* the message is true but *in* God, the God of the Old Testament and the one who acted in Jesus. The result is that what is of God (though of course not *all* that is of God) is transmitted to the person of faith. In both the Old Testament and the New the Rock gives a rock-like quality to believers so that at the end of the day they will not be shaken.

A Methodist theologian puts the matter like this:

The ground of faith is God's revelation of Himself, and offer of salvation, through Jesus Christ.

Jesus Christ is presented to man, first in human form then in the content of the preached word. This word demonstrates Christ's fulfilment of Old Testament prophecy and preparation, affirms His Messiahship and the coming of the Kingdom of God in Him, describes His saving work as the only ground of our approach to God, explains why it is so and exhorts men to repent and believe.

To believe is to accept as trustworthy the Person of Christ as revealed in His earthly ministry and declared in the gospel message. It is so to be convinced about His trustworthiness as to seek a relationship with God through Him. It is decisively to commit oneself to Him, trusting only in Him for salvation, entering into the meaning of His death and resurrection, yielding one's allegiance to Him. It is to see the realities of eternal life which are invisible to the human eye and to experience divine power in one's daily life.[9]

[9] Donald English, 'Faith in the New Testament', *About Faith* (Local Preachers' Department of the Methodist Church 1972), p. 53.

(2) Faith in daily life

The previous paragraphs, sketchy as they are on a subject on which volumes could be written, may be of more assistance to the person who finds it best to move from revelation to daily life than to the person who does the journey the other way round. What is faith for the latter?

At this point, in order to elucidate what is meant by faith in a twentieth-century setting, it is necessary to draw the distinction between faith and belief. That distinction exists in the New Testament but is not always apparent because the verb that could be translated as 'have faith in' could also be, and often is, translated 'believe in'. It is therefore preferable to keep to modern usage. It is common, though by no means universal, to associate belief with propositions, i.e. belief *that* such and such a thing is the case. Consider:

I believe that crime does not pay
I believe that Jesus walked on the water
I believe that all good people go to heaven.

And contrast these sentences with the two with which this section began:

I put my faith in herbal medicines
I have faith in God.

Although the use of 'that' in the first group and 'in' in the second is not decisive[10] it is significant. 'That' introduces a proposition to be accepted or denied, but 'in' introduces a comprehensive process, much better described by the word 'faith'. If I really have faith in herbal medicines I not only accept the proposition that they are beneficial (I believe *that* they are): I talk about them and I stake the health of my body on them, drinking raspberry tea instead of going to the doctor. Faith in God is similarly comprehensive; it evokes commitment. Faith so conceived is the basic stance of a whole person towards something or somebody; it can, but it need not, include belief in the sense in which, for convenience, it has been described.

[10] One can say 'I believe in God' and mean 'I believe that God exists'.

If we think in these terms it is faith, not belief, that emerges from daily life. A person may have all sorts of doubts about his belief and may be prepared to say 'I believe *that* x or y is the case' about very little, if anything. But he has faith in something or somebody for sure. He has a stance in life. He is committed, in word and deed. The object of it may be Sunday school teaching or greyhound racing, social work or making money, God or the workers' revolution. He does his own thing, in faith.

At this point the contribution of the biblical revelation is not to leap in and demand that faith must immediately issue in belief in this or that proposition as being true, though this has its importance. Rather it is to exemplify what faith (in God in this case) can mean in action—what life-style is involved, to use twentieth-century words. Not for nothing is Abraham the great exemplar of faith in the Bible. He 'believed God' (Rom. 4:3) and 'by faith . . . obeyed when he was called to go out to a place which he was to receive as an inheritance; and he went out, not knowing where he was to go' (Heb. 11:8). This is the lifestyle of the pilgrim, of a person who is not shackled to the old, familiar places, who can shake the dust from off his feet and move on to new pastures with no regrets. It is still around in modern times: at one level there was little Edith Piaf refusing to be shackled by her past and putting her entire self into her song, *Je ne regrette rien*; at another there are names on the *In Memoriam* boards of theological colleges, of men who left the shelter of their studies to go as missionaries to West Africa when the life-expectancy there was five years at the most. Supremely there was Jesus, detached and free, having faith in God.

There are two elements in this life-style of faith that need specific reference. One is *trust*. Those who live by faith refuse to be mastered by their own suspicious natures. They trust other people. They ask few questions. They believe the best even when they fear the worst. Consequently they are of all men the most vulnerable, and the vulnerability would seem to be a mark of sanctity. This is indeed the place where the saints come marching in, for trust is indivisible and the people who give themselves away to others are so often those who give

93

themselves away to God. They are rewarded with his dependability, his unshakeability.

> He only is my rock and my salvation, my fortress;
> I shall not be greatly moved.—(Ps. 62: 2)

The other element is *obedience*. Another great twentieth-century theologian once wrote in an exposition of what it means for a Christian to keep the First Commandment: 'Faith is obedience—nothing else—literally nothing else at all'.[11] In the light of the other things that have been said this must be reckoned an exaggeration. It is however one that has to be made from time to time to save faith, not only from being equated with holding right beliefs or enjoying religious experience, but from becoming simply the doing of one's own thing. God is the object of Christian faith and the consequent life-style is not something Christians invent for themselves. It is what happens in practice when they take God seriously and, like Abraham, obey.

Trust and obedience are essential to the daily life of faith. Yet they take us back to the Bible, back to the Psalms, back to Abraham. Experience and revelation, living and theology, have their meeting place in the man of faith.

B. HOPE

It would not be difficult to structure this section exactly as the last one. It could begin with the difference between 'hoping' and 'the Christian hope', then turn to the usages of the words translated 'hope' in the Old and New Testaments and finish with some paragraphs on hope in daily life. There are, however, two reasons for not doing it in this way. One is that, with 'love' still to follow, tedium may set in. The other is that the intimate relationship between theology and living may be the more clearly demonstrated, not by keeping them separate, but by mixing them up.

[11] Emil Brünner, *The Mediator* (Lutterworth 1934), p. 592.

(1) The Last Things now

At one time every theological textbook ended in the same way. After treating of God, Man, Sin, Christ, the Holy Spirit, the Trinity, the Church and the Kingdom, it finished with a chapter that turned from the life here to the life hereafter. The final chapters of four textbooks for Methodist preachers a generation ago carried the titles 'The Last Things', 'Things to come', 'The things that shall be' and 'The Christian Hope'. The subject is known as eschatology from a Greek word meaning 'last' or 'end'. It covers such matters as the Second Coming of Christ (the Parousia), Death, Judgement, Heaven, Hell, the Resurrection of the Body and the Life Everlasting. Not surprisingly it was thought that a treatment of these subjects was a splendid way to end a book on theology. As with the book of Revelation, you finished up in the new Jerusalem.

This book, however, will not conclude like that. Not because these subjects are not of critical importance, but for precisely the opposite reason: they are *too* critically important to be left to a final chapter at which the reader arrives with most of his thinking done. One of the insights of theological study in our own time is that all theology has to be done in the light of 'the Last Things'. The final chapter should be written into every chapter. Jürgen Moltmann, a theologian who has commanded much attention in this field, puts it like this:

From first to last, and not merely in the epilogue, Christianity is eschatology, is hope, forward looking and forward moving, and therefore also revolutionizing and transforming the present. The eschatological is not one element *of* Christianity, but it is the medium of Christian faith as such, the key in which everything in it is set, the glow that suffuses everything here in the dawn of an expected new day.[12]

This view clearly gives us a new perspective in theology. What *will* happen affects profoundly what *is* happening now. The fact that a train is passing through Peterborough and

[12] *Theology of Hope* (S.C.M. 1965), p. 16.

95

not Wigan is determined partly by its having come from Leeds but, just as significantly, by its making for Kings Cross. To put it another way, every event can only be known and understood in terms of its consequences.

What then is the effect of the future on the present? Here is how a Methodist theologian sees this working out in the lives of Abraham and Moses:

> It (the 'living for the future' of Abraham and Moses) is not a future hope which deprives the present of its meaning, which turns it into an unpleasant interim, something to be lived through. It is a future hope which *makes sense of* the present. Abraham and Moses have got that look in their eye because what they are doing now makes sense in the light of what is to come, and what is to come makes sense in the light of what they are doing now.[13]

But how precisely does the future 'makes sense of' the present? What is meant by the phrase that John Robinson used in this context: 'The lastness of things'?

(2) Priorities

One meaning is that the knowledge that certain events are going to happen, events of immense significance both for the individual and the whole creation, and the knowledge that they could happen at any moment (I could be dead before I have finished writing this paragraph; the second coming of Christ could be on Friday week) is of considerable use in deciding priorities. If *the* crisis, either for us or for the world, is imminent (as it could be) then, as Dr Johnson said about the man who was to be hanged in a fortnight, it concentrates the mind wonderfully. If we have three months to live how shall we spend those three months? This was the kind of question that determined what the first Christians did with their time, though with them it was not so much that the End *could* come at any moment but that it *would*. They settled for the things of which they believed their Lord would approve (Mark 13:35–7; Matt. 24:42–7; 1 Thess. 5:1–11).

[13] Henry McKeating, *God and the Future* (S.C.M. 1974), pp. 23–4.

(3) Living in hope

There are two misconceptions to avoid if we are to see 'the lastness of things' in terms of a life full of hope. One is that 'hope' in English can be used in a very feeble sense (I hope that I can call to see you next time I am in town; I hope we shall have a white Christmas this year). Consequently to live in hope is thought to be a rather vague, tenuous procedure without much body to it.

The other is that some of the Last Things for which as Christians we are to hope are on the whole slightly forbidding if not actually grim. Death, Judgement, Hell and the End of all things do not sound cheerful prospects. How can we be expected to live in hope, which one thinks of as a positive, joyous activity, if the things hoped for are sombre and funereal?

The theologian welcomes the raising of such misconceptions as it gives him the opportunity of pointing out that the Last Things are entirely in the hands of God, both as to how they happen and when they will happen. He sits on the great white throne and he names the day. The kind of hope, therefore, that 'the lastness of things' makes possible is a hope in God. And what kind of a hope is that? Here the theologian brings the past to the help of the present and the future. He turns to his Bible and points out that the hope of Israel for a glorious future, under God, lay in their experience of what, in good times and bad, God had already done for them (Isa. 49:8-11). It was the God who delivered them at the exodus who would bring them to the Promised Land and establish his glorious kingdom on earth (Deut. 7:6-19; Micah 4:1-4). The God who had proved himself in the past had the future (and so the present) under control. In all these immense activities God is *for man*. In which case, the hope of what he will do for man in and through the Last Things is a good deal more than dreaming of a white Christmas and much more cheerful than the sort of undertaker's paradise referred to above. It is the sure and certain hope that what God has prepared for us out in the future is far, far more than either we could desire or (more obviously) deserve, *because he is*

97

that kind of God (1 Cor. 2:9; Col. 1:5; Titus 2:13). This is not knowledge. Nor is it faith. But it is hope, for sure.

(4) Life-style

To use this modern expression again, if the present is affected by a future of that kind, and if hope consists of being so affected, then hope, like faith, will have its own life-style. Such a life-style will not be a writing-off of the present, a concentration upon 'pie in the sky when you die' with a reluctant acceptance of bread and butter in the meantime. On the contrary it will be a life-style of affirmation, of confidence, of optimism, of good humour. Sin does not diminish it either, for it is the presence of hope that turns remorse into repentance. Jürgen Moltmann, has this fine paragraph on the subject:

> Does this hope cheat man of the happiness of the present? How could it do so! For it is itself the happiness of the present. It pronounces the poor blessed, receives the weary and heavy laden, the humbled and wronged, the hungry and the dying, because it perceives the parousia of the kingdom for them. Expectation makes life good, for in expectation man can accept his whole present and find joy not only in its joy but also in its sorrow, happiness not only in its happiness but also in its pain. Thus hope goes on its way through the midst of happiness and pain, because in the promises of God it can see a future also for the transient, the dying and the dead. That is why it can be said that living without hope is like no longer living. Hell is hopelessness, and it is not for nothing that at the entrance to Dante's hell there stand the words: 'Abandon hope, all ye who enter here.'[14]

As Moltmann suggests, such a life-style has its own attitude to the one certain thing about life—that it will come to an end. It approaches death, not with the negative resignation of 'when we're dead we're done for', nor with the brash assertion that beyond all possible doubt the trumpets will sound for us on the other side, but with *hope*. It may be so, it may not be so,

14 *Theology of Hope*, p. 32.

but, with some reason and confidence, we hope that it is so. Such hope pervades dying as well as death. Hopes that on this day a particular visitor may come, that this new drug will ease the pain, that the rose the other side of the window will not drop its petals before the weekend, are not inconsistent with the hope that death will be swallowed up in victory.

(5) A social hope

This section so far reads as if hope were only a matter of the individual's present and the individual's future. This is inadequate and certainly unbiblical. The hope of the Old Testament is the hope of Israel (Isa. 40:1-5; 44:1-5). Sometimes this is expressed in the this-worldly terms of political, economic and military success (Isa. 61:5-6; Amos 9:13-5), sometimes in the out-of-this-world language of the writers of the apocalyptic passages (Dan. 7-8), but the primary reference is to the chosen people of God, not to the individual Hebrew. In the New Testament hope is even more expansive: it is a cosmic hope (Eph. 1:3-10; Col. 1:15-20). This will be enlarged upon in the chapter on the Kingdom of God, but for the present it is enough to realize that the hope described in the Bible, the hope for which these paragraphs are contending, is not so much a matter of personal devotion and individual destiny, though these are certainly involved. It is a hope cherished by men together; it is a hope for society; it is a hope for all creation.

(6) Consummated in Christ

The Christian inevitably and properly relates his hope to Jesus Christ. If he is, as the Christian believes, the risen, ascended and reigning Lord, the judge of all men, the one who will come again in the Parousia, then what hope the Christian has for the Last Things will be determined by what hope he has in Christ. The Last Things now make sense for him because the one at the end of time is the one of whom he has present experience. His priorities are determined by what he sees in Christ; Christ is for him the supreme demonstration that God is indeed *for man*; his life-style is, as far as may be, an expression of his discipleship; his anticipations are the anticipations of the new Israel. The Christian's hope is in Christ, raised from the dead, and in what God will yet do for man through him.

C. LOVE

The consideration of 'Faith' began with the Bible and proceeded to daily life, the consideration of 'Hope' intertwined the two, so the consideration of 'Love' will begin with daily life and proceed to the Bible.

(1) Love in daily life

(i) The word
The Greek in which the New Testament was written had different words for different kinds of love. In English we are not so lucky. Consider the following:

I love Paris in the spring
Making love should be forbidden in films
She loved the baby as if it were her own
If men loved one another there would be no more war
I love bread and butter pudding.

Romantic, sexual, maternal, human (not the best of words), gastronomic—each lays claim to the use of the word and this inevitably means that the sense of one intrudes into another. For example human love (the 'goodwill among men' kind of love) is sometimes affected by the romantic, even the sexual, usage and becomes tinged with the sentimental. The use of the word 'love' is, however, unavoidable and all one can hope to do is to be as exact as possible in saying what is meant when it is used.

Christians frequently refer to human love, as they try to practise it, as 'Christian love'. This is permissible in two ways. One is that love of this kind is an identifiable part of the Christian tradition, advocated in the Christian Scriptures as

100

the Christian way of living; the other is that the motivation for such loving is a specifically Christian one, e.g. to please the Lord Jesus Christ, to bear the fruit of the Holy Spirit. What it would be presumptuous to claim (in the writer's view at least) is that the actual quality of loving in Christian love is superior to that found in all other human love. One just cannot go into a hospital ward and pick out the Christian nurses by the quality of their love (their nursing service, in practical terms) for the patients. There may be a different motive present (though that is by no means as simple as it sounds), but the test of love is in its fruits. On these assumptions the adjective 'Christian' will be dropped for the rest of this section.

(ii) Love is unselfish
In two ways at least it is. All the time, as a permanent stance, a continuing attitude towards mankind, it is concerned with other people. Those who live in this style are not therefore perpetually on the defensive, always making sure that their own position and rights are safeguarded. Such people can easily be caught out, for in the absence of careful self-interest they become vulnerable. They are the people who do not act swiftly against the 'hogger' in the bus queue nor speak incisively when another car makes a dent in theirs, not because of apathy or cowardice but because they do not go around this world poised for action in their own interests. Ruefully they think afterwards of all the things they could have said and done to put the aggressor in his place, but their pistols were not cocked. One hopes it is some consolation to know that this is the price they pay for loving their fellow men. It is because they are open to the rest of humanity and quick to see a human need that they do not excel at looking after themselves.

Love is also unselfish because it operates for the good of the person being loved, not the person doing the loving. Much of what masquerades under the name of love is selfish. The Victorian father in *The Barretts of Wimpole Street* doted on his invalid daughter, loved to sit by her bed and talk with her, prohibited friends and visitors and anything that might have brought a breath of life into her stuffy room. And when

101

at last the girl's lover outwitted him, the father's so-called love turned to furious hatred. His care and concern for his daughter would pass for love anywhere, but one does not need to be a psychologist to understand that Elizabeth Barrett's father loved her because of the comfort, the pleasure and the deep self-satisfaction that *he* found in it. Real love is for the sake of the beloved, not the lover.

(iii) Love is for the unlovable

This takes the matter even further. Love is for the sake of the person being loved even if there is nothing lovable about that person at all. Maternal love was included in the list and it is often spoken of as the deepest kind of love there is. But is it? When we see a baby in a pram, his podgy legs and hands, his bright eyes and clear skin, his eloquent gestures and winning smiles, we cannot help loving him and if he were our own flesh and blood we would be monsters not to. Babies seem to draw out of us the stare of affection that is part of our nature. In most cases we do not love babies deliberately but because we cannot help it. The test of real love is very different. It is all about the way in which we build up our relationships with the people we do not like and who do not like us, the hateful, unpleasant people who make life hard for us. Love is for them. Remember the story of Hosea and Gomer?

(iv) Love may not be successful

Sometimes it may. Persistent loving, even of the unlovable, may sometimes work. It can break down the psychological walls that people build up to protect themselves from others and establish new, creative relationships. It can help those who are seeking their identity to find it. But clearly we cannot be certain of this. If we could be then love would pay off every time. It would, so to speak, be good business—investing affection for a good return. The point is that what gives love its quality is that it goes on regardless of what the end will be. Failure does not deter it. Nothing does.

Love has so far been written of as a personal quality active in personal relationships. It also has a reference in social,

102

political, international spheres. Though still carried out by persons, for only persons can love, in these areas it is translated into other terms: the struggle for justice and freedom, for example. And here again it persists through failure. There are revolutionaries incarcerated in prisons in many parts of the world of whose violence we may disapprove but whose will for justice and freedom in the context of oppression is indomitable. What the crucifix does for the devout Catholic the poster of Che Guevara does for the revolutionary: it signifies that, whether in personal or social terms, there is no end to loving.

(v) Love as the sole motive

There are those who are so convinced of the truth of what has so far been said, and of much more besides, that they contend that in any situation all that matters is what love is compelled to do. Over the last decade or so this has been evident in a debate between those who believe in acting according to fixed principles and those called 'situationists' who believe that in any given situation one can only ask, and do, what love demands.[15] The chief situationist of our times can speak for himself:

> ... *Christian* situation ethics has only one norm or principle or law (call it what you will) that is binding and unexceptionable, always good and right regardless of the circumstances. That is 'love'—the *agapē* of the summary commandment to love God and the neighbour. Everything else without exception, all laws and rules and principles and ideals and norms, are only *contingent*, only valid *if they happen* to serve love in any situation. Christian situation ethics is not a system or program of living according to a code, but an effort to relate love to a world of relativities through a casuistry obedient to love. It is the strategy of love.[16]

Thus, for example, one does not say 'Abortion is wrong in principle. Therefore she must have the baby'. One asks 'Does

---

[15] It is doubtful whether anyone can be a hundred per cent one or the other.

[16] Joseph Fletcher, *Situation Ethics* (S.C.M. 1966), pp. 30–1.

103

love for the mother, the father, the family, the unborn child and society as a whole demand, in this particular situation, abortion, or not?'

There are obvious objections to situationism: not knowing how anybody is going to behave until he actually does, the confusion of many motives in the omnibus term 'love', and the desirability of having guidelines, if not hard and fast principles, to help in the delicate and complicated processes of decision-making. The equally obvious factor in its favour is the primacy it gives to love.

(vi) Love and theology
As Christians try to love people in the fashion described they are in fact expressing their theology. They are stating in the clearest possible way, by their deeds as well as by their words, what they believe. For them this has the stamp of that which is *ultimate* upon it or, to put it more colloquially, this is what it's all about. Does the Bible confirm them in this view?

(2) Love in the Old Testament

This paragraph is designed simply to put right a misconception: that love only enters religion with the New Testament; that before Jesus Christ men only feared God; that their relationships with one another in Old Testament times were determined by law. A glance at the entry under 'Love' in any concordance of the Bible will quickly disprove this, though love of God for men and love of God by men are more evident than love of men for one another. The book of Deuteronomy, for example, has a dozen or so references to the love of man for God and about half that number of the love of God for man. It includes a passage which, after asking Israel what God requires of them but that they should love him (10:12) as he had loved them (10:15), goes on to assert that God also loves the sojourner (the non-Israelite) (10:18) and therefore Israel should do the same (10:19). Love is also an Old Testament word.

104

(3) Love in the New Testament

It is in the New Testament that the word comes into its own. The Greek word for sexual love does not appear in the New Testament but two words, both translated 'love', do. The following paragraph, culled from a Greek lectionary, makes the matter clear to all, whether they have little Greek or none at all:

> *Agapao* (one of the words) is commonly understood properly to denote love based on esteem,[17] as distinct from that expressed by *phileo* (the other word), spontaneous natural affection, emotional and unreasoning. If this distinction holds, *agapē* is fitly used in the New Testament of Christian love to God and man, the spiritual affection which follows the direction of the will, and which, therefore, unlike that feeling which is instinctive and unreasoned, can be commanded as a duty.[18]

The love referred to in this chapter is that denoted by the word for 'spiritual affection' (*agapao*—verb; *agapē*—noun and this determines the passages of the New Testament that can be quoted in support (e.g. Matt. 5:43 but not 10:37; Mark 12:30 but not John 11:36). About these passages three things can be said.

(i) Love is nowhere better summarized than in 1 Corinthians 13. Love (*agapē*) that is unselfish, that is for the unlovable, that is undeterred by failure, is there. There are those who will be content to accept the ruling of the Greek lexicon and see this as a quality that follows the direction of the will and can be commanded as a duty. There are others who see such love as either the fruit of the Spirit (Gal. 5:22) or the supreme gift of the Spirit (Paul following the gifts of 1 Cor. 12 with the 'still more excellent way' of 1 Cor. 13) but in either case as the gift of God. There are others who will want to bring both these into their understanding.

---

[17] The reason for the esteem may lie in the nature of the lover, rather than in the intrinsic worth of the loved, as with God's love for man.

[18] G. Abbott-Smith, *A Manual Greek Lexicon of the New Testament* (T. and T. Clark 1921).

(ii) In the New Testament love is personalized in Jesus. Whether Paul had Jesus in mind when he wrote 1 Corinthians 13 or not, the love that is there described is embodied in the Christians' Lord. Jesus 'provides in himself the values by which Christians should live';[19] he was 'God himself in human form, the complete and final revelation.[20] Both of these positions imply that Jesus is the incarnation of love (love 'in a bodily form', to use the dictionary definition of 'incarnation'). All that has been said of love Christians would say of Jesus. They see in his life, and most certainly in his death, the meaning of love. This is one of those many points where theology merges into devotion, for to say that Jesus is love is very close to beginning to love Jesus. So the verse of a hymn sums up the Christian view:

> Jesus, Love and Life art Thou,
> Life and Love for ever.
> Ne'er to quicken shalt Thou cease,
> Or to love us, never.
> All of life and love we need
> Is in Thee, in Thee indeed.[21]

(iii) Behind and within the love of Jesus there is the love of God. This is implicit in the doctrine of the Incarnation. In the New Testament it is the love of God that sends Jesus into the world (John 3:16) and that is the pattern of Jesus's own love for men (John 15:9). It is because of the love of God in sending 'his only Son into the world' (1 John 4:9) that Christians ought to love one another (1 John 4:11). These are quotations from the Johannine literature, but Paul's position is the same. The Christian life is possible because 'God's love has been poured into our hearts through the Holy Spirit which has been given to us' (Rom. 5:5). This is the same love that lies behind the life and death of Christ (Rom. 5:8–10).

So love, the greatest of the three, is in the Christian's life and in the Christian's book.

[19] See p. 49.
[20] See p. 78.
[21] Horatius Bonar, MHB, 95, v. 3.

DOING THEOLOGY

Faith, hope and love make up the basic stance of the Christian. Believing, trusting, obeying, hoping, loving—these are the verbs that direct his life. Various images have been used to attempt to sum this up: the Christian is the pilgrim, the happy warrior, the troubadour, the clown. They are perhaps slightly romantic—it would seem not always easy to be both a happy warrior and an income tax inspector, a troubadour and a platform porter for British Rail—but the main thrust of what they have to say is clear enough. The person who lives in faith, hope and love lives in a fundamental, unshakeable optimism.

This is enough for most people, but this book is being written for preachers, and for preachers who are studying theology. To them— to you and me, that is—is given the task of reflecting (in study) and expressing (in sermons) a practical theology[22] by which those who listen may both believe and live. This chapter has sought—in these three critical areas at least—to guard the preacher against two opposite mistakes. One is to ignore life as it is being lived for the revelation of the Bible or the massive theological system, inviting a theology that is fossilized and sermons that may be of interest to God alone. The other is to ignore the revelation, setting up a particular part of twentieth-century experience as the arbiter of eternal truth. In both cases the hungry sheep look up and are not fed. Doing and preaching theology means that, wherever we may begin (and that, as we have seen, is variable), revelation and experience, theology and living have to be brought together and kept together.

[22] See pp. 82–3.

107

Part II

Chapter 4

God

A. THE FOUNDATION DOCUMENTS

The Apostles' Creed[1]

I believe in God, the Father almighty, creator of heaven and earth. . . .

The Nicene Creed[2]

We believe in one God,
the Father, the Almighty,
maker of heaven and earth,
of all that is, seen and unseen.

The Thirty-nine Articles[3]

I. *Of Faith in the Holy Trinity*
   There is but one living and true God, everlasting, without body, parts, or passions; of infinite power, wisdom, and

---

[1] So called, not because it was composed by the apostles, but because it summarizes the apostolic faith. It had assumed its present form by the middle of the fourth century.

[2] See footnote, p. 48.

[3] The set of doctrinal formulae, finally accepted by the Church of England in 1571, attempting to define the position of that church in relation to the theological controversies of the sixteenth century.

goodness; the Maker, and Preserver of all things both visible and invisible. . . .

The Deed of Union

Clause 30[4]

Explanatory Notes upon the New Testament (John Wesley)

Commentary on Matthew 6:9

I. *Our Father*—Who art good and gracious to all, our Creator, our Preserver; the Father of our Lord, and of us in Him, Thy children by adoption and grace; not *my* Father only, who now cry unto Thee, but the Father of the universe, of angels and men: *Who art in heaven*— Beholding all things, both in heaven and earth; knowing every creature, and all the works of every creature, and every possible event from everlasting to everlasting; the almighty Lord and Ruler of all, superintending and disposing all things: *In heaven*—Eminently there, but not there alone, seeing Thou fillest heaven and earth.

Sermon IX: The Spirit of Bondage and of Adoption (John Wesley)

. . . He [the natural man] at last sees the loving, the merciful God is also 'a consuming fire'; that He is a just God and a terrible, rendering to every man according to his works, entering into judgement with the ungodly for every idle word, yea, and for the imaginations of the heart. He now clearly perceives, that the great and holy God is 'of purer eyes than to behold iniquity'; that He is an avenger of every one who rebelleth against Him, and repayeth the wicked to his face; and that 'it is a fearful thing to fall into the hands of the living God'. . . .

His eyes are opened in quite another manner than before, even to see a loving, gracious God. While he is calling, 'I

4 See pp. 53, 74.

110

beseech Thee, show me Thy glory!'—he hears a voice in his
inmost soul, 'I will make all My goodness pass before thee,
and I will proclaim the name of the Lord: I will be gracious
to whom I will be gracious, and I will show mercy to whom
I will show mercy'. And it is not long before 'the Lord
descends in the cloud, and proclaims the name of the Lord'.
Then he sees, but not with eyes of flesh and blood, 'The
Lord, the Lord God, merciful and gracious, long-suffering,
and abundant in goodness and truth; keeping mercy for
thousands, and forgiving iniquities, and transgressions, and
sin'.

The Senior Catechism of the Methodist Church

5. WHAT DO WE MEAN WHEN WE CALL GOD THE FATHER
ALMIGHTY, MAKER OF HEAVEN AND EARTH?
He creates all things and sustains and loves all that
He has made.

6. WHY DO WE CALL GOD ALMIGHTY?
He is the Eternal Ruler of the universe, and has all
power to fulfil His purpose.

The Methodist Service Book

Lord God, heavenly King,
almighty God and Father,
we worship you, we give you thanks,
we praise you for your glory.

(The Sunday Service, p. B6)

Holy, holy, holy Lord,
God of all power and might,
heaven and earth are full of your glory.

(The Sunday Service, p. B13)

Let us adore the Father, the God of love.
He created us;
he continually preserves and sustains us;

111

he has loved us with an everlasting love, and given us the light of the knowledge of his glory in the face of Jesus Christ.

(The Covenant Service, p. D3)

The Methodist Hymn Book

Praise the Lord who reigns above,
    And keeps His court below;
Praise the holy God of love,
    And all His greatness show;
Praise Him for his noble deeds,
    Praise Him for His matchless power:
Him from whom all good proceeds
    Let earth and heaven adore.

(14, v. 1) (Charles Wesley)

B. THE DOCTRINE OF GOD[5]

The above foundation documents are given that term because they express in creeds, sermons, notes or liturgical forms the basic theology of a Christian community, in this case the Methodist. They reveal how these people speak of God. That theology must now be set out more systematically, as it has been traditionally understood, giving special attention to its Biblical origin.

Before this can be done, however, it is necessary, in the case of the doctrine of God, to raise what is probably the most important question in theology, and certainly the most difficult. It has to do with the use of the word 'God'.

We know what we mean by 'a being'. We call people 'human beings'. We think of our pet spaniel lying on the carpet as a being. Nor should we confuse one another if we extended the use of the word to things: inanimate beings we might call them. The lawn, the lamp-post and the empty milk bottles are beings in this sense.

The normal use of language enables us to make statements about beings that convey our meaning with no trouble at all. Indeed, this is what language is for. We say 'that man is a careless driver' or 'my

[5] In terms of the doctrine of the Trinity (chapter 7) 'God' in this chapter is 'God the Father'.

spaniel is brown' or 'the milk bottles belong to the Express Dairy' and the operation works perfectly. We mean exactly and precisely what we say.

Now this process works very well in the case of God as long as he too is regarded as a being. He may well be thought of as the most exalted being that could possibly be, but a being nevertheless. When he is conceived of in this way, it is possible to make the kind of statements about him that are made about beings: that he is creator, personal, holy and so forth. This is indeed exactly what will be done in this section of this chapter—describing the being, God, as Christians have traditionally understood him. And that makes sense, just like saying that the milk bottles belong to the Express Dairy.

But suppose, as the great theologians of the Church have argued, that there is *that which enables beings to be beings at all*, what then? Well, it is possible to follow the theologians and use the word 'Being' (with no article) but there is then the considerable difficulty that language which communicates meaning when used about beings is quite meaningless when used about Being. (One cannot say, for example, that Being 'exists', for only beings exist). Furthermore, if the word 'God' is the one we want to use for the ultimate reality, then we shall want to use it for what we have called 'Being'. Does this mean then, that we can say virtually nothing that has meaning about God?

This is a question that cannot be answered though attempts have been made along the lines of saying what God is not, rather than what he is. The important thing, however, for all who speak about God, is not to answer the question, but to raise it. We have to be *aware* that when we speak of God as creator, personal, holy and so forth we are using the word 'God' as a kind of sign, a piece of shorthand, for the God whom no words can adequately describe. We are speaking of a Being (with a capital 'B' for his supremacy) simply because we cannot speak of Being in our language. On this assumption we can go ahead and talk about God.

(1) God is creator

The Old Testament proclaims that the world was created by God. The two accounts of creation in Genesis 1:1–2:4a and 2:4b–25, though different in style and content, are united in their affirmation that the world, and everything within it, was made by God. But it must not be thought that, because the Bible begins with creation stories, the Hebrews gave first place in their theology to a doctrine of creation. On the contrary, though they celebrated it in their ritual, they said little about it for a long time. Then, during the Babylonian Exile,

113

the writer of Isaiah 40–55 gave it a significant place in his preaching:

> To whom then will you compare me,
>   that I should be like him?
>   says the Holy One.
> Lift up your eyes on high and see:
>   who created these?
> He who brings out their host by number,
>   calling them all by name;
> by the greatness of his might,
>   and because he is strong in power
>   not one is missing.

(40:25–6)

Again,

> I form light and create darkness,
> I make weal and create woe,
> I am the LORD, who do all these things.

(45:7)

It was in the light of such preaching that the more recent of the two Genesis accounts (1:1–2:4a) was formed and treasured.

The Psalms express the same theology in the language of devotion:

> The earth is the LORD'S and the fulness thereof,
>   the world and those who dwell therein;
> for he has founded it upon the seas,
>   and established it upon the rivers.

(24:1–2)

Traditionally two further truths have been affirmed of God's creative activity.

(i) It is creation *out of nothing*. Genesis 1 gives the impression of a watery chaos 'existing' before creation and Genesis 2 of a barren wasteland. The biblical view of creation is that there is no existence independent of God.

114

Thus says the LORD,
  the Holy One of Israel, and his Maker:
'Will you question me about my children,
  or command me concerning the work of my hands?
I made the earth,
  and created man upon it;
it was my hands that stretched out the heavens,
  and I commanded all their host. . . .'

(Isa. 45:11–12)

Everything and everybody is a creature (Heb. 11:3). This truth has found expression in the traditional doctrine of 'creation out of nothing'.

(ii) Creation, or creative activity or to be precise, is *continuous*. Notice the present tense of Psalm 118:24:

This is the day which the LORD has made . . .

Similarly the future tense of Isaiah 41:18 f. is significant:

I will open rivers on the bare heights,
  and fountains in the midst of the valleys;
I will make the wilderness a pool of water,
  and the dry land springs of water . . .
that men may see and know,
  may consider and understand together,
that the hand of the LORD has done this,
  the Holy One of Israel has created it.

The New Testament confirms this continuous activity (John 5:17; Matt. 5:45b; 6:26–30).

To speculate whether God, the continuous Creator, was busy creating something else before he created our universe is a waste of words. We do not know. What we do know is that God's dynamic work of creation goes on and on. Physically and spiritually God is still bringing order out of chaos.

(2) God is personal

A living, personal God is not at all the same thing as a person. Persons are *people* with all the limitations and perversities of

115

people, and to fasten such a label on God is not the intention of this doctrine. It is true that in some of the early stories of Genesis God is thought of as a bigger and more impressive version of a man:

> And they heard the sound of the LORD God walking in the garden in the cool of the day, and the man and his wife hid themselves from the presence of the LORD God among the trees of the garden. But the LORD God called to the man, and said to him, 'Where are you?' (Gen. 3:8-9).

> And the LORD came down to see the city and the tower, which the sons of men had built (Gen. 11:5).

But the Old Testament makes it very clear that God is no mere person (refer again to the Isaiah passages in the previous section). The suggestion that in the magnificent poetry of chapters 38 and 39 poor Job is confronted by another *person* is unacceptable.

What the doctrine of God insists upon is that, though God cannot be confined within personality, the nature of his relationships with men is never less than personal. He must never be reduced to an impersonal force. He must never be spoken of as 'it'. The God who thundered at Job and asked him if he could bind the chains of Pleiades or loose the cords of Orion (38:31) is also the God who says:

> How can I give you up, O Ephraim!
>   How can I hand you over, O Israel!
> How can I make you like Admah!
>   How can I treat you like Zeboiim!
> My heart recoils within me,
>   my compassion grows warm and tender.
> I will not execute my fierce anger,
>   I will not again destroy Ephraim;
> for I am God and not man,
>   the Holy One in your midst,
>   and I will not come to destroy.
>
> (Hos. 11:8-9)

He is the God who spoke with Moses 'as a man speaks to his friend' (Ex. 33:11).

116

The ultimate justification for the Christian using personal terms of God is that for him God is most fully known in and through a person, Jesus Christ. 'The light of the knowledge of the glory of God' shines 'in the face of Christ' (2 Cor. 4:6) (see also John 14:9b).

(3) God is holy

The original meaning of 'holiness' in the Bible is not 'goodness' but 'separateness', 'remoteness'. Such holiness was a frightening and dangerous affair. Exodus 19:16–25 describes exactly how the Israelites experienced it: God present in the thunder, the lightning, the volcanic eruption, the blaring trumpet and the dire warning that if anybody tried to look, he would die. For any dealings at all to take place between such a separate, awesome, holy God and mortal men, elaborate regulations had to be observed. For instance, whoever was 'unclean' by touching a dead body had to go through a prescribed ritual. Otherwise such a person 'defiles the tabernacle of the Lord, and that person shall be cut off from Israel' (Num. 19:11–13). There was not much justice in all this as poor Uzzah discovered (sic) when he 'tried to steady the ark of God as the oxen stumbled' (2 Sam. 6:6–9).

It was therefore a fuller understanding when the separateness and remoteness of God were understood in moral terms rather than in physical, ceremonial or even magical ones. It was Isaiah (the author of chapters 1–39, or most of them) who proclaimed the (still terrifying) moral holiness of God. The prophet's call by the holy God in chapter 6 is a classic case, but the thunderings of chapter I against those who must

> cease to do evil,
> learn to do good;
> seek justice,
> correct oppression;
> defend the fatherless,
> plead for the widow (v. 17)

are even more emphatic.

117

After the Exile physical separateness and remoteness reasserted itself. God's name could not even be spoken and he was thought to be so far away that intermediaries appear. Angels, Wisdom, the Spirit of Yahweh, the Word of God were supplied, so to speak, by one side and priests were supplied by the other, to help bridge the gap.

The Church has traditionally understood the holiness of God to be indeed moral excellence,[6] but to include that sense of the wholly 'Other' over against man without which God would not be God.

(4) God is righteous

A God of righteousness is one who makes moral demands upon his people, and this Yahweh certainly did. The second half of the Ten Commandments is concerned with ethics. When Nathan the prophet rebuked David for his moral fault,[7] he began his denunciation with the words 'Thus says the Lord, the God of Israel' (2 Sam. 12:7). It was the righteous God who was angry. And David simply said 'I have sinned against the Lord' (v. 13).

Amos also insists that righteous behaviour is the requirement of a righteous God. In chapter 5 the *ethical* sins of Israel are specified and denounced:

> Therefore because you trample upon the poor
>   and take from him exactions of wheat,
> you have built houses of hewn stone,
>   but you shall not dwell in them,
> you have planted pleasant vineyards,
>   but you shall not drink their wine.
> For I know how many are your transgressions,
>   and how great are your sins—
> you who afflict the righteous, who take a bribe,
>   and turn aside the needy in the gate (vv. 11–12)[8]

---

[6] This does not mean that there is some standard of moral excellence to which God has to conform. It is moral excellence precisely because God is like that.

[7] See p. 51.

[8] Cf. Matt. 19:17.

There is an appeal for better ways:

> Seek good, and not evil,
> that you may live (14).

Finally, Amos issues a powerful warning that the practices of the cult are no substitute for righteousness:

> I hate, I despise your feasts,
>   and I take no delight in your solemn assemblies.
> Even though you offer me your burnt offerings and cereal
>   offerings,
>   I will not accept them,
> and the peace offerings of your fatted beasts
>   I will not look upon.
> Take away from me the noise of your songs;
>   to the melody of your harps I will not listen.
> But let justice roll down like waters,
>   and righteousness like an ever-flowing stream (21–24).

This position, so forcibly proclaimed by Amos, became the orthodoxy of Israel.

The Old Testament writers, however, do not oppose God's righteousness to his mercy. His saving activity, like his judgement, is an expression of his righteousness:

> Gracious is the LORD, and righteous;
>   our God is merciful (Ps. 116:5)

Paul in Romans makes the same point (5:18–21). The righteous God is the Saving God, and to be saved is to be made righteous.

(5) There is only one God

Israel began with a tribal deity and this situation pertained at the time of Moses, though the great leader himself paid little attention to other gods. It was generally taken for granted that Melkart was the god of Tyre, Chemosh the god of Moab and so forth. When Israel came into Canaan she encountered 'Baal

119

worship', that is to say, fertility cults involving sexual practices in a magical attempt to make the crops grow. The Baalim were considered as rivals of Yahweh (1 Kings 18:17-40). This worship of one god out of many was known as 'monolatry'.

It was Deutero-Isaiah (the author of chapters 40–55) who first denied the existence of other gods:

Is there a God besides me?
There is no Rock; I know not any (44:8).

This belief in the one and only god (called monotheism) was laudable since the normal evidence for the supremacy of a god was the success in battle of his supporters, and Deutero-Isaiah was a prophet *of the Exile*, the time of Israel's greatest humiliation. As a result of this achievement the writers of the New Testament were able to assume monotheism (see Mark 12:32; 1 Tim. 1:17; Jas. 2:19).

(6) God is eternal

This raises the fascinating question of the relation of God to time. A preacher once began the opening prayer of a service with the words: 'O Thou who knowest all that has happened in the week that has gone and who knowest all that will happen in the week that is to come....' Was he right?

It might be thought that the point here is the *omniscience* of God, that he knows everything. Certainly this is so, and the traditional Christian view is that God is omniscient (See Ps. 139:1-6). What, however, now concerns us is that in order to know everything God has to stand in a special relation to time. If he knows 'all that will happen in the week that is to come' then, in some way or another, for God the week that is to come has already come. In what way?

We are not entirely limited by time ourselves. If you are standing on a cold, draughty platform waiting for a train that is already half an hour late, every minute seems like an hour. But if you are at a party, having a rollicking time and thoroughly enjoying yourself, you look at the clock and say,

120

'Good gracious, it's half-past-eleven. It seems as if we've only been here for ten minutes'. Time is indeed that which is registered on the face of a clock. But the nature of our experience can make the passage of time mean very different things. At the party it is the intensity of the experience, the sheer enjoyment of what is going on and the large extent to which we are taken out of ourselves that make every hour seem like a minute. And it is the absence of these on the station platform that makes every minute seem like an hour.

There may be a clue here to the way in which God transcends time. Might not his 'intensity of experience' and his 'sheer enjoyment of what is going on' be of a kind that releases him from the tyranny of the clock? And is he not completely taken out of himself in out-going love? This kind of thinking may well be considered idle speculation in the light of the traditional Christian view that God created time. Creation was not an event in time. Time was part of creation. So inevitably God transcends time. This the Church has always believed. It has not been able to conceive that there was a time when God was not, nor that there will be a time when he will not be. In other words, he is eternal. The Christian God is 'the eternal King, the undying, invisible and only God' (1 Tim. 1 : 17, *Jerusalem Bible*).

The outstanding problem is to reconcile belief in a God who transcends time and knows everything with genuine human free will. If next week has already come for God, how can we be free to do next week anything other than that which, as far as he is concerned, we have already done? Some have tried to resolve this problem by arguing that God knows all that *could* happen rather than all that *will* happen: all the possibilities, not all the actualities. But how can we ever know?

Finally, being eternal does not mean that time has no significance for God. He does not, so to speak, sit cross-legged and inscrutable while time goes by. Eternity is different from mere everlastingness. Time has significance for God, not only because he created it, but also because he acts within it. 'In the beginning God created . . .' (Gen. 1 : 1); 'But when the time had fully come, God sent forth his Son . . .' (Gal. 4 : 4).

121

(7) God is spirit

He is other than man, who is flesh (Isa. 31 : 3) and he is mysterious, like the wind (the same Hebrew word is translated 'wind' and 'spirit'). God is a spirit (John 4 : 24).

Just as there is a link between God as eternal and the attribute of omniscience, so there is a link between God as spirit and the attribute of *omnipresence*. If God is spirit, then he must be everywhere (Ps. 139 : 7). Some people expected the first astronauts to meet him the other side of the moon— or, rather, asserted that if they did not there was no God to be met. This notion of God pervading everywhere, spread out through space like a vast holy fog, has no support either in the Bible or in the traditional teaching of the Church.

The Christian view of omnipresence is simply that God can do what he decides to do *wherever he wants to do it*. In any place whatsoever, he can encounter man and act for his salvation (see Ps. 139 : 7–12). He is sovereign over space. From man's point of view this means the total availability of God. No considerations of space need ever prevent man from turning to him and finding him.

This is possible only because God is spirit. Christians have always believed that though God is present in the man Jesus Christ (John 1 : 14–18; 2 Cor. 4 : 4; Col. 1 : 15) and, as those in the Catholic tradition believe, localized in the bread and wine of the eucharist, these special physical manifestations in his presence are in no way inconsistent with the fact that he is spirit. The truth remains that 'no one has ever seen God' (John 1 : 18).

(8) God is almighty

This is often taken to mean that God can do anything. It is allied with the attribute of *omnipotence*, which means, by derivation, 'all-powerful'. If God cannot do everything, then how can he be God? This is the popular form of the question as it is often put by those who have become disenchanted with religion or have been (as they believe) jilted in prayer. It has found expression as a serious argument in a dilemma first formulated by Epicurus (340–270 BC) but re-stated briefly and in modern terms by John Hick:

> If God is perfectly good, He must want to abolish all evil; if He is unlimitedly powerful, He must be able to abolish all evil: but evil exists; therefore either God is not perfectly good or He is not unlimitedly powerful.[9]

Christians have replied to this with two assertions:

(i) God cannot do everything, he can only do those things which his nature allows. For example, the God of truth cannot do what is contradictory. As Augustine said, it is not possible for God to die, to make what is done undone, or what is false true. Again, the God of love (1 John 4:16) cannot cease to act in love. He cannot, to put it colloquially, hate the guts of a man, no matter how sinful he may be. And it could be that his nature will not allow him—perhaps in the interest of human freedom—to abolish evil and suffering 'at a stroke'.

(ii) The dilemma of Epicurus is only a genuine dilemma if the omnipotence referred to is coercive, dictatorial power, the power that says to everybody and everything, 'Do this' and it is done. With that sort of power it is not possible to be both perfectly good and omnipotent if evil and suffering are allowed to persist. But Christians hold that God's power is the power of love, and this inevitably means that men are not coerced to do the right and the good but given freedom to do the wrong and the bad if they so choose. With that kind of omnipotence-in-love, it is indeed possible to be perfectly good and yet not to prevent suffering and evil in the world.

The Christian assertion of the omnipotence or 'almightiness' of God is an assertion of his sovereignty. He cannot do anything, for some things he does not, and indeed cannot, will to do (Jas. 1:13). But he is in control. All things are in his hand. 'The Lord reigns; let the earth rejoice' (Ps. 97:1; cf Rev. 1:8; 19:6).

[9] *Evil and the God of Love* (Collins 1968), p. 5. John Stuart Mill put it more briefly: Either God is good and not powerful, or else powerful and not good.

(9) God is a father

This statement comes so easily to Christian lips that we need to remind ourselves that we are using the word 'father' as an analogy, an illustration, an indication, rather than as a plain fact. Literally speaking, God is not anybody's father. But as a statement revealing the true nature of God, this is as far as biblical, traditional language (and many would say *any* language) can take us.

It is asserted that two classes of people have special difficulties with the fatherhood of God. There are those whose human fathers have not loved them, and no love has been given in return. It is said that they cannot think helpfully of God as Father. Martin Luther's father was so severe on him that he found difficulty in praying the Lord's prayer and calling God 'Father'. But he won through! And there are those who are bothered because male chauvinism is so deeply entrenched in theology. It has to be pointed out to them that when the term was first used in the biblical tradition fatherhood embodied the ideas that people had about God—authority and originative power particularly—and motherhood did not.

To be fair to the Jews, or other religions for that matter,[10] we cannot pretend that Jesus was the first person to address God as 'Father'.

Deuteronomy 32:6 uses the word and Psalm 68:5 runs:

Father of the fatherless and protector of widows
is God in his holy habitation.

In Psalm 89 God puts into the mouth of David:

Thou art my Father,
my God, and the Rock of my salvation (v. 10).

Jeremiah says, simply and profoundly:

For thus says the Lord:
I am a father to Israel (31:7, 9) (cf. Isa. 63:16).

[10] One of the titles ascribed to Zeus, for example, was 'Father of men'.

124

Nevertheless, God as Father comes into unprecedented prominence with Jesus. It is the Father's kingdom he proclaims (Matt. 13:43, Luke 12:32), the Father's 'fatherliness' and providential care that he preaches (Matt. 5:45; 6:26). To have an insight into what the fatherhood of God meant to Jesus, it is only necessary to read and meditate upon the two versions of The Lord's Prayer, the 'Our Father' as it is called in some Churches (Matt. 6:9–13; Luke 11:2–4), or to recall the unique way in which Jesus spoke personally and intimately to God, using the word *abba* for 'Father'. This word has been rendered by some as 'Dad' or 'Daddy'.

Moreover, Jesus brought a new dimension into our understanding of the fatherhood of God through his own unique relationship to the Father. Hence the fatherhood of God is to be understood in the light of the sonship of Jesus. Or to put it less ponderously: what sort of father must God be if this man is his 'well-beloved son'? The first Christians were able to give themselves a highly satisfactory answer to this question, consequently their distinctive name for God was 'the God and Father of our Lord Jesus Christ' (2 Cor. 11:31; Eph. 1:3; Col. 1:3).

There has been a good deal of theological argument as to whether, if God is our Father, we are his children or whether that is something we become, either by our obedience (Matt. 5: 44–5) or by the redemptive activity of God (Gal. 4:4). This is largely a question of defining the senses in which we use the words 'children' and 'sons'. What is not in dispute is the Christian belief that God is Father to us, whether we realize and acknowledge it or not.

(10) God is love

The Jews believed, and still believe, themselves to be the Chosen People. The source of that election lay in the love of God. He chose them because he loved them and having chosen them he vowed to bring them to prosperity, to success, to independence, to the Promised Land. For their part, they must be obedient. This was the celebrated Covenant, and its basis was the covenant-love of God, translated as 'lovingkindness'

in the A.V. and R.V. and as 'steadfast love' in the R.S.V.
As the book of Hosea makes clear, the covenant-love of God
persists through the sin of Israel. Its answer to apostasy is:

> How can I give you up, O Ephraim!
> How can I hand you over, O Israel! (11:8).

The love of God is combined with, and is not in opposition
to, his righteousness. The combination saves it from becoming
a pampering indulgence and accounts for the stern words of
Hosea and the even sterner ones from Amos.

'God is love' is implicit throughout the New Testament,
though that precise form of words occurs only in 1 John 4:

> God is love, and he who abides in love abides in God and God
> abides in him (v. 16).

The verb 'to love' is more commonly used than the noun:

> God so loved ... that he gave ... (John 3:16).

The Christian God is the God of holy love.

God's holy love cannot make light of sin, but neither can it
be defeated by it. The vindication of these truths is in the life
and death of Jesus.

(11) God is a mystery

Having said ten things about God, and taken three thousand
words to say them, the impression may be given that there is
nothing more to be said. Now we know all about God; we
have 'done' him just as a certain type of American tourist
'does' London, Edinburgh, Paris, Rome and Vienna in a week.
To correct this impression it is necessary to point out that
there is much more that could be added about God, but even
if it were *all* added it would still be necessary to say that God
is a mystery.

The word 'mystery' is not an easy one. Its modern meaning
is 'obscure', 'difficult to understand', as in the sentences:

126

To most people the international monetary system is a mystery.

Why my daughter is a vegetarian is a mystery to me.

But to say that God is a mystery does not mean that he is obscure or difficult to understand. It means that when all there is to be said has been said, when the entire revelation is, so to speak, spread out before us and comprehended by us, there is much more that could be revealed but is not. The Greek word from which 'mystery' is derived referred originally to the secrets in some forms of religion that were known only to the initiates and could not be revealed to others. Christians took over the word and used it to proclaim that God *had* revealed his secrets, his mysteries, in Jesus Christ (Eph. 1:9). The Gospel is an open secret. But beyond what is known there is what is not known. The ten sections above do not by any means provide a complete answer to the question of the Second Isaiah:

> To whom then will you liken God, or what likeness compare with him? (Isa. 40:18).

C. PRESENT CONSIDERATIONS

So far many readers, perhaps most, will have had no problems. They will not wish to quarrel with what has been asserted about God. They will not question the underlying assumption of this chapter: that there is in fact a God about whom such things can be written. This is predictable in a readership largely composed of aspiring preachers.

The truth is, however, that many people in the European tradition, including some who are not without commitment to Jesus Christ, would find the previous sections of this chapter problematical, to put it mildly. If they were to flick over the pages and read the headings, 'God is Creator', 'God is Personal', 'God is Holy', and so forth, all on the assumption that there is a God in the first place, they would be inclined to say 'It's all too neat and tidy. You've got God organized. And we simpy can't believe it'. Moreover, even if they were referred back to the carefully built up argument of chapter 2 and were to be told, 'It has been revealed in the Bible and tradition, and both reason and experience support it'[11] they would still, one suspects, not be deeply impressed. They would still place an enormous question mark against God.

Some of these people may be found in churches, or so it is asserted by the provocative theologian, Alistair Kee:

> ...fewer and fewer people today have any knowledge of God. There does not seem to be any way in which the Church can enable them to come to belief in God. But most of all, living without God has now become a feature not only of those outside the Church, but of many within it. A significant number of Christians now find themselves without any experience of God. I do not see how it is possible to deny that this is the situation in which we live today. It is either a quite new situation, or it is the first time in history that we have been able to recognize it. We are not dealing with intellectual atheism, a strident or belligerent denial of the possibility of God. It is a much more calm atmosphere, in which many people find nothing in their lives which would enable them honestly to speak of belief in God.[12]

Others may be found in the thick of theological debate: how else should we find books in theological libraries with such titles as *Guide to the Debate about God*,[13] *God the Problem*,[14] *The Eclipse of God*?[15] What debate? What problem? What eclipse? To these questions we now turn.

(1) Secularization

It is not possible in the space available to give a comprehensive account of why many modern people have difficulties in believing in God, particularly as Christians understand him. Attention can only be drawn to two or three factors that seem more obvious than the rest. Secularization is the first of them. The sociologist, Peter Berger, offered this definition:

---

11 See p. 70.
12 *The Way of Transcendence* (Pelican 1971), pp. 77–8.
13 D. Jenkins (Lutterworth 1966).
14 Gordon Kaufman (Harvard University Press 1972).
15 Martin Buber (Gollancz 1953).

By secularization we mean the process by which sectors of society and culture are removed from the domination of religious institutions and symbols.[16]

The process to which he refers is a fascinating one. As the Scottish theologian, John Baillie, pointed out some years ago,[17] during the Middle Ages pursuits such as art, music, painting, science, travel and invention were regarded as innocuous diversions from the one serious business of life, which was to prepare the soul for its eternal destiny in heaven. The Renaissance was the movement that gave to such pursuits a serious importance in their own right, and in doing so began their detachment, so to speak, from religion and so, inevitably, from God. The scientific and technological revolution—and much more for which there is no space—speeded up the process. Scientists were able to explain the rainbow, the fatal disease, the energy of the sun, without recourse to God, and the best answer to drought was to irrigate the land, not pray for rain.

It is a familiar theme and there is no need to pursue it. Exaggerations have taken place. One is the assertion of some philosophers that unless a statement be confirmed by the experience of the senses it is nonsense ('God is our Father' is obviously out, but so is 'it is wrong to falsify your income tax returns'). Another is what is known as 'secularism', the deliberate attempt to exclude religious considerations from the entire human scene. Christians may reject these exaggerations while acknowledging secularization as a fact of life. Some positively welcome it, for they believe with Dietrich Bonhoeffer that, in these respects, what God is teaching us is that we must live as men who can get along very well without him.[18]

Whether we enthuse about secularization or sigh for the good old days when God was God and everybody knew it, it is hard for any of us to deny that it has made it more difficult to believe in God, to talk about God and to experience God.

[16] The Social Reality of Religion (Faber and Faber 1967), p. 107.
[17] And the Life Everlasting (O.U.P. 1934), p. 9.
[18] Letters and Papers from Prison (S.C.M. 1953), p. 10.

129

The truly secular man, the humanist, would find the first two sections of this chapter very much against the grain.

(2) Evil and suffering

If secularization is a recent factor in making it hard for people to believe in God, the presence of evil and suffering in the world must be the oldest. We have already referred to the trouble it caused Epicurus three hundred years before Christ.[19] For many people that situation has not changed.

Some are appalled by the total, vast extent of evil and suffering. It is true of course that no one person can *experience* it all. If twenty thousand people suffer and die from cancer of the lung there is no one person existing who can suffer more than his own individual share of the pain. No one can die twenty thousand deaths. Even so the bare contemplation of *the fact that* there is so much diabolical evil, so much agonizing suffering is enough to put some people off God for good.

When evil and suffering are focused in one person the reaction is often bitter and intense. A man calls to collect the money from the gas meter at a house in Belfast, triggers off a bomb, and both his legs are blown off. A beautiful and brilliant 'cellist develops multiple sclerosis and will never play again. It would not be surprising if those very close to such were to find it hard to believe in a good and loving God (though some of them do, nevertheless).

When unbelief occurs in such circumstances it would seem that, understandably, the emotions have much to do with it. People *feel* that they just cannot bring themselves to believe in God. In other, not so personally harrowing, circumstances, it is possible to reach the same conclusion by a less emotional route. People can discern that the presence of evil and suffering is an enormous problem, not to the unbeliever, but to the believer. As John Hick puts it:

> For the atheist is not obliged to explain the universe at all. He can simply accept it at its face value as an enormously complex natural fact. It constitutes an environment that is for him partly

[19] See p. 123.

pleasant, partly unpleasant, and partly neutral; but he need find no special intellectual problem in its pleasantness or unpleasantness.... It is the Christian theist (among others) who claims that the situation is other than it appears, in that there is an invisible divine Being who is perfect in goodness and unlimited in power. And the problem of evil arises at this point as a genuine difficulty that he is bound to face.[20]

The answer is simple. If you do not want the problem, you do not believe.

(3) Unhelpful notions of God

(i) The big, bad God of the Bible

Some unbelievers are disillusioned refugees from our teaching of the Bible to children. By failing both to understand and to interpret what the Bible has to say about God, Christians have made him quite incredible to more children than one cares to think of. The uninterpreted, literally-presented God of the Old Testament is the one who looks after his favourites (those who have faith and are obedient): Noah, Abraham, Elijah, David and the rest. He is the ogre of the Flood, a story loved by children because of the animals, that as likely as not begins 'Once upon a time all the people in the world were so wicked that God decided to drown them'. The God behind the stories of the plagues in Egypt virtually turns the notion of the Christian God upon its head. Is it surprising that, having been told these tales just as they are, children grow up to assume that God rewards the good and punishes the bad? And is it not this that leads to the cry of unbelief: 'What have I done to deserve this?' We have succeeded in purveying a God in whom people do not *want* to believe. Maybe we ought not to exempt from censure our failure to interpret the New Testament also, as a result of which a child mind comes to see God as the ogre, not only of the Flood, but of the Passion, letting Jesus die, and in some theologies actually sending him and willing him to die. Who wants to believe in a God like that? Educationists may have exaggerated all this. It is difficult to deny that there is some truth in it.

[20] *Evil and the God of Love*, p. 11.

131

(ii) The Old Man in the sky

It is part of traditional theology to assert that God is both immanent and transcendent. These technical words mean that God is present in his creation (immanence) and that he is also separate from it (transcendence). Both notions can be exaggerated and distorted, the first leading to what is known as pantheism (the doctrine that God and the universe are identical so that God is everything and everything is God) and the second leading to deism—to what has been called 'The Old Man in the sky'. Immanence seems not to have troubled modern people very much. Transcendence certainly has.

This was the point at which that *enfant terrible* of theological books, *Honest to God*, began in 1963. It started by dismissing as quite incredible the *literal* view of the

Friend for little children
Above the bright blue sky . . .[21]

This in itself was a blow to the faith of some for, as John Robinson admits:

Whatever we may accept with the top of our minds, most of us will retain deep down the mental image of 'an old man in the sky'.[22]

But to make matters worse (from the point of view of those holding an uncritical faith) Robinson went on to expose the difficulties of believing in a God who was thought to be, not literally, but spiritually, metaphorically 'out there'. He meant our 'mental picture' of:

a God who 'exists' above and beyond the world he made, a God 'to' whom we pray and to whom we 'go' when we die.[23]

In other words we are not allowed to have even a metaphorical Old Man in a metaphorical sky. God 'out there' shares the same fate as God 'up there'. Like the Christians of

21 MHB 839.
22 *Honest To God*, (S.C.M. 1963), p. 13.
23 P. 14.

132

1963, we may find this devastating or exhilarating. But there can hardly be two views about Robinson's assessment of the resulting situation. If God cannot be thought of as a Being separate from his creation, either 'up there' or 'out there', then:

There is a double pressure to discard this entire construction, and with it any belief in God at all.[24]

(iii) The interfering God

A generation or two ago one of the most popular sermon illustrations on faith, prayer, the providential care of God (it could do a turn for most things) was the story of Muller's Orphanage at Bristol. Its gaunt buildings, now occupied by a polytechnic, still line one side of the county cricket ground. Muller had no resources of money or of food. None at all. He had hundreds of orphans under his care yet he literally did not know where the next meal was coming from. So what did he do? He prayed. And unfailingly (literally) the food or the money, or whatever it was he lacked, somehow arrived just in time.

It is a remarkable story and has doubtless stimulated many towards faith and prayer. Yet its effect on some, perhaps many, of our contemporaries, were they to hear it, would be exactly the opposite. For it raises the problems they find in the claims made by religious people as to what God is prepared to do on their behalf, e.g. 'God kept my son on the right road', 'God saved me from redundancy', 'God cured me of my arthritis', and so forth.

The dilemma for the secular man, the humanist, is this. If the person is wrong in making such claims, what sort of credence can you give to his religion? On the other hand, if he is right, what sort of God is it who intervenes to adjust matters on behalf of those who ask him and presumably not on behalf of the rest?: certainly not one they can believe in.

Maybe the matter ought not to be put in such black-and-white terms, for this does not give enough importance to the *interpretation* of events, but this is simply an attempt to

---

[24] P. 16.

describe the scene. And the kind of God some religious people have in fact succeeded in portraying—an interventionist, an interferer—has not invited modern believers. Muller's story made faith easier for my grandfather. It makes it more difficult for my children.

These are some of the factors making for disbelief in God. Taken with others[25] they produce what has been called the experience of 'the absence of God'. This was expressed by some theologians, mostly American, in the 1960s, by the adoption of the title 'Death of God'. It was their way of saying —and a very confusing way it proved to be—that their experience was one of the absence of God. Indeed they claimed that God had actually died.

It is possible not to be affected very much by such factors oneself and therefore at least to be tempted to adopt a 'take it or leave it' approach to those who are. To say 'I believe in God because of my personal experience' or 'You've just *got* to believe' may be true enough, but such statements do not make for the most constructive approach to people struggling to believe, whether they are inside or outside the Church. The preacher should be able to meet unbelief not only with the counter-assertion of his own faith (though that will often be called for) but also by being able to communicate those contemporary theological insights, those present considerations, that may help people to believe in God. Most of them have been written for that precise purpose. The remark that theologians once wrote to persuade others to believe, now they write to persuade themselves, is not entirely true.

Intimations

Perhaps it is possible to focus upon ordinary, non-religious experiences (using 'religion' in the narrower sense of chapter 2) and to find there some considerations for believing in God? Certainly the possibility has been suggested.

---

[25] It might be helpful to re-read at this point the section on Expression (Language) in chapter 1, with God in mind.

GOD

(1) Indicator experiences

In the book *Doing Theology*[26] David Deeks examined a number of common experiences under this head. He enquired whether in the experience of personal relationships, in encountering other people 'at depth' there is not some indication of how we can encounter God. He examined awe, with its twin elements of exhilaration (on top of a mountain) and terror (down in the pothole again!) and suggested that this was the way we meet the supernatural and the holy. Moral demand was another such experience. If I pick up a £5 note on the pavement and spend it on golf balls instead of taking it to the police station, I sense that something, somebody, is *getting at me*, holding me accountable. There are those who will say that it is simply the way my mother brought me up, but it does not *feel* like that kind of experience. There are those who will say that I have been indoctrinated with a father figure, and I can never get out of his clutches. It is good of them to warn me (leaving aside the question that absence of need for a father figure does not determine whether he exists or not) but it makes no difference. I have an inescapable sense that if I know what is right (for me, in those circumstances) and do what is wrong, I am answerable.

The search for meaning is another indicator experience. People everywhere try to find it—lonely old people living in discomfort in their tiny flats seek a meaning to their existence; so do humanists as they throw off the (to them) trappings of religion, believing that the proper study of mankind is man; so do Communists as they try to change the world. Perhaps, then, there is a meaning to be sought?

It would be easy to add very many to this list of indicator experiences, only to be told that they were all explicable in terms of themselves. The hope is that some would find them otherwise.

(2) Signals of transcendence

In his book *A Rumour of Angels* Peter Berger defined these as follows:

26 (Local Preachers' Department 1972).

135

By signals of transcendence I mean phenomena that are to be found within the domain of our 'natural' reality but that appear to point beyond that reality.[27]

He then spells out some of them, of which the following are two examples, though it should be noted that 'pointing beyond that reality' could well stop short of Christian faith in God. One is the argument from ordering, the other the argument from damnation.

(i) The argument from ordering

Berger points out that man has a faith in order as such, grounded in a trust that everything is 'all right', 'as it should be', both for himself and for the society in which he lives. This faith cannot of course be proved, it can only be experienced, but it points beyond the experience. Here is the precise illustration:

A child wakes up in the night, perhaps from a bad dream, and finds himself surrounded by darkness, alone, beset by nameless threats. At such a moment the contours of trusted reality are blurred or invisible, and in the terror of incipient chaos the child cries out for his mother. It is hardly an exaggeration to say that, at this moment, the mother is being invoked as a high priestess of protective order. It is she (and in many cases, she alone) who has the power to banish the chaos and to restore the benign shape of the world. And, of course, any good mother will do just that. She will take the child and cradle him in the timeless gesture of the Magna Mater who became our Madonna. She will turn on a lamp, perhaps, which will encircle the scene with a warm glow of reassuring light. She will speak or sing to the child, and the content of this communication will invariably be the same—'Don't be afraid—everything is in order, everything is all right'. If all goes well, the child will be reassured, his trust in reality recovered, and in this trust he will return to sleep.[28]

Then Berger continues:

All this, of course, belongs to the most routine experience of life and does not depend upon any religious preconceptions. Yet

[27] Penguin 1969, p. 70.   [28] P. 72.

136

this common scene raises a far from ordinary question, which immediately introduces a religious dimension: *is the mother lying to the child?* The answer, in the most profound sense, can be 'no' only if there is some truth in the religious interpretation of human existence. Conversely, if the 'natural' is the only reality there is, the mother is lying to the child—lying out of love, to be sure, and obviously *not* lying to the extent that her reassurance is grounded in that fact of this love—but, in the final analysis, lying all the same. Why? *Because the reassurance, transcending the immediately present two individuals and their situation, implies a statement about reality as such.*[29]

(ii) The argument from damnation

Berger's point here refers to 'experience in which our sense of what is humanly permissible is so fundamentally outraged that the only adequate response to the offence as well as to the offender seems to be a curse of supernatural dimensions'.[30] His illustration is that of the Nazi war criminals and Eichmann in particular. Without any trace of sadism, Berger is able to say that 'No human punishment is "enough" in the case of deeds as monstrous as these'.[31] In other words, human wickedness points men to that which is beyond themselves.

Again, one must emphasize that this is not a matter simply of believing or disbelieving in God. In some circumstances it may be a matter of people strengthening the tenuous hold they already have on him and in others of being willing to think again.

(3) Disclosures

Disclosures may well prove to be more than 'Intimations' but not always so, and they are best included here.[32]

Paradoxically, one cannot always be sure beyond all doubt as to who or what is being disclosed. It is easier with people, of course, like the man in Ian Ramsey's *Religious Language*[33]

---

[29] Pp. 72–3 (author's italics).
[30] P. 84.   [31] P. 87.
[32] The student should re-read the brief section on theology as disclosure at the end of chapter 1.
[33] P. 28.

who is known simply as the man who orders 'Double Diamond', does *The Times* crossword in fifteen minutes, has a wife and three children and too much herbaceous border to weed in the evenings but who discloses himself by offering his hand and saying, 'Look here—I'm Nigel Short'. But God does not act in quite that manner, not even in Exodus 3, and the response required is always that of faith.

The field for disclosure is wide. If God has created all things, then anything could be the medium of disclosure. If God has created people, then any person can be the means of disclosure, to himself or to others. If everything that happens is the concern of a loving Father, then every human experience, not least the most distressing ones, may be, for a particular person at a particular time, a disclosure of God. And the role of the preacher is not to introduce people to a God with whom they have no relation, but to help them recognize the God who is already active in their lives? In other words, to lead them *from what has happened to them* to faith.

(4) Less unhelpful notions of God

Under this deliberately modest title a small number of 'present considerations' can be mentioned. The fact that they are 'present' is of some importance, for the way in which we think and speak about God is much affected by the culture of which we are a part.

(i) Transcendence

The problem here is how to make it clear that God really is God, without using such spatial expressions as 'up there' or 'out there' that seem to invite disbelief.

Some theologians have expressed the big difference between God and man in terms of quality of character, of holiness. The difference is essentially a religious one. So Gustav Aulén:

> It is perfectly clear to faith that the divine presence at the same time accentuates the separation between the divine and the human. The more faith perceives the presence of God and

138

experiences the fellowship, the more definitely appears also the distance between God and man.[34]

That this is part of religious experience few would deny, and it may therefore solve the problem for some. But is it the whole truth about God's transcendence, his otherness?

In *The Remaking of Christian Doctrine*[35] Maurice Wiles contends for belief in a transcendent creator by producing two arguments, well known to theological students, and showing their point for today. One is the *cosmological* argument (that the universe must have a sufficient cause and this can only be found in God). This means that when we use the word 'God' we are referring to that which is ultimate, absolute, the creator, the source and the ground of all that is. And we may do this, argues Wiles, as it is a way of indicating that reality to which we trace the ultimate dependence of ourselves and all that is; a way of expressing our wonder that there should *be* anything at all. Can one think of God in any other way?

The other argument from the book is the *teleological* one (that as there is evidence of order and design in the world there must be a Designer). This dwells on those purposes, large and small, that fill our lives and lead us to suppose that we do not inhabit one vast madhouse. Presumably therefore there is purpose in the overall relationship of God to the world and Christians may fairly claim to have some insights into what it is.[36] It is not reckoned by Wiles to include those personal interventions that we recorded as stumbling blocks to faith. But it is enough to come to the conclusion that there is ultimate sense in things and that is part of the experience of a transcendent God.

(ii) Depth
The key passage here is from Paul Tillich.[37] No one can study theology post 1963 without paying attention to this passage:

The name of this infinite and inexhaustible depth and ground of all being is *God*. That depth is what the word *God* means. And if that word has not much meaning for you, translate it, and speak of the depths of your life, of the source of your being,

[34] *The Faith of the Christian Church* (S.C.M. 1954), p. 154.
[35] S.C.M. 1974.
[36] As with moral excellence (footnote, p. 118) this does not mean that there is a fixed order and purpose to which God has to conform. Order and purpose are what they are precisely because they are found in God.
[37] *The Shaking of the Foundations* (Pelican 1962), pp. 63 f.

of your ultimate concern, of what you take seriously without any reservation. Perhaps, in order to do so, you must forget everything traditional that you have learned about God, perhaps even that word itself. For if you know that God means depth. you know much about him. You cannot then call yourself an atheist or unbeliever. For you cannot think or say: Life has no depth! Life is shallow. Being itself is surface only. If you could say this in complete seriousness, you would be an atheist; but otherwise you are not. He who knows about depth knows about God.

The obvious charge that to switch God from 'up there' to 'down there' is simply a change of metaphor is one that John Robinson meets in *Honest to God*. He contends that 'depth' has richer, profounder associations than height'. More importantly he stresses that when Tillich speaks of God in 'depth' he is not really referring to another Being at all.[38] Rather he is speaking of the 'infinite and inexhaustible depth and ground of all being', of our 'ultimate concern'. To put the matter more simply, he has in mind the answers to the two questions: 'What is life all about?' and 'To what am I prepared to commit myself without reservation?' You might of course ask what has happened to the personality of God in this magnificent conception and you would be right to enquire, for theologies of immanence do tend to present God as pervasive rather than personal. The answer is that the ground of *all* being sustains personal being as well as every other sort.

To believe in God so conceived is not simply being willing to acknowledge the existence of the Deity. 'I believe that there is a God' will not do at all. No:

It is a question of openness to the holy, the sacred, in the unfathomable depths of even the most secular relationship.[39]

Does this make it easier to believe in God?

(iii) God as Being
The idea quoted from Tillich, going back at least to Thomas Aquinas,

38 See p. 113.
39 John Robinson, *Honest to God*, p. 48.

that God is not *a* Being, but Being itself takes us back to the start of the chapter. There Being was referred to as 'that which enables beings at all'. This is the theme of the Anglican theologian, John Macquarrie, in his *Principles of Christian Theology*. He says:

The expression which I prefer to use, however, to point to the characteristic of being as the condition that there may be any particular beings, is 'letting be'. Being, strictly, 'is' not; but being 'lets be'.[40]

Then, in the rest of the book, he writes of God in terms of holy Being who 'lets all else be'.

We only call him 'God' and recognize him as holy Being, calling forth our worship, because he pours out Being.[41]

He enables us to be.

God is absolute letting-be and letting he is the ... foundation of love.[42]

These concepts and this language are not easy, so it is necessary to stop short, hoping that for some people struggling to believe, 'God as Being' is for them one of the 'less unhelpful notions'.

In this chapter, as in subsequent ones, the last section must remain unfinished, for there will be fresh present considerations with every year that passes. Theology is a dynamic study. The responsibility of the preacher is to hold together the truth that comes out of the past and the truth that is being disclosed in the present.

[40] P. 103.
[41] P. 138.
[42] P. 278.

Chapter 5

Jesus Christ

A. THE FOUNDATION DOCUMENTS

The Apostles' Creed

I believe in Jesus Christ, his only son, our Lord.
He was conceived by the power of the Holy Spirit and born
of the Virgin Mary.

The Nicene Creed

We believe in one Lord, Jesus Christ,
the only Son of God,
eternally begotten of the Father,
God from God, Light from Light,
True God from true God,
begotten, not made,
of one Being with the Father.
Through him all things were made.
For us men and for our salvation
he came down from heaven:
by the power of the Holy Spirit
he became incarnate from the Virgin Mary, and was made
man.

The Thirty-nine Articles

II.   Of the Word or Son of God, which was made very Man
The Son, which is the Word of the Father, begotten from

everlasting of the Father, the very and eternal God, and of one substance with the Father, took Man's nature in the womb of the blessed Virgin, of her substance: so that two whole and perfect Natures, that is to say, the Godhead and Manhood, were joined together in one Person, never to be divided, whereof is one Christ, very God, and very Man; ...

The Deed of Union

Clause 30.[1]

Explanatory Notes upon the New Testament (John Wesley)

Commentary on John 10:30
I and the Father are one—Not by consent of will only, but by unity of power, and consequently of nature.
Commentary on John 14:10
I am in the Father—That is, I am one with the Father in essence, in speaking, and in acting.
Commentary on Philippians 2:7
Being made in the likeness of men—A real man, like other men.

Sermon V. Justification by Faith (John Wesley)

In the fullness of time He was made man, another common Head of mankind, a second general Parent and Representative of the whole human race.

Sermon IX. The Spirit of Bondage and of Adoption (John Wesley)

The man under grace 'sees the light of the glorious love of God, in the face of Jesus Christ'.

[1] See pp. 53, 74.

The Senior Catechism of the Methodist Church

7. WHY IS JESUS CALLED CHRIST?

He fulfilled God's promises made to mankind through the Hebrew people that a king would come to reign in righteousness and peace.

8. HOW IS JESUS CHRIST THE ONLY SON OF GOD?

In His nature and being He is eternally one with God the Father.

9. WHY DO WE WORSHIP HIM AS LORD?

He is to be worshipped and obeyed as the Lord of all because He is one with the Father and was born, lived, died and rose again, and ever lives and reigns.

10. WHAT DO WE MEAN BY 'CONCEIVED BY THE HOLY GHOST, BORN OF THE VIRGIN MARY'?

It was by the power of the Holy Ghost that Jesus was born of His human mother, and He was in Himself both human and divine.

The Methodist Service Book

For you alone are the Holy One,
you alone are the Lord,
you alone are the Most High,
Jesus Christ, with the Holy Spirit,
in the glory of God the Father.

(The Sunday Service, p. B6)

Jesus Christ is holy, Jesus Christ is Lord
to the glory of God the Father.

(The Sunday Service, p. B15)

Almighty God, who wonderfully created us in your own image and yet more wonderfully restored us through your Son Jesus Christ: grant that as he came to share in our humanity, so we may share the life of his divinity; who is alive and reigns with you and the Holy Spirit, one God, now and for ever.

(Collect for Christmas Day, p. C12)

144

The Methodist Hymn Book

Let earth and heaven combine,
  Angels and men agree,
To praise in songs divine
  The incarnate Deity,
Our God contracted to a span,
Incomprehensibly made man.

(142, v. 1) (Charles Wesley)

B. THE DOCTRINE OF THE PERSON OF JESUS CHRIST

(1) Theology and history

Theology is made all the more interesting by its encounters with other subjects. Already this book has flirted with anthropology (the look at religion as it has occurred in the life of man) and with philosophy (the brief references to 'being'); a relationship must now be formed with history. Christianity, as has been said so often, is a historical religion. This means that its distinctiveness lies in the central position and importance it gives to a series of events which, so it is asserted, occurred in Palestine within a specified period that can be marked on a calendar. Jesus of Nazareth was a figure of history. Theology has therefore to know something about history and the way in which historians do their work.

(i) Event
History is in the first place concerned with what actually happened. In 1066 William the Conqueror came, in 1666 the Great Fire of London raged—this is part of the recital of events that has made many a schoolboy's life a misery. To pass school history examinations you have at least to know your dates. This is history in a very raw state, for a moment's reflection shows that simply to date an event is not to say very much about it.

When one probes a little deeper in search of what actually

145

happened in any given event, one is just as likely to find questions as answers. A few years ago there was a sustained correspondence in *The Times*, and a television programme, about the massacre of Polish officers in the Katyn Forest during the Second World War. It had happened. The bones had been uncovered. But who did it? The Germans? The Russians? And why was it done? We do not know the answers with certainty, and probably never shall.[2] Hence it is not surprising that history is regarded by some as the study of probabilities.

Theology has an intense interest in the events surrounding the appearance in history of Jesus of Nazareth. That he lived, and at a time that can be dated within a few years, no responsible historian would deny. But over 'what actually happened' in its precise detail, the exact words and deeds of Jesus, there is much argument.

Apart from scholars, who have a professional interest in such questions, some Christians regard these matters as more crucial for their faith than do others. They view with misgiving, even with alarm, the ease with which other Christians regard this or that event or this or that saying in the New Testament as expendable. They look to archaeology to substantiate the events recorded in the Bible. They would be predisposed to believe that bearded priest in Samaria who, for a consideration, drops a stone for every party of tourists to prove that 'the well was deep'. Of course they have a point: a historical religion must be concerned about its history. Other Christians, however, are not willing to give such weight to historical questions; they feel that to do so is to substitute evidence for faith and to sell out theology to the historians. The student may see these two positions as complementary.

(ii) *Interpretation*
If it is difficult to find out 'what actually happened' it is even more difficult to reach agreement about the meaning of what happened. People see events so differently. There are two

[2] The subject received publicity again in 1976 with the erection of a Katyn memorial in West London. This memorial assumes Russian guilt, but the Russians insist that the Germans were to blame.

146

ways of looking at the First World War: the way of the War Memorial that speaks of 'the glorious and immortal dead who gave their lives for freedom so that the world could grow old in peace'[3] and the way of *Oh What a Lovely War* which sees it as a foolish and unnecessary mistake, prosecuted with a half-witted fanaticism. The same events, but a very different interpretation.

The matter does not, however, stop there. A circular process is involved for, having interpreted an event or a series of events in a particular way, that way will undoubtedly influence the judgement made on any fresh material purporting to add to our knowledge of 'events'. Thus, to refer to our previous example, Russian *émigrés* did not take much convincing that the Katyn Forest murders were perpetrated by the Russians. Is it too cynical to suggest that their minds were made up before they looked at the evidence?

Interpretation is a central issue in the case of Jesus. Of course it is true that people interpreted him differently: some saw him as a threat to the religion of Israel, others acclaimed him as Messiah and Lord. It is also true that facts are presented in the light of the interpretation. As it is sometimes put, the Gospels are confessional documents. This means that the writers were not as much interested in circulating an impartial biography or recounting the events of a story (though these certainly had their place: Luke 1:1–4) as in persuading people to believe that the claims they made about Jesus were true. As Morna Hooker has put it—'the gospels are recognized as "propaganda" ',[4] or as John 20:31 has it, 'these are written that you may believe that Jesus is the Christ, the Son of God, and that believing you may have life in his name'.

New Testament scholarship concerns itself with this whole area of enquiry, studying the reciprocal relationships between the events and the interpretations. As a result we have constantly to be looking in new ways at the evidence concerning Jesus.

We now turn to the questions: 'What do the New Testa-

[3] So Burton upon Trent.
[4] 'What do we preach about Jesus Christ?' *Epworth Review*, Vol. 3, No. 7, January 1976, p. 50.

ment and the traditional theology of the Church have to tell us about Jesus of Nazareth?' 'How do they see the facts?' 'What is the interpretation they offer us?'

(2) Jesus was a man

The first Christians knew Jesus as a human being and spoke of him as such. Peter's sermon on the day of Pentecost cannot be interpreted in any other way:

> 'Men of Israel, hear these words: Jesus of Nazareth, a man attested to you by God with mighty works and wonders and signs which God did through him in your midst, as you yourselves know—this Jesus, delivered up according to the definite plan and foreknowledge of God, you crucified and killed by the hands of lawless men. . . .' (Acts 2:22-3).

The Gospel of Mark refers to a man: his anger (3:5), his indignation (10:14), his surprise (6:6), his compassion (6:34), his disappointment (8:17; 9:19), his lack of knowledge (13:32). This was the man about whom it had been said:

> Is not this the carpenter, the son of Mary and the brother of James and Joses and Judas and Simon, and are not his sisters here with us? (Mark 6:3).

The Church has been so seized of the importance of maintaining the true humanity of Jesus that it has pounced on views that suggested the contrary. One of the first heresies to arise, and that before the New Testament was completed, was *Docetism*: that Jesus only *appeared* to be human (the Greek word *dokein* means 'to seem'); his body was in fact a phantom. The resistance to this probably accounts for the emphasis upon the sheer physical nature of Jesus in the Fourth Gospel. The story of doubting Thomas:

> Put your finger here, and see my hands; and put out your hand, and place it in my side (20:27).

was in part a refutation of the first heresy.

148

From that day to this Christian orthodoxy has insisted on the full humanity of Jesus. A modern theologian sums it up:

> *Jesus is truly human.* However we may think of the ways in which we come to know about him, and whatever reliance we may be prepared to place upon the details of the narratives found in the gospels, there can be no Christianity without the humanity of Jesus. He was born, he lived and worked, he suffered and died; and all this as a man.[5]

(3) What more does the New Testament say about Jesus?

Before answers to this question are given, one point must be made clear. It is not a matter of looking at the titles and attributes of Jesus (Messiah, Son of God, inaugurator of the kingdom, sinless, and so forth) and then affirming that a person so categorized must obviously be more than a man. The process worked the other way round. It was precisely the unique impact of Jesus in his human life that made the first Christians look around for such expressions to use about him. That was how, for example, they came to call him Lord. To put the point technically, the assertions are Christological before they are historical; to put it simply, the first statements about Jesus were statements, not primarily of history, but of faith. *Only in the light of this understanding can the evidence of the New Testament be considered.*

(i) Jesus was Messiah

'Messiah' means 'Anointed' and was translated into Greek as 'Christos', but it soon came to be used as a proper name. It is true that Jesus is not (save in John 4:25-6 and that in private) represented as claiming to be Messiah and only with some hesitation does he accept the title when it is thrust upon him. (Mark 8:29-30; Matt. 16:16, 20; Luke 9:20-1; Matt. 26:63-4 (but see Mark 14:61-2); Luke 22:67-8). It was, however, a title that the Christians of the early Church gladly accorded him, particularly the Jewish ones who knew what it meant. Indeed, as we have noticed, the Fourth Gospel was

[5] W. Norman Pittenger, *The Word Incarnate* (Nisbet 1959), p. 11.

written precisely so that people could believe he was just that (John 20:31). What did his followers mean when they called him Christ?

In popular Jewish expectation, Messiah was thought of as, among other things, 'Son of David', a powerful king who would deliver captive Israel and enable her to realize her destiny as the Chosen People of God. It seems as if both political independence and religious aspiration were mingled in such a hope: certainly it was much more than jingoistic tub-thumping. God himself was coming to reign, in a new and more direct way, and Messiah was his herald. So when Jesus came into Galilee saying:

The time is fulfilled, and the kingdom of God is at hand (Mark 1:15)

it is not surprising that the question of Messiahship should at least be raised.

The question of the way in which Jesus himself may be said to have viewed his Messiahship is a vexed one among scholars. Much of the argument has centred around the use by Jesus of the term *the Son of man*. Some think 'the Son of man' is a re-interpretation of the suffering servant of Isaiah 52:13–53,[6] but this view has been contested.[7] In the Old Testament the term is used as a synonym of 'man' (Ps. 8:4; Ex. 2:1) but in Daniel 7:13 f. 'one like a son of man' signifies a figure representative of a renewed Israel appointed by God to bring in his kingdom. In the Jewish book of Enoch the term describes the figure who is to be the instrument of God's judgement and rule. Against this background Jesus uses the term of himself.

It is because he is the Son of man that Jesus claims authority; it is his obedience as Son of man that involves him in suffering;

[6] E.g. Vincent Taylor, *The Gospel According to St Mark*, (Macmillan 1955), pp. 119 f.
[7] See Morna D. Hooker, *The Son of Man in Mark* (S.P.C.K. 1967), pp. 187–8.

it is the fact that he is Son of man that is the ground of his faith and his ultimate vindication.[8]

The term 'the Son of man' was not generally used by the early Church to express its view of Jesus (Acts 7:56; Rev. 1:13; 14:14 are the only cases) because he had by then already been exalted and vindicated by God. 'Messiah' was a better word for the first Christians and they used it to express their conviction that Jesus was a unique human being of extraordinary significance.

(ii) Jesus was the inaugurator of the kingdom[9]
Mark 1:14–15 is the slogan. As the Jerusalem Bible has it:

'The time has come', he said, 'and the Kingdom of God is close at hand. Repent and believe the Good News.'

on which C. H. Dodd's paraphrase is:

Here is God in all his power and majesty, confronting you where you live! What are you going to do about it?[10]

What was the nature of the person about whom it could be said that the reign of God had begun *with him*? Granted that it was the Father's good pleasure to give the kingdom (Luke 12:32), Jesus was clearly reckoned to be instrumental in the operation in a unique fashion. He was in the prophetic tradition, to be sure (Mark 6:15), but more than that needed to be said. Matthew 12:28 and Luke 11:20 say it. Jesus is the inaugurator of the kingdom of God.

(iii) Jesus was sinless
This assertion appears in the New Testament and in much traditional theology.

---

[8] Hooker, pp. 190–1. There is a clear and brief summary of the complicated 'Son of Man' situation in Hans Küng, *On Being a Christian* (Collins 1977), pp. 289–90.
[9] See also chapter 9.
[10] *The Founder of Christianity* (Collins 1971), p. 56.

GROUNDWORK OF THEOLOGY

For our sake he made him to be sin who knew no sin (2 Cor. 5:21).

He committed no sin: no guile was found on his lips (1 Pet. 2:22).

One who in every respect has been tempted as we are, yet without sinning (Heb. 4:14).

During the greater portion of Christian history...it has been taken for granted that He was without sin; this being the very least that has been spontaneously conceded by any affecting to believe on Him in any sense.[11]

It has to be admitted that sinlessness is a negative concept, but it has been thought necessary to maintain it on two counts. One is that though it cannot possibly be demonstrated, for we have no access to the secret thoughts of Jesus, it is an essential part of the impression Jesus made on his contemporaries. The New Testament attributes no consciousness of sin or guilt to him. The other consideration is a theological one: that a spotless victim was a requirement for any sacrificial theory effecting man's salvation.

The difficulty of course is to reconcile being sinless with being a real man, for no other real man we have ever encountered in history or experience has been sinless. This difficulty has usually been met by the assertion that Jesus possessed the freedom to sin or not to sin and at every temptation chose not to do so. As a result:

We know of no situation which could shake the truth of these words: 'yet without sin'.[12]

This provides further support for the use of the word 'unique' in describing Jesus.

[11] James Stalker, 'Sinlessness', *Dictionary of Christ and the Gospels* (T. & T. Clark 1908), Vol. II, p. 637.
[12] Emil Brünner, *The Christian Doctrine of Creation and Redemption* (Lutterworth 1952), p. 324.

152

(iv) Jesus was born of a virgin

Roman Catholic theologians make a distinction between the Immaculate Conception (the doctrine that from the first moment of her conception Mary was kept free of all stain of original sin), the Virgin Conception (that the agent in pro-creation was the Holy Spirit) and the Virgin Birth proper (that by a supernatural stretching of the hymen Mary was in every respect a virgin when Jesus was born). Most Protestants under-stand the Virgin Birth to be the second of these three. It is a doctrine about which differing views are held.

In his note on the Virgin Birth in *Introducing Theology*[13] (a predecessor of this book) Munsey Turner listed the arguments for and against the doctrine as follows:

The basic arguments which underlie the doctrine are:

(1) The Birth narratives of Luke 1:26–38 and Matthew 1:18–25 clearly point to a virgin birth.

(2) Judaism, on the whole, did not in any way exalt virginity over marriage, yet the virgin birth tradition appears in a distinctively Jewish and probably Palestinian stratum of the New Testament.

(3) No doctrinal use appears to have been made of the tradition in the rest of the New Testament, so that it does not appear to have been invented as a Christological argument during the N.T. period.

(4) The doctrine appears early on in non-canonical writing in Ignatius (*c.* AD 110) and Justin Martyr (*c.* AD 150) though the latter clearly speaks of Christians who do not hold the doctrine.

(5) The doctrine appears in the principal Christian creeds and doctrinal statements.

On the negative side we can say:

(1) Some scholars believe that mythological and legendary elements are present in the birth narratives.

(2) The virgin birth does not feature in the basic apostolic *kerygma* or preaching.

(3) The virgin birth tradition does not appear in very large portions of the New Testament—Mark, Paul, John, the Letter to the Hebrews make no mention of it.

(4) There are several ancient manuscripts which speak of Joseph as Jesus's father, i.e. they do not appear to know of a virgin birth tradition.

[13] Pp. 56–7.

153

(5) The argument from the prophecy of the coming of Emmanuel in Isaiah 7:14 is confused. The original word in the Hebrew means 'young woman', though in the Greek translation of the Old Testament (The Septuagint) the word used does mean a virgin.

(6) The genealogies of Jesus trace his descent through *Joseph* and he is claimed to be of the House of David through him.

(7) Jesus is referred to in the Gospels in a way which suggests normal parentage (Luke 2:27, 41; Matt. 13:55; John 6:42).

There are further important questions to be thought about. Is the doctrine primarily a way of expressing the truth that 'God was in Christ'? Or is its point the initiative of God, not man, in the plan of salvation? In either case, the doctrine is primarily Christology (a statement about the significance of Jesus) rather than history (a statement about how Jesus was conceived and born).

(v) Jesus performed miracles

Men of Israel, hear these words: Jesus of Nazareth, a man attested to you by God with mighty works and wonders and signs which God did through him in your midst, as you yourselves know ... (Acts 2:22).

This is the primitive Christian tradition: that Jesus performed miracles. For those first Christians, whose spokesman Peter was, the matter was beyond doubt. Jesus himself is recorded as making reference to his miracles in two passages 'which are accepted by almost all scholars as authentic'.[14] One is the answer to the question of John the Baptist, 'Are you he who is to come, or shall we look for another?':

Go and tell John what you hear and see: the blind receive their sight and the lame walk, lepers are cleansed and the deaf hear, and the dead are raised up.... (Matt. 11:3–5; Luke 7:20, 22)

The other is part of the Beelzebub controversy (Matt. 12:24–8; Luke 11:15–20):

[14] J. P. M. Sweet, 'Miracle and Faith (2): The Miracles of Jesus', *Epworth Review*, Vol. 3, No. 2, p. 83.

But if it is by the Spirit of God that I cast out demons, then the Kingdom of God has come upon you (Matt. 12:28).

There is therefore a solid tradition in which the important question was not whether the miracles happened or not but under whose authority and power they happened. This was important because the alternatives were genuine possibilities: they could have been done under Satan or under God. Hence Jesus specifically refutes the possibility of Satan's casting out Satan (Matt. 12:24–7; Luke 11:15–19) and the first Christians are careful to attribute the miraculous works of Jesus to the power of God (Acts 10:38).

Behind these assertions of Jesus and his first followers lay a definite view of the purpose of God. God had made man in his own image and he had given him dominion over the beasts of the field and the fowls of the air (Gen. 1; Ps. 8). As long as he discharged his stewardship in fidelity and obedience, all was well. But once he rebelled and insisted on going his own way he brought upon himself and upon the entire creation nothing but trouble. This was not seen by the Jews as a piece of theology to be argued about at the gate of the village at the end of the day; it was intimately linked with the political fate of Israel and its oppression by one alien empire after another.

Every pious Jew looked for the deliverance of Israel, in terms of both political freedom and the restoration of that proper standing with God, the loss of which had preceded the political disasters. God would restore the (whole) kingdom to Israel. And part of the evidence that he was actually doing so would be signs and wonders performed under his authority and power. Hence the miracles of Jesus are in intimate relationship to the place he had in God's plans for the redemption of Israel, and of all mankind. They are the signs of the new order driving out the old, under God's new Messiah.

Why then was Jesus so cautious about his miracles, refusing to do them to order? There are two traditional answers. First, that he wished to avoid that blaze of publicity which would probably have frustrated his primary work of preaching and teaching the good news of what God was doing. Secondly,

155

that a response based predominantly upon having seen a miracle was likely to be lacking in depth. Jesus countered the latter danger by an insistence that miracles, like everything else, should lead to faith in God.

(vi) Jesus was the Son of God

In the Old Testament Israel is referred to as a son of God (Ex. 4:22; Hos. 11:1) as is the person with a special mission from God (2 Sam. 7:14; Ps. 2:7; 89:26). 'Son of God' expresses not physical descent but reflection of character, just as 'Son of Belial' is a comment not on a man's ancestry but upon his wickedness. The title is used of Jesus in association with moments of deep awareness of God, e.g. baptism (Mark 1:10), transfiguration (Mark 9:7). The Fourth Gospel, particularly, is full of references to 'the Son' (1:18, 34, 49; 3:16, 17, 18, 35, 36, etc.) and the Son is the revealer of the Father. Other New Testament writers see Jesus as the Son of God from whom their own sonship is derived (Rom. 8:14 ff.; Gal. 4:6 ff.; 1 Cor. 1:9; Heb. 1).

Furthermore, there is associated with 'Son of God' the notion of pre-existence, though that is an incidental rather than a primary idea in the New Testament. The Acts 2 quotation refers to 'the definite plan and foreknowledge of God' (v. 23) and this came to be understood as implying the existence of Christ with God, before the birth to Mary at Bethlehem. Most of us are familiar with the idea from the great prologue to the Fourth Gospel, but it is in Hebrews as well. It is also in Paul.[15]

The answer to the question 'What did the New Testament *mean* by referring to Jesus as the Son of God?' is a complex one, for different writers and readers understood different things by the expression. It meant one thing to the first Palestinian Christians, another to the writer and readers of the Fourth Gospel.[16] There is, however, common ground. It is to be found, not in the notion of a divine being descending from

---

[15] See Phil. 2:5–7; 2 Cor. 5:21: Rom. 8:3–4.

[16] The whole subject is worked through very thoroughly in R. H. Fuller, *The Foundations of the New Testament Christology* (Collins Fontana 1969).

heaven, but in the belief that in Jesus of Nazareth God was accomplishing the salvation of the world.

(vii) Jesus was Lord

If there was one word more than another that summed up the reactions of the first Christians to Jesus, it was the word 'Lord'. It was used very early in the life of the Church (1 Cor. 16:22), in credal statements (Rom. 10:9; 1 Cor. 12:3) probably made at baptisms (Acts 8:16).

For those Jews who knew Greek the significance of the word (Kurios in Greek) was that in the Greek translation of the Old Testament it translates the Hebrew words for 'God'. For those Greeks who were pagans the word was used of divinities in their own mystery religions.[17] To use the word of any man, therefore, was to attribute to him what had previously been attributed to divinity.

It would be a mistake, however, to jump to big conclusions, for in the New Testament the word is also used as a general title of courtesy or as a name for a master or owner (Matt. 21:30; Luke 13:8) and as a form of direct address to Jesus in a context that would not seem to imply divinity.

It is interesting that the use of the title with the definite article, 'the Lord', for Jesus occurs almost entirely in the two later Gospels, Luke (eighteen times) and John (twelve times). This suggests a development in the use of Kurios among the first Christians in the direction of divinity.

(viii) Does the New Testament call Jesus 'God'?

The following passages expose some of the difficulties that are to be found in answering this question.

Rom. 9:5 The point here is whether the doxology is to be attributed to Christ (as A.V., R.V. and Jerusalem) or to God (as R.V. margin, Moffatt, N.E.B.). It is uncertain.
Heb. 1:8–9 This is a quotation from Psalm 45:7–8 which is applied

[17] 'The mystery religions promised their members salvation, both in the sense of deliverance from life's misfortunes and in the ultimate sense of immortality and the salvation of the soul. As the name suggests, the mysteries were characterised by secret rites and formulae known only to the initiated.'—Eric Lord and Donald Whittle, A Theological Glossary (R.E.P. 1969), p. 77.

to Christ to show his superiority to the angels. The divine name (God) appears to be there simply because it is part of the quotation. But some[18] argue that this verse is applied to the Son precisely because it contains the reference to 'God'.

John 1:1–18 Scholars disagree about the meaning that should be given to Jesus the Word in this passage, and particularly in verses 1 and 18. VINCENT TAYLOR[19] notes that in v. 1 the definite article is not used in the final clause. For this reason, he says, it is generally translated 'and the Word was divine' (Moffat) or is not regarded as God 'in the absolute sense of the name'. The New English Bible neatly paraphrases the phrase in the words 'and what God was, the Word was'. As for v. 18, Taylor points out that the textual evidence for 'only-begotten God' is stronger than that for 'only-begotten Son'. His conclusion is:

> In neither passage is Jesus unequivocally called God, while again and again, in the Gospel He is named 'the Son' or 'the Son of God'.

C. K. BARRETT, however, accounts differently for the omission of the article in v. 1:

> The absence of the article indicates that the Word is God, but is not the only being of whom this is true[20]

Barrett says that if the article had been written, the implication would have been that no divine being existed outside the second person of the Trinity.

OSCAR CULLMANN[21] insists that v. 1 ought not to have its absoluteness and sharpness weakened (this is what Vincent Taylor did), for the Word is not subordinate to God, he is God himself in so far as God speaks and reveals himself. (This emphasis on the *action* of God as the essential character of the Word is important and will be taken up later in the chapter.)

As for v. 18 C. K. Barrett admits the textual point made by Vincent Taylor, but adds:

> The sense is substantially unaltered by the textual variation. The Son is the Word and the Word has already been declared to be *theos* (God).[22]

John 20:28 This verse expresses worship and devotion to the risen Christ as God.

Titus 2:13 There is argument as to whether the correct translation is:

[18] Oscar Cullmann, for example, in *The Christology of the New Testament* (S.C.M. 1959), p. 310.
[19] *New Testament Essays* (Epworth 1970), pp. 85–6.
[20] *The Gospel according to St John* (S.P.C.K. 1958), p. 130.
[21] *The Christology of the New Testament*, p. 265.
[22] P. 141.

the glory of our great God and Saviour Jesus Christ (R.V., R.S.V., N.E.B., Jerusalem),
or
the glory of our great God, and of our Saviour Jesus Christ (A.V., R.V. Margin).

It would appear from these passages, and from others with which there is no space to deal, that the New Testament is reticent in the matter of calling Jesus 'God'. One factor in this state of affairs would seem to be that the intense monotheism of the Old Testament made the writers of the New Testament reluctant to take such a revolutionary step. But, more importantly 'Was Jesus God?' is not a question the New Testament itself asks. The concern of John 1, for instance, is rather to express the one purpose of God in speaking, acting and revealing himself in and through Jesus.

(4) Development of the Doctrine of the Person of Christ

The problem the first Christians had to face soon emerged. For them three things were true:

1. There was only one God
2. Jesus was a real man
3. They were worshipping and praying to Jesus, as if *he* were God.

How then could 3 be reconciled to 1 and 2?

As they tried to find the answer all kinds of suggestions were made but invariably they stressed one of the numbers (1–3) to the exclusion of the other two or two to the exclusion of the other one. Here are two examples:

Docetism

See p. 148. The human body of Jesus was thought to be only a phantom, an appearance. This asserts 1 and 3 but denies 2.

Adoptionism

It is easy to understand how the first Christians, so close to

159

the human life of Jesus, could come to think of God 'adopting' him into Messianic, or even higher status. There is the suggestion of such a view in Acts 2:36 and Romans 1:4. Adoptionism asserts 1 and 2 but puts 3 at risk. Paul of Samosata (third century), one of the exponents of this view, believed that, though Jesus *became* the Son of God, in his nature he differed only in degree from the prophets.

The debate went on. The theologians associated with Alexandria (CLEMENT, AD 150–212, and ORIGEN, AD 186–254 were the most prominent) stressed the Word (*logos*) that became flesh (so placing the emphasis on our 3). The theologians associated with Antioch (PAUL OF SAMOSATA was one) stressed the humanity of Jesus (our 2). Then came the conflict between ARIUS (AD 250–336), for whom Jesus was a kind of demi-god in a human body (denying our 2), a doctrine he expressed in popular songs, and ATHANASIUS (AD 295–373). The latter's views were adopted by the Council of Nicea (AD 325) and expressed first in a short creed and then in the expanded one that we still use. Here, Christ is 'of one Being with the Father', i.e. he is not just 'like God' (Arius), he is 'God from God, Light from Light, true God from true God'. Yet he was made man. It was a bold attempt to keep our 1, 2 and 3 together.

The arguments about the divinity and humanity of Jesus did not then die down. APOLLINARIUS (AD 310–390) denied that Jesus had a complete human nature. In him the eternal Word took the place of the human mind. The Council of Constantinople in AD 381 rejected this view. NESTORIUS, bishop of Constantinople (d. *c.* AD 451) had his name attached, perhaps a little unfairly, to the view that there were not only two natures in Christ, one divine and one human, but also that he was in fact two Persons. The Council of Ephesus in AD 431 rejected this view. EUTYCHES (*c.* AD 378–454), head of a monastery at Constantinople, went to the opposite extreme and declared that there was only one nature in Jesus, that of God become flesh.

The Church sought to settle all the arguments at the COUNCIL OF CHALCEDON in AD 451 and this is what was said:

We, then, following the holy Fathers, all with one consent, teach men to confess one and the same Son, our Lord Jesus Christ, the same perfect in Godhead and also perfect in manhood; truly God and truly man, of a reasonable[23] soul and body; consubstantial[24] with the Father according to the Godhead, and consubstantial with us according to the manhood; in all things like unto us without sin; begotten before all ages of the Father according to the Godhead, and in these latter days, for us and for our salvation, born of the Virgin Mary, the Mother of God, according to the manhood; one and the same Christ, Son, Lord, Only-begotten, in two natures, inconfusedly, unchangeably, indivisibly, inseparably, the distinction of natures being by no means taken away by the union, but rather the property of each nature being preserved and concurring in one person, and one substance, not parted or divided into two persons, but one and the same Son and only-begotten, God the Word, the Lord Jesus Christ; as the prophets from the beginning have declared concerning Him, and as the Lord Jesus Christ Himself has taught us, and the creed of the holy Fathers has been handed down to us.

This then was, and is, the orthodox Christian position. Out go Arius (by 'Jesus is consubstantial with the Father and consubstantial with us'), Apollinarius (by 'truly man'), Nestorius (by 'not parted or divided into two persons') and Eutyches (by 'in two natures'). The Christian faith is that the one God is incarnate in the real man, Jesus Christ.

C. PRESENT CONSIDERATIONS

It is necessary to look now at some of these questions as they are thought about and discussed in our own time. In doing so we have to try to avoid the arrogance which assumes that the latest is invariably the best, that the wisdom of the present is always to be preferred to that of the past. At the same time we have to realize why the operation is necessary. Jesus Christ may be the same yesterday and today and for ever, but man's understanding and interpretation of him are always on the move, changing with the changes of thought and language and culture generally. The debate will be about the same subjects, but it will be *our* debate, carried on in the terms of our understanding and our interpretation. 'What is bothering me incessantly', wrote Dietrich Bonhoeffer,[25] 'is the question... who Christ really is, for us today'. It has to bother us too.

[23] Reasonable = rational.
[24] Consubstantial = of one substance or being.
[25] *Letters and Papers from Prison* (S.C.M. 1967), p. 152.

(1) The historical Jesus

Attention has been drawn to the importance of historical questions,[26] and this is recognizable in the modern debate about Jesus. Indeed the course of the debate can be traced in terms of the changing, developing attitudes towards Jesus as a historical figure.

(i) The Jesus of history movement

During the nineteenth century, and for some years into this one, there took place what is known as 'the quest of the historical Jesus'. That is in fact the English title of a book, published in 1906, by Albert Schweitzer, in which the great man undertook the task of assessing all that had been written on the life of Christ (mainly in Germany) for over a century. Although to generalize is a risky business, one might say that the aim of many of the writers considered by Schweitzer was to get behind the interpretations of Jesus, the preaching of the first Christians, the writings of Paul, the doctrinal statements of the Councils of the Church, to Jesus *as he actually was*. Schweitzer came to the conclusion that the writers had failed, and failed because the materials for writing a systematic biography of Jesus simply do not exist. The so-called lives of Jesus told the reader more about the authors than they did about the subject. But attempts continued. In 1923 a book by A. C. Headlam, Bishop of Gloucester, was published under the title *The Life and Teaching of Jesus Christ* and the author had this to say about it:

> Our purpose was to construct a life on the basis of the material before us, without presuppositions either positive or negative; not to assume what Christian tradition has taught about Jesus, but not to deny it.[27]

Before critical comments are made it must be acknowledged that these authors did well to be so concerned with history,

---

[26] See pp. 145-6.

[27] P. 313 of the book. Quoted in Stephen Neill, *The Interpretation of the New Testament* 1861–1961 (O.U.P. 1964), p. 129.

for Christianity is a historical religion. But in two ways the ongoing debate has pointed to their failure.

(a) The gospel records

The 'Jesus of history' writers assumed, particularly in the case of the Gospel of Mark, that they had a factual account of the precise words and deeds of Jesus. Now before any reader dismisses this paragraph as damnable modernism rearing its ugly head it must be stated clearly that modern scholarship, far from debunking the gospel records, has made them altogether more credible. It has unearthed the foundation upon which they rest—the setting forth, the proclamation, of the significance of Jesus. At the same time scholarship has delivered us from having to believe six impossible things before breakfast and has given us a picture of Jesus upon which we can rely. We may not know to the letter what he said and did, but we know beyond doubt the kind of man he was. A writer as critical as Maurice Wiles,[28] after pointing out that 'New Testament scholars have sharpened their tools to an extreme degree of precision' states that the application of these tools gives us 'a reasonable degree of reliability in the gospel records'. But this is not enough on which to write a big biography. When Harold Wilson left No. 10 Downing Street for the last time the TV news had a shot of the furniture men loading some very large filing cabinets into their van. 'For the benefit of future historians', the newsreader said. There is nothing like that in the case of Jesus. And books written on the assumption that there is will be viewed with a critical eye by every student of theology.

(b) Interpretation

The 'Jesus of history' movement did not give enough weight to the process of interpretation,[29] and in more than one way. The writers failed to see the size of their own interpretations in their work (once described by a critic as an author looking for Christ but seeing only his own face as at the bottom of a

[28] *The Remaking of Christian Doctrine*, p. 47.
[29] See pp. 145–8.

deep well).[30] They also failed to grasp the importance of interpretation in the New Testament itself.

> Even the earliest Gospel (Mark) was not a simple historical narrative but was impregnated with the theological interpretation of the Christian community.[31]

Such a judgement comes, of course, from a situation in which the significance of interpretation is fully recognized.

(ii) The Apostolic preaching

It was in the preaching of the first Christians that the work of the interpretation of Jesus began. If the scholars are to be believed, much of the material in the Gospels was preached again and again before it was written down and in these early 'sermons' Jesus was interpreted to the hearers. In *The Apostolic Preaching and its Development*, C. H. Dodd outlined, as he saw it, the content of those first sermons. It was an interpretation of Jesus in terms of what God had done, and would do, for men through him. This was the *Kerygma*,[32] the proclamation, the good news. We note that such preaching was not an exercise in biography, nor yet a history lesson; it was *theology* or, to be precise, *Christology*, the interpretation of Jesus.

(iii) The debate continues

Modern study of the historical Jesus is indeed a debate, for there is division of opinion wide and deep, and it is a debate studded with the great names of New Testament scholarship. The issue being debated has been clearly stated by a Roman Catholic biblical scholar, XAVIER LÉON-DUFOUR:

> Over the last seventy years it has become customary to draw a distinction between 'the historical Jesus' and 'the Christ of faith'. Though the terms can be used with varying nuances, 'the historical Jesus' generally denotes Jesus as he can be known by the historian, and 'the Christ of faith' stands for the concept of Jesus as the co-

[30] G. Tyrrell of Harnack, *Christianity at the Crossroads* (Longmans 1909), p. 44.
[31] Harvey K. McArthur, *In Search of the Historical Jesus* (S.P.C.K. 1970), p. 5.
[32] See p. 328.

eternal Son of God, adored by the early Church. The issue debated among theologians revolves round this distinction: some maintain that the early Christians created the idea of the Christ of faith by idealizing and deifying Jesus of Nazareth, and that it is impossible to discern from the early Christian writings what Jesus of Nazareth was really like. Can this position be maintained?[33]

KARL BARTH preferred not to be involved in 'the quest for the historical Jesus'. Such detachment was not due to a lack of concern as to what Jesus was actually like. There were at least two reasons for it. One was that he recognized how difficult, if not impossible, it was to disentangle the Jesus of history from the Christ of faith. The other was his un-willingness to deliver Christian faith into the hands of historians. The believer's primary interest must be in the Christ of faith who comes to him through the preaching of the Gospel, from faith to faith.

RUDOLF BULTMANN took a thoroughly radical view:

I do indeed think that we can now know almost nothing concerning the life and personality of Jesus, since the early Christian sources show no interest in either.[34]

Historians can only know what ideas the first Christians themselves had about Jesus (the *existence* of Jesus Bultmann of course takes for granted) but believing Christians can know Christ through faith. What Bultmann has to say about the resurrection is typical:

Nothing preceding the faith which acknowledges the risen Christ can give insight into the reality of *Christ's resurrection*. The resur-rection cannot—in spite of 1 Cor. 15:3-8—be demonstrated or made plausible as an objectively ascertainable fact on the basis of which one could believe. But insofar as it or the risen Christ is present in the proclaiming word, it can be believed—and only so can it be believed.[35]

Others would answer Léon-Dufour's question differently. JOACHIM JEREMIAS would:

Underlying our protest against the equating of the Gospel and the Kergyma[36] is a concern for the concept of revelation. According to the witness of the New Testament there is no other revelation of God but the incarnate Word. The preaching of the early Church, on the other hand, is the divinely inspired witness *to* the revelation, but the Church's preaching is not itself the revelation. To put it bluntly, revelation does not take place from eleven to twelve o'clock

---

[33] *The Gospels and the Jesus of History* (Collins 1968), p. 272.
[34] *Jesus and the Word* (Ivor Nicholson and Watson 1935), p. 8.
[35] *Theology of the New Testament* (S.C.M. 1952), Vol. 1, p. 305.
[36] So Barth and Bultmann.

on Sunday morning.[37] Golgotha is not everywhere, there is only *one* Golgotha, and it lies just outside the walls of Jerusalem.[38]

One of the interesting turns the debate has taken goes under the title of a book by JAMES M. ROBINSON, *A New Quest of the Historical Jesus*.[39] This sees history in terms of the disclosure, in what is recorded, of the intentions, the commitments and the understandings of the person about whom the record is made. In the case of Jesus his self-hood, the kind of person *he actually was* can be discerned from those recorded events and sayings that almost all scholars regard as authentic. This is different from the mere recital of events and sayings as if, strung together, they made up a biography. It is to treat them as evidence for the kind of person we are encountering when we study the New Testament.

So the debate goes on.

(2) Starting with the man

Though it is both traditional and orthodox to begin Christology with the humanity of Jesus, this has to be worked out afresh in every generation. Why? Because, as Dorothy Sayers discovered years ago when she set about writing *The Man Born to be King*, worship and devotion do things to a man. Put him in stained-glass windows, sing your hymns and say your prayers to him and in no time you have a divine being on your hands. This may well be the proper and inevitable result of having anything to do with Jesus but it makes life hard for those beginning the study of theology. They have to start with the man. For the next few paragraphs (only!) they need to smash the stained-glass windows and give up praying to Jesus.

(i) The humanity of Jesus
In his book *The Humanity and Divinity of Christ*[40] John Knox asserts that to call Jesus a man 'would mean nothing at all if we did not mean "a man like other men" '. He then continues (and this paragraph is considered so significant by John

[37] Bultmann is reported to have said that the resurrection happened every time he climbed the pulpit steps on a Sunday morning.
[38] *The Problem of the Historical Jesus* (Fortress 1964), p. 23.
[39] S.C.M. 1959.
[40] O.U.P. 1967, p. 67.

166

Robinson that he quotes it in full in *The Human Face of God*):

Because of the importance, and the difficulty, of being understood on this point, I want to state my meaning as clearly as I am able. I should say that the assertion of Jesus' humanity implies something rather definite about his self-consciousness and also about the actual anthropological, biological and sociological structure of his being. As regards the latter, an affirmation of Jesus's manhood is an assertion that he was born out of, and into, humanity in the same sense every man is; that he was a son of Abraham, just as every man participates in his own race or nation or culture; and, more important, that he was a son of Adam, as all men are, regardless of what their culture, nation or race may be. There is no other conceivable way of being a man. Not only is it impossible, by definition, that God should become a man, it is also impossible, by definition, that he should 'make' one. A true human being could not be freshly created. Such a creation might look like a man and even speak like a man. He might be given flesh like a man's and a man's faculties, but he would not *be* a man. He would not be a man because he would not belong to the organic human process, to the actually existing concrete entity in nature and history, which is, and alone is, *man*.

(ii) What marks him as a man?
(a) Growth
In an article in the *Epworth Review*[41] Ronald Williamson writes:

The experience of growth, or development. If one were to encounter a being who had never grown, physically, mentally or spiritually, especially if it were because there was no need for growth, if maturity in all its aspects had been present from the start, there would be a strong inclination to conclude that such a being was not a *human* being, not at any rate of the kind we are.

Williamson then proceeds to argue from such passages as Luke 2:52, 22:28, Hebrews 2:10, 2:17 and 5:8 that Jesus

41 'How human was Jesus?', Vol. 3, No. 1, January 1976.

did in fact grow. He also makes the interesting point that the use of parables, with their ambiguities and enigmas, by Jesus could be an indication that he was himself engaged in the search and struggle for truth and that he had not at that point found all the answers.

(b) Sex

The question of the sexuality of Jesus is sometimes raised in this context. It is a delicate and controversial matter. People who suggest the possibility (not the actuality) of heterosexual experiences in the life of Jesus often incur the wrath of the devout. It is all part of the stained-glass window image. But surely, if he was a real man, he had a real man's body?

(c) Death

Certainly he experienced a real man's death, and the New Testament is not silent about that (Phil. 2:8; Acts 2:9 and of course the accounts of the crucifixion). No divine intervention saved him from the common end of all men.

(d) Self-consciousness

In one of his earlier books,[42] Knox has written more about the self-consciousness of Jesus:

Unless he had a human consciousness, he was not a man. If he did not think and feel, about himself and others, as a man does; if he did not take man's lot for granted as being intimately, entirely, and irrevocably his own; if he did not share, at the very deepest levels of his conscious and subconscious life, in our human anxieties, perplexities, and loneliness; if his joys were not characteristic human joys and his hopes, human hopes; if his knowledge of God was not in every part and under every aspect the kind of knowledge which it is given to man, the creature, to have—then he was not a true human being, he was not made man, and the Docetists were essentially right. If by being 'more than a man' we mean that he lacked the normal self-consciousness of a man, then we are saying that he was less than a man. We are rejecting his humanity at the really decisive point. It may be possible to think of him as being 'more than a man' in ways which permit us to think of him also as being a

42 *The Death of Christ* (Abingdon, Nashville, Tenn. 1958), p. 70.

man, but we cannot think of him as *knowing* he was more than man without denying that he was man at all—that is, a true, sane man.

(e) Sin

The matter of the sinlessness of Jesus has already been considered,[43] but the modern debate has thrown up the possibility that sin might be one of the marks that made Jesus a man. Certainly the point made above about growth might be held to imply that a life without sin was attained only after a struggle. As Williamson comments[44] with reference to the phrases in Hebrews, 'learned obedience' and 'was made perfect', how can someone learn obedience and become obedient if he was wholly obedient to begin with? How can someone perfect to begin with be made perfect? Paul and the author of Hebrews were both aware, as we are, of the tension between the asking of such questions and the insistence on the sinlessness of Jesus. Perhaps it is helpful to separate the subject into the two questions--Could Jesus sin? Did Jesus sin? If we are dealing with a real man the answer to the first must be 'yes'. There is no evidence at all for giving the same answer to the second.

(iii) The man

There is no doubt that for modern Christians, as for ancient ones, Jesus is all that man can ever be. 'Perfect' is a rather bloodless word suggesting artistic or aesthetic or scientific completeness. We call statues, pictures, roses, suspension bridges, solutions to problems in mathematics, 'perfect'. It is the wrong word for Jesus. But in the context of obedience, commitment to others, courage, freedom, self-sacrifice, in sum *being a man*, we want to say, in our modern idiom, 'Jesus is the greatest'. There is no one else who can express for us the fullness of humanity. As one of our modern hymns puts it:

> Word that ends our long debating
> Word of God that sets us free,

43 See pp. 151–2.
44 *Epworth Review*, Vol. 3, No. 1, p. 44.

> Through your body re-creating
> Man as he is meant to be.[45]

Some would go even further than that. Leonard Hodgson speaks for them:

> To the Christian believer His was the only human life that has ever been lived which had at its centre a fully real *hypostasis*.[46] The mistake we make is to take our humanity as the standard and measure His manhood by ours. We ought rather to measure ours by His, for His humanity, so far from being less real than ours, was more so.[47]

(iv) And ending with?

If we start with the man, do we end with him? Has this section now said all that modern Christians need to say about Jesus? Or does the main stream of Christian tradition prevail: that what must be said about this man can only properly be said in the language of divinity? If so does that make him divine? And if it does, what has happened to the man who was 'one of us'?

These questions belong to the next section. The attempt to find answers to them may be suitably prefaced by a quotation from John Robinson. He argues that we are not dealing with one super-human person with two natures, one human, one divine, but with:

> one human person of whom we must use two languages, man-language and God-language. Jesus is wholly and completely a man, but a man who 'speaks true' not simply of humanity but of God. . . . He is a man who in all that he says and does as man is the personal representative of God: he stands in God's place, he is God to us and for us.[48]

(3) Insights into incarnation

At this point modern Christians are in virtually the same

---

[45] Ivor H. Jones, *Hymns and Songs* (Methodist Publishing House 1969), No. 10.
[46] Hypostasis = Person.
[47] *For Faith and Freedom* (S.C.M. 1968), Vol. II, p. 85.
[48] *The Human Face of God* (S.C.M. 1973), pp. 113–14.

170

predicament as that in which the first Christians found themselves.[49] Twentieth-century theologizing has confirmed first century experience—that Jesus was a real man. But modern Christians, like early ones, have been led to the brink of using God-language about him. Can the former now follow the latter and use it, speaking of Jesus as both human and divine?

(i) Chalcedonian problems

The Definition of Chalcedon[50] presents Jesus as a pre-existing divine being. He is 'perfect in Godhead', 'consubstantial with the Father', 'begotten before all ages of the Father according to the Godhead'. At the same time it insists on his humanity. He is 'truly man', 'consubstantial with us, in all things like unto us without sin'. This means that he must have *two* natures not one, and from this conclusion Chalcedon does not shrink: 'in two natures, ... the distinction of natures being by no means taken away by the union'. But the two natures are together in *one* person: 'not parted or divided into two persons, but one and the same Son and only-begotten, God the Word, the Lord Jesus Christ'.

A pre-existing divine being becoming a real man, two natures in one person; can a modern Christian believe all this?

(ii) Language

It is frequently pointed out that some of the words used did not then mean what they now mean with the implication, presumably, that if they did the Chalcedonian Fathers would not have used them. *Substance* meant for them the permanent, underlying reality contrasted with its visible and changing properties (that which makes a horse a horse, and not anything else whatever). For us, in colloquial speech at least, it means almost exactly the opposite: 'Bostik is a sticky substance sold in tubes', though when we say 'the substance of his sermon was heretical' we are nearer their meaning. *Person* seems to have been used in a less individualistic and atomic sense than we would use it. It would be more abstract too, lacking the direct, psychological reference that it now has. Nature meant for them the qualities attributed to a substance whereas, again, for us, it can mean almost the opposite—the essence of something, e.g. the nature of a church spire is that it points to the sky.

These differences may soften the blow a little, but not much. Even if nature did mean qualities, how can one man have the qualities of both man and God? Even if person was less intensely personal than now, the reference is to Jesus who plainly was a person in our sense as well as theirs; as for substance, in which their meaning was

[49] See p. 159.   [50] See p. 160.

fuller than ours, the point is that they used the word *in their sense*, and the offence, if offence it be, remains. The linguistic argument really solves very little.

(iii) The incredibility

The Incarnation belongs to the realm of the apparently incredible: Jesus the God-man, the person who, because he has the nature of man, experiences growth, is limited in power and can only be in one place at one time, is yet also the person with the nature of God, who is all-knowing, all-powerful and can be anywhere at any time.

The fact that there was a need for creeds and definitions does not make them easier to accept. With the rise of heresies about Jesus the Church *had* to say that he was truly God, that he was truly man, that he was one person. What it was necessary to say about Jesus was said. By the creeds and definitions all future statements about him could be tested. But necessity does not make the incredible credible.

Nor does the 'explanation' that goes under the name of *kenosis*, self-emptying, solve the problem. Philippians 2:5–11 is a key text for this doctrine, the basic idea of which is that Jesus divested himself of the trappings of divinity, so to speak, in order to become man. There is a superb poetic expression of the doctrine in Milton:

> That glorious Form, that Light unsufferable,
> And that far-beaming blaze of Majesty
> Wherewith He wont at Heaven's high council-table
> To sit the midst of Trinal Unity,
> He laid aside; and, here with us to be,
> Forsook the courts of everlasting day,
> And chose with us a darksome house of mortal clay.[51]

But what precisely was laid aside and what precisely was not?[52] Surely what led to Jesus being accepted and proclaimed as the Son of God was not the recognition of what he had left behind but the recognition of what he was. That which men

[51] *Ode on the Morning of Christ's Nativity*, v. 2.
[52] For a critical approach to the doctrine of *Kenosis* see D. M. Baillie, *God was in Christ* (Faber and Faber 1948), pp. 94–8.

wanted to call divine was that which they had seen in him. If, as Charles Wesley says, he

'emptied Himself of all but love',[53]

that love was acclaimed as divine. In any case, who can be satisfied with a deity sliced in two?

(iv) Was it a story?
How then can twentieth-century man find his way through this situation? Reference has already been made to John Knox, and his contribution at this point is to see the doctrine of the Incarnation in terms of a story. After referring to the problem he continues:

> Now I should say that this impasse comes about because we do not recognize clearly enough that a story is a *story* and that its truth is its own kind of truth. One must not expect a story of a deed of God—a story bound to be in some degree mythological —to be true in the same way narratives of actual incidents may be true, not to speak of scientific or metaphysical propositions.[54]

Knox then unfolds the precise story:

> A divine being, God's own Son, most high in the glory of God the Father, surrenders not only his status but his very being as divine (one might soon say, 'as God') in order to become a man and to stand with his brothers against man's demonic enemies, sin and death, who held him in grievous bondage. As a man he suffers the ultimate in deprivation, pain and shame. But instead of succumbing to his foes, he conquers them and sets man free. Here are expressed the heights and depths of the divine *agape*, the full meaning of the Incarnation, the wonder of the event, the reality of a new health and a new hope—in a word, the content, the inner substance, of the Church's life. It is, I say again, the perfect story; and in the prayers and hymns of the Church it is allowed to be the story it is.[55]

[53] MHB 371, v. 3.
[54] *The Humanity and Divinity of Christ*, p. 96.
[55] Pp. 97–8.

173

If one were to start arguing that this is a story in the kenosis tradition and therefore open to the objections cited above, he would probably say that you do not haggle about such things when you are dealing with a story. Stories are there to be told, to be sung, to be confessed, to be part of the liturgy of the Church, and only then are they to be interpreted to the best of our ability. In other words, the story is a *symbol*, representing for us the truth that we know is there, but which our minds cannot comprehend. Is this infidelity to the Gospel? Or is it a shaft of light in a dark place?

(v) God in action

Norman Pittenger's book *The Word Incarnate* contains the following paragraph:

> To sum up, we may say that the Word or External Self-Expression of God—who alone pre-exists, for the human life (body, mind, and soul) of Jesus was born in time and thus came into existence in time—through the 'operation of the Holy Ghost' clothed himself with humanity in such wise that a complete human life—including a human 'person' in our modern sense—was open to his action. Thereby man was given the manifestation of God in human terms in a distinctive and definitive manner in *this* one human life. It is in this sense that we can say that here we have 'God living a human life', but living it in such a way that it is still and always human.[56]

Two things may help us here, though they are only insights, not solutions. One is the insistence that pre-existence is *not* to be attributed to Jesus of Nazareth but to the Word that became flesh. This saves us from trying, against all reason, to believe that the Jesus about whom we read in the New Testament was once, hammer and nails and all, in the heavenly places from which he came bursting in on the human scene. The title of Pittenger's book is itself significant.

The other truth to be pondered upon is that in the incarnation a complete human life was open to the action of God. This in itself is no new thought. As D. M. Baillie says:

[56] P. 183.

174

Whatever Jesus was or did, in His life, in His preaching, in His cross and passion, in His resurrection and ascension and exaltation, it is really God that did it in Jesus: that is how the New Testament speaks.[57]

But some old thoughts are more useful to modern man than others. One of the major difficulties that twentieth-century people have with the ancient creeds is that they are entirely in static terms. That is to say, they state what is the case or what is not the case; they are concerned with propositions. Unlike the New Testament they say very little about what has happened and what will happen. They are short on action; they are not *dynamic*. Our own orientation to life is just that; for us everything is on the move. The words of our time are change, flexibility, decision, ongoing, existential, situational—ugly enough, but descriptive of what life is for us.

The incredible becomes credible for us when we see Christology in these, our own terms. The divinity of Jesus, as moderns might understand it, is not his nature, still less one half of his nature, but what God was *doing* in and through him. The uniqueness of Jesus is not that he was a heavenly being in an earthly body but that God was acting in and through him in a unique way.

The precise nature of the divine action in and through Christ is the subject of the next chapter.

[57] *God was in Christ*, p. 67.

175

Chapter 6

The Death and Resurrection Jesus of Christ

I. THE DEATH OF JESUS CHRIST

A. THE FOUNDATION DOCUMENTS

The Apostles' Creed

He suffered under Pontius Pilate,
was crucified, died, and was buried.

The Nicene Creed

For our sake he was crucified under Pontius Pilate;
he suffered death and was buried.

The Thirty-nine Articles

II. Of the Word or Son of God which was made very Man
... whereof is one Christ, very God, and very man; who
truly suffered, was crucified, dead, and buried, to reconcile
his Father to us, and to be a sacrifice, not only for original
guilt, but also for all actual sins of men.

The Deed of Union

Clause 30.[1]

---

[1] See pp. 53, 74.

Explanatory Notes upon the New Testament (John Wesley)

Commentary on Rom. 6:10
He died to sin—To atone for and abolish it.
Commentary on 1 Cor. 1:17
Lest the cross of Christ should be made of none effect—
The whole effect of St Paul's preaching was owing to the
power of God accompanying the plain declaration of that
great truth 'Christ bore our sins upon the cross'.

Sermon V. Justification by Faith (John Wesley)

In the fullness of time He was made man, another common
Head of mankind, a second general Parent and Representative of the whole human race. And as such it was that 'He
bore our griefs', 'the Lord laying upon Him the iniquities
of us all'. Then was He 'wounded for our transgressions, and
bruised for our iniquities'. 'He made His soul an offering for
sin': He poured out His Blood for the transgressors; He
'bare our sins in His own body on the tree', that by His
stripes we might be healed: and by that one oblation of
Himself, once offered, He hath redeemed me and all mankind; having thereby 'made a full, perfect, and sufficient
sacrifice and satisfaction for the sins of the whole world'.

The Senior Catechism of the Methodist Church

36. WHAT DID JESUS DO FOR US ON THE CROSS?
He atoned for our sins, that is, He reconciled us to
God and obtained for us all the benefits of salvation.

The Methodist Service Book

Lord Jesus Christ, only Son of the Father,
Lord God, Lamb of God,
you take away the sin of the world:
(The Sunday Service, p. B6)

177

When we had fallen into sin, you gave your only Son to be
our Saviour.
He shared our human nature, and died on the cross.

(The Sunday Service, pp. B12–13)

The Methodist Hymn Book

O Love divine! what hast Thou done?
The immortal God hath died for me!
The Father's co-eternal Son
Bore all my sins upon the tree;
The immortal God for me hath died!
My Lord, my Love is crucified.

(186, v. 1) (Charles Wesley)

B. THE DOCTRINE OF THE ATONEMENT

Event and interpretation

We begin on familiar ground: the interaction of events and
interpretation. To refer to one of the previous illustrations:
the Second World War was an event; the interpretations varied
from *Oh What a Lovely War* to the words inscribed on their
war memorial by the good burghers of Burton upon Trent.[2]

The death of Jesus was an event. Though there are the
discrepancies one would expect over the record of the precise
manner and timing in which things happened, and over the
inclusion or exclusion of various features, the crucifixion of
Jesus is attested more widely and at greater length than any
other event in the New Testament. Though the tourist in
Jerusalem may well have his qualms about the golden hole on
show there as the actual hole into which the cross of Jesus
was slotted, he can be sure that not very far from where he
stands there was a real hole, for a real cross.

The interpretation of that event began at once and has continued ever since. The Gospel of Mark, for example, which
was once thought to give a plain, unvarnished account of the

2 See p. 147.

events of the crucifixion (as of the ministry of Jesus) is now reckoned to include 'certain material of an interpretative and didactic kind'.[3] That is to say, woven into Mark's account of the events can be discerned the meaning that those events were beginning to have for him and for the Christian community in which he lived. This is inevitable, entirely proper, and universal. As the writer of a fine modern study of the Atonement put it:

> But we nowhere see this death (and resurrection) as bare, isolated, disinterestedly-reported event. Every witness to it moves within a certain 'theory': it may be the theory of Jesus' Messiahship, it may be the theory of a new redemption, it may be the theory of a new covenant. The fact is set within the framework of the theory but simultaneously the theory is affected by the introduction of the new fact. So the mysterious dialectical[4] relationship between fact and theory, between event and interpretation, may be said to have been operating at the beginning and to have continued in operation ever since.[5]

It is necessary to look now at the main directions the interpretation has taken.

(1) What did Jesus think?

It is not immediately obvious that Jesus held a specific theory of the meaning of his own death. The difficulty here is not that there are no 'Passion sayings' in the Gospels that can be explored. Mark 8:31; 9:12, 31; 10:33–4, 45; 14:24; Luke 17:25 are such. The difficulty is to know whether they were the words of Jesus or the expression of the theology of the primitive Church. The Methodist scholar, Vincent Taylor, argued vigorously[6] for the authenticity as Jesus-sayings of Mark 8:31; 9:12, 31; 10:45; 14:24; Luke 17:25, and contended that they have as their background reflection upon the

---

[3] C. F. Evans, *The Beginning of the Gospel* (S.P.C.K 1968), p. 78.
[4] This is the interaction referred to above.
[5] F. W. Dillistone, *The Christian Understanding of Atonement* (Nisbet 1968), p. 23.
[6] In *The Cross of Christ* (Macmillan 1956), p. 15 f.

teaching about the Servant of Isaiah 53. This latter view as was noted above,[7] has been strongly contested.

Jesus gives no comprehensive statement of the meaning of his death. But the words in the Gospels are not at odds with later and fuller interpretations.

(2) The action of God

For Christians, the inheritors of the Old Testament, the interpretation must begin (as it must have begun with Jesus himself) with the recognition that in the death of Christ God was at work. Such a statement raises obvious questions: Do we mean that God *planned* that Jesus should die on the cross? Did he *will* him, and therefore *want* him, to do so? Does not this mean that God is an ogre? No wonder the little girl in the novel *The Story of an African Farm* exclaimed, 'I love Jesus but I hate God'.[8]

The traditional answer is that God himself was in Christ, sharing in all that happened.

We must make it unmistakably clear that we are dealing, not with the human effort of a very brave and good man to put us right with God, but with God's initiative, God's activity, for our salvation. '*God* was in Christ, reconciling the world unto himself' (2 Cor. 5:19). '*God* commendeth his own love toward us, in that, while we were yet sinners, Christ died for us' (Rom. 5:8). '*God* so loved the world that he gave his only-begotten Son, that whosoever believeth on him should not perish, but have eternal life' (John 3:16). The Biblical message is not that God was persuaded to relent towards us when He saw the heroic self-sacrifice of Christ, but that He Himself set on foot the whole process of the Incarnation, Life, Death and Resurrection of Christ with the sole purpose of saving us from our sin.[9]

Whether or not the traditional answer is thought to be satis-

7 See p. 150.
8 Quoted by J. Munsey Turner. *Introducing Theology*, p. 38.
9 Rupert E. Davies, 'The Work of Christ', *Approach to Christian Doctrine* (Epworth 1954), p. 73.

factory depends on the extent to which one has come to terms with the issues raised in the last chapter. If God was acting in and through Jesus Christ, and in a unique way, then presumably he was at work in and through his death. But how? What is the interpretation?

(3) Participation

Paul was the first theologian to offer a significant interpretation of the death of Christ. It has been argued by D. E. H. Whiteley,[10] with widespread acceptance, that the essence of this interpretation is best expressed by the word 'participation'. Human beings, according to Paul, die in Adam (1 Cor. 15:22), such death being the result of sin. But in order to save us from our predicament Christ shared our human life and death. He participated in our condition. This enables participation to take place in the opposite direction, so to speak. Christian believers may, by their human nature, be members of Adam and share in his death but, through their baptism, they are also members of Christ and they share in *his* death. Furthermore, in the latter case, there is an additional dimension. If believers share in Christ's death, they share too in his resurrection.

> For if we have been united with him in a death like his, we shall certainly be united with him in a resurrection like his (Rom. 6:5).

Dying in Adam, believers live in Christ. Christ, having shared our life and death, enables us to share in his, to participate in his death and resurrection. In this participation is our deliverance (see Rom. 6:5–11; 2 Cor. 5:14–15, 21; Gal. 3:13–14).

(4) A sacrifice

Everybody interprets the meaning of events in terms of their own cultural background. Heavy rain after a long drought would lead some Christians to thank God for answering prayer.

[10] *The Theology of St Paul* (O.U.P. 1964), chapter 6.

181

But any Marxists around would grin, and talk of meteorology. In interpreting the death of Jesus, the category of thought that would come readily to the minds of people brought up on the Old Testament, as the first Christians were, was sacrifice. The Epistle to the Hebrews demonstrates this very clearly. Jesus is 'a merciful and faithful high priest in the service of God, to make expiation for the sins of the people' (2:17). He has 'put away sin by the sacrifice of himself' (9:26). The work of Christ is seen in Hebrews in terms of the Day of Atonement (see Leviticus 16), the day when the High Priest sprinkled the sacrificial blood in the Holy of Holies. In the heavenly places he sprinkled his own blood for the purification of mankind. His work is also seen (9:18-21) as the sacrifice inaugurating the new covenant as the sacrifice of Moses (Exod. 24:4-8) inaugurated the old.

Two words are used of such a sacrifice. One is *propitiation*, and it has to do with establishing a right relationship between God and the sinner. The sacrifice turns aside God's wrath, and the punishment so richly deserved by the sinner is not meted out. The way is then open for a right relationship. *Expiation* is more concerned with seeing that amends are made for the offences committed. Through the sacrifice of Christ, amends that the sinner cannot make for himself, are made for him.

In either case Christians assert that three things are true:

(i) Christ's sacrifice was an act of self-offering, the sacrifice 'not of a reluctant beast but of a voluntarily surrendered human personality'.[11] It was an offering of willing obedience.

(ii) It was a sacrifice to supersede all sacrifices, a once-for-all offering (Heb. 7:27; 9:26); 'by his one oblation of himself once offered', as the 1662 Holy Communion has it, driving the point home.

(iii) It resulted in forgiveness for the sinner, and reconciliation with God. One liturgical formula through which Christians have recited their faith since the sixth century, the *Agnus Dei*, addresses Jesus (in the traditional English translation):

[11] C. F. D. Moule, *The Sacrifice of Christ* (Hodder and Stoughton 1956), p. 25.

182

'O Lamb of God, that takest away the sins of the world.' They are taken away because, by the sacrificial act of the cross, they are forgiven. And a forgiven sinner is one reconciled to God. The relationship, broken by sin, is restored.

(5) Christ the conqueror

The Devil and his attendant demons have been a feature of the Christian cultural background for many centuries, so it is not surprising that they have their place in interpretations of the death of Jesus. The theory that on the cross Jesus paid a ransom, not to God, but to the Devil, was widely believed for a thousand years. (God double-crossed him at the Resurrection.) Straining the imagination less was the classic view that through his cross Christ became the conqueror of the hosts of evil (see Col. 2:14–15). His death liberated men and women from the bondage in which they had been held by the powers of darkness.

This understanding of the Atonement was Martin Luther's approach to the subject.[12] In the twentieth century it has been re-stated by the Swedish theologian Gustav Aulén, in his book *Christus Victor*. In the closing paragraphs he asserts that if, as he hopes and believes, the classic idea of the Atonement again resumes a leading place in Christian theology:

> We shall hear again the old realistic message of the conflict of God with the dark, hostile forces of evil, and His victory over them by the Divine self-sacrifice; above all, we shall hear again the note of triumph.[13]

It has of course been asked why, if evil was so thoroughly defeated, it is still operating so effectively. The traditional answer is that on the cross evil was *decisively* but not *finally* beaten. The 'mopping-up' of the enemy still goes on. This, it need hardly be said, is the answer of Christian faith, not of incontrovertible fact.

12 See M.H.B. 494.
13 S.P.C.K. 1931, p. 176.

(6) Satisfaction for God

A further example of the way in which interpretations are culturally conditioned can be seen in the view of the death of Jesus set out by Anselm (1033–1109), once Archbishop of Canterbury. He lived in a culture deeply influenced by Roman law, in which offenders received the punishment they so justly deserved, and in a feudal society of vassals and lords, in which honour had to be given to those to whom honour was due. His doctrine of the Atonement was not unaffected by such considerations. Man is God's creation and as such must offer his creator total obedience. God's honour will not be satisfied until such obedience is given. Alas, man, through his sin, is disobedient and as a result accumulates an ever-increasing debt of honour to God. What can be done? Straightforward forgiveness is not possible, for God's honour would remain unsatisfied; neither is punishment for then man would be destroyed. The only way is for an equivalent compensation, or satisfaction. But man is in no state to offer it. So Christ does. He pays the debt upon the cross and the honour of God is satisfied.

Though those of us little influenced by Roman law and feudal society can cheerfully refrain from believing all this, we should be unwise to disregard the traditional Christian doctrine to which, in its own way, it bears witness: that men and women are guilty before God, that God cannot forgive without cost, that Christ on the cross paid the price of sin.

Closely related to this is the theory of penal substitution,[14] developed at the time of the Reformation and still held by some. Christ is the sinner's substitute, facing in his stead the anger and judgement of God and bearing the just punishment for sin.

> In my place condemned he stood;
> Sealed my pardon with his blood.[15]

[14] Some Christians see substitution not so much as another theory, but as a factor in most other theories.
[15] MHB 176, v. 2.

(7) Moral influence

A distinction is sometimes made between objective and subjective views of the death of Jesus. The former stressed that the cross brought about an actual change in the nature of things and not least in God himself (being 'satisfied' for example) and the latter emphasized the effect of the cross on man. This is an artificial and too rigid distinction, not heard much of these days but, when it was made, pride of place in the subjective field was always given to Peter Abelard (1079–1142). His view is that Christ reconciles men to God by revealing God's love on the cross, thus causing men to love God in return.

The story of Abelard's romantic love, saturated in tragedy, is well enough known,[16] and his theology does not contradict his life. Looking at the cross he, and all men, can see the love of God (John 12:32) and they respond in love. This view has been criticized as inadequate on the grounds that it takes no account of guilt, underestimating the power of sin to hold men captive and making the efficacy of the work of Christ depend on man's response to it. Maybe so, but Abelard marks the change from thinking of God engaging, through the cross, in a transaction affecting humanity as a whole, to a concern with the profound effect of the cross on each individual person. He realized that what was most likely to turn every man from sin was the love of God in Christ crucified.

C. PRESENT CONSIDERATIONS

If people in past cultures looked at the death of Jesus in the light of the beliefs and pre-suppositions of their own time, so do people today. Twentieth-century man sees the cross through twentieth-century eyes. What does he see? Or perhaps the prior question is 'How does he see?' Furthermore, do such questions imply that none of the traditional ways of interpreting the death of Jesus is of any use in the dialogue between Christians today and their contemporaries? And for Christians

---

[16] In Helen Waddell's *Peter Abelard* (Constable 1933) and in the play *Abelard and Heloise*.

themselves when they struggle to believe? It is necessary to look briefly at the main ones.

(1) Participation

The notion of participation is certainly not foreign to our culture. To hear the shrieks of teenage girls at a pop concert given by their latest idol, to observe the faces (not least the female ones!) of the audience at a wrestling match, to watch a demonstration making for Trafalgar Square, to see the posters going up one after another in the windows at a general election is to be aware of participation. 'Get involved' is one of the slogans of our time. And modern people, no less than their predecessors, share in one anothers' sorrows and joys.

It is not the notion that is foreign, but its association with ideas that for so many people appear to have lost their meaning. Adam and Eve make a beautiful story, and one not without point. But participating in Adam's sin and death is not the way that modern man would express his predicament. That Jesus shared our human life and participated in our condition would be acceptable, but to speak of sharing in his death and resurrection is to speak the strange, esoteric language of religion. The pop idol, the wrestlers, the demonstrators, the political leaders, the person in sorrow or in joy, can be seen and heard. But where is Jesus with whom we are to die and be raised? And what can dying and rising *mean* beyond the alternating moods of depression and exhilaration, of pain and pleasure that are the mark of all human life? These are the questions Christians have to answer. To sell the notion of participation presents less formidable problems.

(2) Sacrifice

Does modern man speak the language of sacrifice? Frances Young does not think so:

> For the early Church, sacrificial imagery was powerful and inevitable. For us, it is by no means inevitable, and far from

powerful—indeed, it is more often an offence and a stumbling block.[17]

Young goes on, however, to argue that the human drives and emotions which were focused in and satisfied through traditional sacrifice are still there and perhaps through literature and drama the old sacrificial symbolism can live again for us. It is a subject worth exploring. Modern equivalents for the scapegoat (Lev. 16:5-10, 20-2) would certainly not be difficult to find, beginning with blacks or Irish or homosexuals. Perhaps too there is a deep, instinctive response to the good man crucified as 'the timeless symbol of reconciliation through sacrifice'.[18] But the Epistle to the Hebrews is a foreign language to most twentieth-century people.

Leaving Young's imaginative suggestions to the pursuit of the student, the question then is whether there is a refined form of this interpretation that will make any kind of sense to modern man. Vincent Taylor is one scholar who in modern times (he died in 1968) has attempted to provide such an interpretation.[19] He sees the sacrifice of Jesus as a representative offering with which the worshipper identifies himself. Christ is our representative, he says, 'because in His self-offering He performs a work necessary to our approach to God'.[20] This self-offering has a threefold character: it is Christ's perfect obedience to the Father's will, it is his perfect submission to the judgement of God upon sin and it is the expression of his perfect penitence for the sins of men.[21] It is made 'in the name of men, and with the intention that they should participate therein'.[22] But, as he himself asks, 'Can modern Christianity speak of Christ as man's representative before God?'[23] The answer is that

to 'use such a terminology depends upon our estimate of His Person, our agreement with the witness of the historic Church, our reading of history and of personal Christian experience.[24]

[17] *Sacrifice and the Death of Christ* (S.P.C.K. 1975), p. 103.
[18] F. W. Dillistone, *The Christian Understanding of Atonement*, p. 399.
[19] *The Cross of Christ* (Macmillan 1956), p. 91.
[20] *Jesus and His Sacrifice* (Macmillan 1943), p. 307.
[21] Pp. 307-9.   [22] P. 305.
[23] P. 305.   [24] P. 306.

That is to say, a person soaked in the Christian tradition would have little difficulty in accepting a refined doctrine of sacrifice, an assertion that does not take us very far forward, as far as many of our contemporaries are concerned.

(3) Christ the conqueror

The Devil and the demons may be good for a laugh (though many Christians would doubt it) but what is known as the demonic certainly is not. Some years ago D. E. H. Whiteley wrote an article on Ephesians 6:12[25] in which he defined demonic forces as 'powerful, vital forces outside the control of individuals'. Instead of forcing himself back into the first-century culture, as the exorcists do, he attempted to demythologize, to see the truth through twentieth-century eyes. He did so in terms of compulsive behaviour:

> Before the Second World War it was true to say that the majority of human beings, both in England and in Germany, desired peace; but the event showed that it was dangerous to argue from this fact that war would not break out. Both countries were impelled, although not deterministically, by demonic forces. . . . A secular historian would be unlikely to use the term 'demonic': he would speak rather of group loyalties or of historical and economic factors. But whatever language we may choose to employ, the facts remain: individual goodwill, though valuable, and indeed indispensable, is not enough.[26]

The same kind of possessive force is discernible in the more intimate human relationships. Two people, married to one another, but genuinely incompatible, sometimes find that resolution and determination to get on with each other are just not enough. They keep on trying, but there is a compulsive element in their quarrelling. They may see marriage guidance counsellors, doctors, psychologists and priests, but they still wrangle and fight because, literally, *they cannot help it.*[27]

25 *Expository Times*, Vol. LXVIII, No. 4. January 1957, pp. 101–3.
26 P. 101.
27 See Rom. 7:21–4.

Can we not detect an element of the compulsive in John Donne's verse?:

> Wilt thou forgive that sin where I begun,
> Which was my sin, though it were done before?
> Wilt thou forgive that sin, through which I run,
> And do run still: though still I do deplore?
> When thou hast done, thou has not done,
> For, I have more.[28]

There is obviously more to goodness than simply 'playing a straight bat to the bowling of life', as the school chaplain put it. There are the demons to be dealt with.

Can then a modern person, who cannot make much sense of the death of Christ, seen as a victory over the Devil and the demons, interpret it with more meaning as a victory over the demonic forces so described? He can indeed. The method by which he can is the subject of the next section. Here it is necessary to notice that there is an eschatological element in the victory. The decisive battle has been won, but the victory is not yet final.[29] It has yet to be consummated. The traditional reference here is to the End of the present age:

> Then comes the end, when he delivers the kingdom to God the Father after destroying every rule and every authority and power. For he must reign until he has put all his enemies under his feet (1 Cor. 15:24–5).

But—more intelligibly perhaps to modern man—there is also a sense in which the victory of Christ over the demonic can be appropriated by the Christian at his own end. So John Donne again:

> I have a sin of fear, that when I have spun
> My last thread, I shall perish on the shore
> But swear by thyself, that at my death thy son
> Shall shine as he shines now, and heretofore;
> And, having done that, Thou hast done,
> I fear no more.[30]

28 'A Hymn to God the Father', *The Oxford Book of Christian Verse* (O.U.P. 1940), p. 84.
29 See p. 183.   30 Verse 3.

(4) Satisfaction for God

Satisfaction theories fare worse. Who can take seriously a God who insists on having his honour satisfied, and at such a cost? Moreover, the element of transaction in theories of the Atonement is not now easily understood or accepted. The assertion 'Jesus died on the cross to save you from your sins' is, for many, hard to understand. Any connection between, say, selling a dud second-hand car to an innocent customer, and the death of a Jewish prophet outside Jerusalem nearly two thousand years ago is almost impossible to see. And it is so because in order to see it one has to believe, not only in God, but the kind of God who intervenes directly in human affairs and with whom, to put it colloquially, some kind of deal can be done. Secular man, by definition, does not think in these terms, and it is idle to deny the pervasive influence of secularity. Furthermore, the 'once-for-allness' element with its exclusive claim, is alien to the pluralism that is thought by many to be inevitable and right in a multi-racial society.

Some theologians, however, continue to argue for a substitutionary view of the death of Jesus—Leon Morris is a contemporary example. In *The Cross in the New Testament*[31] he contends that redemption is substitutionary, for it means that Christ paid the price that we cannot pay ourselves. Morris defends the legal terms in which the New Testament speaks of the Atonement and asserts that our salvation is 'legally valid' because Christ 'took our legal liability, took it in our stead'. Reconciliation is offered because, though we could not deal with sin, the cause of the trouble, Christ could and did. He is the propitiation for our sins[32] because he bore the wrath of God for us. All this adds up to a doctrine of substitution, stated by Morris in the strongest terms.

It should be added that Morris does not see substitution as Jesus obtaining salvation for men from a just, but unrelenting Father:

31 Paternoster Press, p. 405.
32 See p. 182.

It must be said as firmly as it can be said that there is no understanding of the atonement at all unless it is seen as a fully divine work. Atonement is wrought basically because God loves men.[33]

Some Christians find this modern restatement of the traditional view helpful in their search for truth. Others do not.

(5) Moral Influence

Of the main ways of interpreting the death of Jesus, this is the one that has the strongest appeal to the modern mind. For one thing, love is more readily understood than sacrifice, satisfaction (using the words in a theological sense) or demons. For another, the significance of Christ's death for the individual person means more than an objective transaction for the whole human race. And for another, the ethical response demanded satisfies (at least in theory) the popular modern view that the value of a religion can be seen in the way its adherents live.

The question raised in the last section was: *how* can the death of Christ bring us the victory? For the Abelardian answer we turn to a modern man, not a theologian and something of a romantic, Victor Gollancz.[34] He is devoted to Abelard, 'one of the great tragic figures of our history, one, I cannot help thinking, whom Christ would specially have loved'.[35] Acknowledging his debt to the Oxford theologian, Hastings Rashdall (1858–1924), Gollancz goes straight to the point, that what the death of Jesus accomplishes depends upon who Jesus was:

His death has been more to Christendom than other martyr-deaths, just because He was so much more than other martyrs, because His life was more than other lives, . . . because, in fact, of all that has led Christendom to see in that life the fullest revelation or incarnation of God.[36]

33 P. 369.
34 I am indebted to Ivor Jones, *Doing Theology*, p. 99, for the lead to Gollancz.
35 *My Dear Timothy* (Gollancz 1952), p. 407.
36 P. 408.

191

Revelation is the key word in this context. The death of Jesus is for us a revelation of the love of God. On the cross we see what God is like. And having seen it, we respond in love. That is the Abelardian (Moral Influence) view that Gollancz is expounding:

> And if the character which is revealed by that Sufferer be the character of God himself, then the love that is awakened towards Christ will also be love of the Father whom in a supreme and unique way Christ reveals. And that love will express itself in repentance and regeneration of life.[37]

The danger here, though Gollancz does not mention it, is that revelation will be thought of in a passive way, as if one could look on the cross as one looks at a great painting, gazing in awe and wonder *at what is there to see.* That may well be part of it, but it is not all. The cross is God in action. It is not only a revelation of what God is like, but also of what he is doing. As Leon Morris says:

> We must not think of God's mighty acts as so much pageantry, a show wherein God simply reveals himself. They are God in action saving man.[38]

The power of the cross to inspire, to evoke the response of human love, lies partly in its disclosure of the divine nature, and partly—and modern people may understand this more readily—in dynamic, active quality. Here is God in Christ, experiencing and overcoming in real life the sin and evil that corrupt the whole creation.

Granted that, then the cross—never separate of course from the rest of the life of Jesus—becomes:

> ...a necessary part of that whole incarnation or self-revelation of God, the object of which was to make known God's nature and His will, to instruct men in the way of salvation, and to excite in them that love which would inspire sorrow for past sin and give the power to avoid sin in the future.[39]

37 P. 408.
38 *I believe in Revelation* (Hodder and Stoughton 1976), p. 127.
39 Gollancz, p. 409.

In the last part of that sentence we can see the signs of victory over what in the last section we discussed as 'the demons'. Their compulsive hold begins to break because this is true:

> Christ's whole life was a sacrifice which takes away sin in the only way in which sin can really be taken away, and that is by making the sinner actually better.[40]

For modern man?

It is likely that a small number of twentieth century people has been brought to a position of Christian faith by the old interpretations of the death of Jesus in their modern dress. The new interpreters have not wasted their time. And preachers will not be wasting theirs if they try, in twentieth-century terms, to make sense for their congregations of the traditional ways of understanding the cross.

But the unpalatable fact has to be acknowledged that all this leaves most of our contemporaries cold. To change the metaphor, the Atonement and the God who atones ring no bells for them. To say to such people, 'Jesus died on the cross to save you from your sins' is to invite the (usually unspoken) reply, 'Quite honestly, I do not know what you are talking about'. Can we say anything that will make sense to them?

Towards the end of *The Human Face of God*, John Robinson faces this situation. He points out that if one is asked 'Do you believe in the Atonement?' (not a New Testament word anyway) it is immediately assumed (rightly, of course) that the questioner is asking about 'something Jesus is supposed to have done on the cross'.[41] This is the sticking point for modern man:

> The whole notion of a transaction once accomplished for us can no longer be taken as an objective description of a happening in which men can be asked to believe as if it has changed their lives.

40 P. 409.
41 P. 231.

Robinson himself believes in the Atonement. He argues strongly that one of the functions of the cross is to bring together the historic death of Jesus and the realities of human experience.[42] His point is that *in order to be heard by modern people* we should *begin* with human experience for of that, at least, they have some understanding. To ask 'Do you believe in the Atonement?'

> removes the reality of Christ from the kind of present where every eye might in fact see him to the distant past or to the remote future or to 'the divine superworld' where Christ lives in a timeless realm.[43]

But to ask 'Do you believe in atonement?' is to ask a much more intelligible question. For that can only be answered in terms of human experience which is for real. At least *as a start* the place of atonement is:

> where atonement actually takes place—namely, where men and women, races, classes and nations are in fact made one, where reconciliation, release, renewal, the reunion of life with life are experienced.... For this actually happens before men's eyes.[44]

The task of the Christian witness, and certainly of the Christian preacher, is to relate the experience of atonement, which is known, to *the* Atonement, which is not known; to point from the factory, the bank or the political party conference to the cross and then to refer back to the theories of the Atonement 'in such a way that men say, "Oh, *that's* what that meant!"'[45]

If we care, as preachers of Christ crucified (1 Cor. 1:23), to think further about this method—and we are hardly in a position to toss it nonchalantly aside—the questions do not take much finding. Is it possible, in any way at all, to use the

[42] P. 234.   [43] P. 231.
[44] P. 233. It might be necessary to begin even further back, with the simple notion that atonement is making amends. 'Greig atoned for his previous mistake by holding a fine catch in the slips.'
[45] P. 233.

experience of participation—in concerts, football matches, demonstrations, in sharing sorrows and joys—to point modern people towards participation in the redemptive acts of God in Christ? How can we interpret sacrifice in human life so that our hearers can understand the sacrifice of the Lamb of God? Is there any element of 'in my place condemned he stood' in human experience that can make the notion of substitution real to our contemporaries? Where is the evidence on the human scene for the breaking of demonic power by the greater power of goodness? Do we have insights into situations where suffering love in action elicits love in response? To try to answer such questions is not to explain the cross in human terms. That cannot be done. It is, more modestly, to teach the language that the cross speaks.

II. THE RESURRECTION OF JESUS CHRIST

A. THE FOUNDATION DOCUMENTS

The Apostles' Creed

On the third day he rose again.
He ascended into heaven,
and is seated at the right hand of the Father.

The Nicene Creed

On the third day he rose again
in accordance with the Scriptures;
he ascended into heaven
and sits at the right hand of the Father.

The Thirty-nine Articles

IV. Of the Resurrection of Christ
Christ did truly rise again from death, and took again his body, with flesh, bones, and all things appertaining to the perfection of Man's nature; wherewith he ascended into Heaven, and there sitteth. . . .

195

The Deed of Union

Clause 30.[46]

Explanatory Notes upon the New Testament (John Wesley)

Commentary on 1 Cor. 15:26
Death He so destroys that it shall be no more.

Sermon VI. The Righteousness of Faith (John Wesley)

'If we believe on Him who raised up Jesus our Lord from the dead; who was delivered' to death 'for our offences, and was raised again for our justification' (Rom. iv. 23–25): for the assurance of the remission of our sins, and of a second life to come, to them that believe.

The Senior Catechism of the Methodist Church

13. HOW DO WE KNOW THAT HE ROSE FROM THE DEAD?
His tomb was empty, He showed Himself to His friends and apostles, and He has been present in His church and with His followers from that day to this.
14. WHAT DOES HIS RESURRECTION PROCLAIM?
It proclaims His final victory over sin and death, and vindicates God's love and justice.
15. WHAT DOES HIS ASCENSION MEAN?
He entered into heaven and reigns with God the Father, still human and divine, still the Saviour of men and the Lord of all.

The Methodist Service Book

You raised him from the dead, and exalted him to your right hand in glory, where he lives for ever to pray for us.
(The Sunday Service, p. B13)

[46] See pp. 53, 74.

We praise you because you have brought him back from death with great power and glory, and given him all authority in heaven and on earth.

(The Burial or Cremation of the Dead, p. F13)

The Methodist Hymn Book

Christ Jesus lay in death's strong bands
  For our offences given;
But now at God's right hand He stands,
  And brings us life from heaven :
Wherefore let us joyful be,
  And sing to God right thankfully
Loud songs of Hallelujah !
      Hallelujah !

(210, v. 1) (Martin Luther tr. Richard Massie)

B. THE RESURRECTION OF JESUS

Paul was the first person to express in writing the fact that the Christian faith stands or falls on the resurrection of Jesus from the dead :

if Christ has not been raised, then our preaching is in vain and your faith is in vain (1 Cor. 15 : 14).

It would therefore have been extraordinarily helpful to believers in general and to students and preachers in particular if the whole matter had been made so plain, so irrefutable, that there could be no argument. To have uncertainty and debate in unimportant matters is of no concern, but to have them right at the centre, when their absence would have made life so much easier, is something of a trial. When, for example, an archbishop of the Church writes :

The Resurrection is something which 'happened' a few days after the death of Jesus.[47]

[47] A. M. Ramsey, *God, Christ and the World* (S.C.M. 1969), p. 78.

197

why does he have to put 'happened' in inverted commas? How much simpler it would be if he could leave them out! But the appeal to have everything simple and straightforward seems to be one that God has turned down, and even his archbishops have to conform. Certainly when we think in terms of event and interpretation, of history and theology, we encounter a glorious muddle[48] and are quite incapable of finally sorting out one from the other.

This is not, of course, to disparage the Christian faith. On the contrary, to have at the centre, not certainty but a far-from-easy choice between acceptance and rejection, is what makes it *a faith*. To believe in the Resurrection must mean the possibility of disbelieving. If this makes this section (and the rest of this book for that matter) less than precise and incontestable one has to assume that the convenience of those reading books on theology was not the first consideration that the good Lord had in mind.

(1) The appearances

The earliest testimony to the Resurrection is in 1 Corinthians 15:

> For I delivered to you as of first importance what I also received, that Christ died for our sins in accordance with the scriptures, that he was buried, that he was raised on the third day in accordance with the scriptures, and that he appeared to Cephas, then to the twelve. Then he appeared to more than five hundred brethren at one time, most of whom are still alive, though some have fallen asleep. Then he appeared to James, then to all the apostles. Last of all, as to one untimely born, he appeared also to me. (vv. 4–8)

Here is what C. H. Dodd calls 'a solid body of evidence from a date very close to the events'.[49] The appearances are there to be read: Jesus suddenly confronting his disciples on the road (Matt. 28:9) (Luke 24:15), on the hillside (Matt.

48 See p. 207.
49 Dating is a precarious exercise but AD 55 would be a reasonable suggestion for the Epistle. Earlier material may well lie behind it.

28:17), in a room (Luke 24:36) (John 20:29,26), by the sea-
side (John 21:1) and doing the same to Paul on the road to
Damascus (Acts 9:1-9, 26:12-18). They are strange stories,
isolated incidents rather than a continuous narrative, giving
impressions of the risen Jesus that lack consistency. Sometimes
he passes through closed doors (John 20:19), sometimes he
eats broiled fish (Luke 24:42-3). There is no consistency of
place either. Matthew refers to Galilee, Luke and John to
Jerusalem. It takes time to recognize who he is (Luke 24:16,
31, 37-39; John 20:20; 21:4). The one thing, however, that
was clear to those involved was that they had 'seen the Lord'
(John 20:25).

It is asserted that these narratives are late. In different ways
both Mark 16:9-20 and John 21 are regarded by some
scholars as appendanges to their respective Gospels. The lake-
side stories and the journey to Emmaus, it is contended, are
literary compositions that must have taken time to produce.
The comment of Avery Dulles, the Jesuit scholar, on the
stories of Matthew 28, Luke 24 and John 20 is:

> Accounts composed so long after an event, which cannot be
> certainly traced to eyewitnesses, are far from ideal historical
> sources.[50]

Against this has to be set the statement of Paul in 1 Corinthians 15, the earliest written evidence.

On the assumption that *something* happened to these people,
what was it? That is was a particularly intensive form of what
we understand by 'Christian experience' seems unlikely. The
appearances were a kind all their own, bound up with the
death and resurrection of Jesus and the emergence of the
Christian community, climactic events that were unique and
unrepeatable. Paul was the last to 'see' such an appearance.

In the context of the period immediately after the death of
Jesus, the resurrection appearances were not entirely alien.
The apostles were doubtless exhausted, bewildered, grieving
and terrified all at once, and therefore more than normally
susceptible to extra-sensory experiences. But this does not

[50] *Apologetics and the Biblical Christ* (Burns and Oates 1963), p. 65.

mean that the appearances can be dismissed as hallucinations for there was the other side to be reckoned with—Jesus.

What was the nature of the risen Christ who appeared? It is of course an unanswerable question but a little can be said. Jesus was not a second Lazarus. It was not a case of reanimation of a corpse; of Jesus, so to speak, carrying on where he had left off when he died on the cross. The words of the apostles to Thomas are highly significant: 'We have seen *the Lord*' (John 20:25; see also John 21:7; Luke 24:34). The Jesus who appeared was the exalted Jesus, now enjoying a new kind of existence. The crucified Jesus has become the present Lord. If this is conceded, then we are not faced with the stark alternatives of either another Lazarus or a completely subjective hallucination, a choice between the physical and the mental. If he really is the Lord, then the categories that bind us do not bind him. He can move more freely on the middle ground.

(2) The empty tomb

The Gospels contain accounts that on the third day the body of Jesus disappeared from his tomb, leaving it empty. They vary in their details. The three women of Mark 16:1 become the two women of Matthew 28:1 and the one of John 20:1; so the young man of Mark 16:5 becomes the angel of Matthew 28:2 and the two men of Luke 24:4. But, allowing for such discrepancies, the main point being made is clear enough: the tomb was empty.

The intrinsic unlikelihood of the story—corpses normally remain where they are put—has produced many alternative 'explanations'. Some of them centre around what might have happened in Jerusalem after the burial of Jesus. In a popular book of a generation ago *Who Moved the Stone?*,[51] Frank Morison listed them:

1. That Joseph of Arimathea secretly removed the body to a more suitable resting-place.
2. That the body was removed by order of the Roman Power.

[51] Faber and Faber 1930.

200

3. That the body was removed by the Jewish authorities to prevent the possible veneration of the tomb.
4. That life was not really extinct, and that Jesus recovered in the cool of the grave.
5. That the women mistook the grave in the uncertain light.
6. That the grave was not visited at all and that the story about the women was a later accretion.[52]

Then, with considerable ingenuity, he attempted to demonstrate that they were all impossible.

A more substantial point is that here we have the supreme example of 'reading back', of expressing in the story of an 'event' the experience of the Christian Church; that belief in the Resurrection created the story of the empty tomb, and not the other way round. This is called 'more substantial' because, unlike the dubious propositions dealt with by Morison, it starts from what is central to the Christian faith—that the Church experienced the presence of the living Jesus. Thus it could be argued that the better Christians they were, the more certain that Jesus was alive, the greater the pressure to relate their faith to the events in Jerusalem after the crucifixion. And this they did in the story of the empty tomb.

Some scholars are unable to accept this account of the matter. John Robinson, for example, defends the traditional view:

If the empty tomb story had really been created subsequently to convince doubters, the church could surely have made a better job of it.[53]

He then points out that the story rested entirely on the testimony of women and in those unenlightened times that did not count for much. And while they were about it, they might have avoided confusion about the number of women and of angels!

Assessing whether the story of the empty tomb is a piece of early or late tradition is another cause for argument (early tradition is, for obvious reasons, reckoned to be more weighty).

[52] P. 83.
[53] *The Human Face of God*, p. 132.

Those who think it late make much of the fact that even in
1 Corinthians 15 Paul does not appeal to it and his belief in
the resurrection of Jesus plainly does not depend upon it.
Those who think it early argue that though the first Christians
(and Paul) knew the tradition it did not add to the message
they wished to convey, and they hardly knew what use to make
of it.[54]

There is no point in pursuing the matter further. It is
basically a historical question and, though history (including
the claim of the empty tomb to be historical) has a considerable
importance for the Christian, it does not have the last word.
To be *sure* that Jesus is alive we have to look elsewhere.

(3) The Ascension

The omission of the word 'Ascension' from the title of this
chapter is deliberate. If the New Testament consisted only of
Luke and Acts, then it could well be included, for the author
of those two books sees the Resurrection and the Ascension
as two events, one following the other after forty days (Acts
1:1–11; see also Luke 24:50–53, taking note of RSV margin).
Each would then have a claim to be treated in its own right.

But other parts of the New Testament give the impression
that the Resurrection and Ascension together form one process,
often described by the word Exaltation. From the dreadful
agony and death of the cross through the Resurrection Jesus
was exalted to the glory of heaven. This is the one process that
God

> accomplished in Christ when he raised him from the dead and
> made him sit at his right hand in the heavenly places (Eph. 1:20;
> see also Col. 3:1)

Indeed, when Luke turns from his history to the beginnings of
theology in the Church he too holds them together (Acts
2:32–3 and 5:30–1).

If therefore we have to expound for our congregations the
meaning of the Ascension we ought not to spend too much

[54] See C. H. Dodd, *The Founder of Christianity* (Collins 1971), p. 167.

time on the details of the 'lift-off' scene in Acts 1. It would be more faithful to the New Testament witness if we tried to probe that Exaltation which embraces both Resurrection and Ascension. Here are three ready-made points!

(i) Exaltation means that Christ reigns. 'Seated at the right hand of God' (Col. 3:1) is the pictorial way of saying just that. In such a position he commands our worship:

> Therefore God has highly exalted him and bestowed on him the name which is above every name, that at the name of Jesus every knee should bow, in heaven and on earth and under the earth, and every tongue confess that Jesus Christ is Lord, to the glory of God the Father (Phil. 2:10–11)

Such worship is possible because the Ascension has universalized Jesus. It enables him to be present, not in Palestine alone, but wherever his name is invoked.

(ii) Exaltation means that Christ is our High Priest, the one who intercedes for us (Heb. 7:23–5—the high priesthood of Christ is often referred to in this epistle). In one of Paul's most splendid verses the intercession of Jesus comes as the climax:

> Who is to condemn? Is it Christ Jesus, who died, yes who was raised from the dead, who is at the right hand of God, who indeed intercedes for us? (Rom. 8:34)

(iii) Exaltation means that our human nature—for Jesus was a real man—has not been rejected by God, but accepted. Back in the 1950s George Macleod wrote a book with the ambiguous title *Only One Way Left*. In it he argued that the ascension of the 'complete humanity' of Jesus meant that 'we with Him are there already'.[55] To use the New Testament terms, as we have died with Christ, so we shall be exalted with him (Rom. 6:5). Macleod expounds the consequences of this for our spiritual, physical and political life and the reason he gives for the radical demands made upon us is: 'There is a Man crowned in Heaven'.[56]

---

[55] *Only One Way Left* (The Iona Community 1954), p. 102.
[56] P. 145.

(4) The experience of the Church

When earlier in this book an attempt was made to form answers to the question 'How do you know that what you assert is true?' one of the grounds to which appeal was made was religious experience, 'what actually happens to people'.[57] There cannot be many Easter sermons that do not hold up before the congregation the transition of the little band of dispirited and defeated men and women huddled together after the crucifixion mourning their leader to the triumphant company, sure of the presence of their risen and exalted Lord, that in the face of opposition and persecution blazed a trail for the Gospel across the known world. (That really is sermon language!) It is a good thing that this is done, for the argument from experience is a strong one.

The heart of the experience was knowing Jesus to be the Lord, the testimony that he was indeed exalted. The first confession[58] made by Christians, their short and simple creed, was 'Jesus Christ is Lord' (Rom. 10:9; 1 Cor 12:3; Phil. 2:9–11). The word 'Lord' had a remarkable part to play in their life. Reference has already been made to the fact that it had associations with the mystery religions of the Greeks and Romans and was therefore familiar to the people to whom they preached. And also, more significantly in this context, to the fact that in the Septuagint (the Greek translation of the Hebrew Old Testament) the word *Kurios* (Lord) translated the Hebrew word *Yahweh*.[59] In other words they were putting the stamp of divinity upon Jesus and for Jews to do this was, to put it colloquially, quite something. This was not, however, done in carefully reasoned statements. There were no treatises in those early days arguing the case (the Church has made up for that since!). Our evidence for asserting that Jesus as exalted Lord was in fact 'the heart of the experience' lies in two areas.

(i) The first is worship: C. F. D. Moule wrote:

---

57 See pp. 68–70.
58 The word in this sense has nothing to do with acknowledging sin. It means the assertion of one's allegiance, i.e. a confession of faith.
59 See p. 157.

204

Nobody reading the New Testament with a grain of imaginative insight could fail to recognize that considerable blocks of its material glow with the fervour of worship.[60]

Moule then points to passages like Acts 4:24 ff. where the worship and prayer make the occasion 'one of exultant spontaneity',[61] and to Revelation 11:15 and 19:6–8, which are triumphant acclamations of Jesus. He says of the latter:

It is hard to doubt that they represent the kind of poetry which Christians actually used in corporate worship.[62]

The eucharist, when the bread was eaten and the wine drunk, would certainly have been the focus of such an experience of the exalted Lord. In the famous *Didaché*, a first-century document that describes Christian worship in the post-apostolic age, the eucharistic[63] prayers begin:

'As touching the eucharist, we give thanks in this manner. First over the cup.
'We give thanks to Thee, our Father, for the holy vine of David Thy servant which Thou hast made known to us through Jesus Thy servant. To Thee be the glory for ever.
'Over the broken bread.
'We give thanks to Thee, our Father, for the life and knowledge which Thou hast made known to us through Jesus Thy servant. To Thee be glory for ever. As this broken bread was scattered over the mountains, and has been gathered together and made one, so may Thy Church be gathered from the ends of the earth into Thy kingdom; for Thine is the glory and the power through Jesus Christ for ever.[64]

The words look cold in print. It seems most unlikely that they were in experience.

[60] C. F. D. Moule, *The Birth of the New Testament* (A. and C. Black 1962), p. 11.
[61] P. 21.
[62] P. 23.
[63] Some think the meal is a love-feast (*Agapé*) despite the use of the word *eucharisteo.*
[64] Quoted in William D. Maxwell, *An Outline of Christian Worship* (O.U.P. 1936), pp. 9–10.

(ii) The other area in which the early Christians expressed their belief in their exalted Lord was the area of *missionary preaching*. They *proclaimed* Jesus as risen from the dead and exalted to God's right hand (Acts 2:32–6; 5:30–1; 10:36–43), and as a result of the proclamation people repented and believed (Acts 2:41; 5:42, 6:1a; 10:44–8), though not invariably, as Paul found out in Athens (Acts 17:31–2). The Resurrection, nevertheless, was the burden of Paul's preaching. The appearance granted to him was 'in order that I might preach him among the Gentiles' (Gal. 1:16). There is an urgent note in the first Christian preaching, and the impression is given that this is the supreme matter about which men have to decide and it is, as we might say, now or never. It is extraordinarily difficult to explain this missionary fervour—the long-term results of which are still with us—if the experience the first Christians enjoyed of the crucified, risen and ascended Lord was totally bogus. If *nothing* happened after the crucifixion, then what in heaven's name was all the fuss about? This question has never been satisfactorily answered.

(5) The action of God

We have to say about the Resurrection what was said about the death of Jesus—that it was due to the action of God. Notice the precise wording of the proclamations in Acts: not 'this Jesus rose' but 'this Jesus God raised up' (2:32); not 'the Author of life, who rose from the dead' but 'the Author of life, whom God raised from the dead' (3:15). The Resurrection was an act of God.

It is necessary to pause for a moment at this term. An 'act of God' may, as with insurance policies, describe an occurrence over which man has no control. If lightning strikes a church spire and a large stone falls on to the vicar's car parked beneath, that is an 'act of God'. (If the vicar was not in the car at the time that might also be construed by some as an act of God, but we cannot stretch our theology that far!) On the other hand, we may think that *all* events are acts of God, in the sense that nothing happens that God does not either will or permit. The Resurrection would qualify as an 'act of God' in both these senses, but that is not to say very much. To say more we have to think in the familiar terms of event and interpretation. There would seem to be no events of any kind which are universally recognized as acts of God without some measure of interpretation. Even to use the insurance policy phrase about the lightning presupposes the belief that there is a God who is in control of the natural forces. In the case of the Resurrection, to assert, as we do, that it was an act of God is to look at the events (some qualifying for this description more strongly than others) of the empty tomb, the appearances and the experience of the early Church and to see in them God at work. The bare events are not enough. They have to be interpreted. We need our theology as well as our history.

How then do we see God at work in the Resurrection? Some, most notably Paul, have answered this question in terms of the vindication of Jesus by God. Not, of course, that Paul thinks crudely that here is God putting right on Sunday something that went wrong on Friday. The meaning of passages such as Romans 1 : 4 and 4 : 25 would appear to be that, although Jesus had been condemned under the Law and suffered a death to which the Law attached a curse, by raising him from the dead God vindicated him. This would seem to be a profoundly significant interpretation for those, like Paul, to whom the Jewish Law was crucial, but hardly so for the rest of us.

Gentiles like ourselves are probably happier in stressing, as indeed Paul did, the aspect of God's creative power at work in the Resurrection; a power resulting in both a risen Lord and a Christian community rejoicing in him. Earlier the mixture of event and interpretation associated with the Resurrection was described as 'a glorious muddle'.[65] This can now be substantiated. The appearances—were they events or interpretations? Some, as we have seen, regard the empty tomb as an event; others, for whom the bones of Jesus may still lie somewhere in Palestine,[66] see it as an interpretation, an explanation of a present experience thrust back into the historical scene. And as for the experience of the early Church, some would regard that as part of the interpretation (the

[65] See p. 198.
[66] R. Gregor Smith, *Secular Christianity* (Collins 1966), p. 103.

event being the Resurrection) and others as part of the event (and the most 'factual' part, as they see it). The point of referring to this variety of understanding here is to emphasize that it is over-arched by the one interpretation on which all Christians would agree: that the Resurrection was a creative act of God. Christians would say together that the raising of Jesus from the dead to be the exalted Lord, acclaimed and proclaimed by the Church, was the act of God's creative power.

C. PRESENT CONSIDERATIONS

This will not be a long section because, as the essence of Resurrection is that Christ is still alive, any discussion (such as the one just concluded) contains 'present considerations'. The risen Lord is acclaimed and proclaimed by the twentieth-century Church as well as by the first century one, and in assessing their experience we are assessing our own. The distinctive contribution the twentieth century can make is probably not momentous and can be considered quite briefly.

(1) The liberated zones

This is the title of a book by a modern theologian[67] and is a reference to those areas in which our contemporaries might be led to an experience of resurrection. Notice that in that sentence (a) the definite article before 'resurrection' has been dropped, (b) the capital 'R' has not been used and (c) there is no reference to Jesus. The question is whether (as with the Atonement)[68] twentieth-century people are more likely to end up worshipping the risen Lord Jesus Christ if they first learn to recognize what resurrection is all about from their own liberating experiences. The pointing-up of such experiences is the theme of a fine and moving book by H. A. Williams of the Community of the Resurrection, *True Resurrection*.[69] After asserting that 'The miracle is to be found precisely within the

67 John Pairman Brown (S.C.M. 1970).
68 See p. 194.
69 Mitchell Beazley, London 1972.

ordinary round and daily routine of our lives,'[70] he gives some concrete examples:

> An artist, at first only painfully aware of an utter emptiness and impotence, finds his imagination gradually stirred into life and discovers a vision which takes control of him and which he feels not only able but compelled to express. That is resurrection. Or a scholar or a scientist as he pursues his research finds a favourite theory breaking up in his hands. He is left with no home in which to house the quantities of evidence he had collected. Then a new more adequate theory gradually takes shape in his mind which makes him more at home with his material even than he was before. That is resurrection. Or a married couple find their old relationship, once rich and fulfilling, slowly drying up into no more than an external observance to the point where it seemed impossible that these dry bones should ever live again. Then a new relationship emerges, less superficially high powered and less greedy than the old one, but deeper, more stable, more satisfying, with a new quality of life which is inexhaustible because it does not depend on the constant recharging of emotional batteries. That is resurrection. Or suffering, a severe illness, or a catastrophe like the premature death of someone deeply loved, such suffering is always destructive. People, we say, are never the same again. Sometimes they shrivel up and atrophy. But appearances here can be deceptive. Under the devastation of their ordeal which leaves its deep and permanent traces, one can be aware that they are in touch with a new dimension of reality. They have somehow penetrated to the centre of the universe. They are greater people. They are more deeply alive. That is resurrection. Or, on a lighter but by no means insignificant level, the prisoner of irritating or confining circumstances, the man who slips on one of the many kinds of banana skin, the man whose great expectations are belied, the man who is tied to triviality, realizes the humour of his situation, and by his laughter shows that he has risen above what cabins and confines him because he can relish the joke at his own expense. That is resurrection.[71]

There are some who will doubtless regard all this as a rather dubious ploy, enabling people to be satisfied with something

---

[70] P. 10.   [71] P. 11.

less than what is *actually* the true Resurrection, the rising again from the dead of the Lord Jesus Christ. Knowing him personally and directly in his risen power, and not looking inwardly at our own liberated zones, is what the Christian faith has to offer. Certainly it is true that believers are able to experience 'resurrections' in their lives because they have first come to know 'the power of his (Christ's) resurrection' (Phil. 3:10). But is there not also the possibility that when people have been led to see Christ in their own 'resurrections', they will be able to see him in his?

(2) New knowledge

There is the possibility that our century could provide new knowledge, for example in the way in which the spiritual and the physical affect one another. We know considerably more now in this area than the first century Christians did—witness the field of psychosomatic medicine. If we discover more, it could well illuminate what, in connection with the appearances, was called 'the middle ground'.[72]

There is also the possibility of understanding more of what John Robinson refers to as 'total molecular transformation'.[73] He explains:

For the power of spirit over matter is still so marginally understood that it would be dogmatic to discount the possibility that 'the next development in man' might be in the direction of the transformation of material energy, and therefore material substance, into spiritual. There are accounts, for instance, of rare but recently attested examples of Buddhist holy men who have achieved such control over the body that their physical energies and resources are so absorbed and transmuted that what is left behind after death is not the hulk of an old corpse but simply nails and hair. An empty tomb would thus be the logical conclusion and symbol of the complete victory of spirit over matter.

These are speculative matters, but they do at least serve to show that all the truth is not yet known.

[72] See p. 200.
[73] *The Human Face of God*, p. 139.

(3) Jesus and the Spirit

It is appropriate to close this section with a mildly provocative paragraph with which Geoffrey Lampe finished an article in the *Epworth Review*.[74] Although in the view of some it does not take the history seriously enough, it suggests one possible way in which this generation can move forward theologically on the subject of the Resurrection and at the same time links this chapter with the next.

If we ask, 'How is Jesus alive today?' 'How do we know he is alive?' 'How can we meet him today?' do we need to give our answers in terms of *resurrection*? Do we, indeed, have to refer to an Easter event, a rising of the crucified Jesus from the grave? Or can the experience of Christians today of encountering the living Christ be adequately and satisfactorily translated into the language of 'God's Spirit' or 'God the Holy Spirit'? Both Paul and John came close to making an identification of the ascended yet present Christ with the present, indwelling and inspiring, yet transcendent Spirit. Can we go further and say that when we speak of meeting Christ today we mean that God who was incarnate in Jesus and made himself known to the world of men in Jesus still encounters us today as that same God? When we say that 'Jesus is alive', do we mean more than that the Spirit (or Word) of God, who was united with man in Jesus, speaks to us and saves us now, reproduces in us in some measure those characteristics of Jesus which Paul calls the 'fruit of the Spirit', and will in the end so transform and take possession of the human community that 'in', rather than 'with', the saints Christ will be manifested in glory, 'coming again' in the mode of the Spirit of God incarnate in the human race?

[74] Vol. 3, No. 3, September 1976, pp. 98–9.

Chapter 7

The Holy Spirit and the Trinity

I. THE HOLY SPIRIT

A. THE FOUNDATION DOCUMENTS

The Apostles' Creed

I believe in the Holy Spirit.

The Nicene Creed

We believe in the Holy Spirit, the Lord, the giver of life, who proceeds from the Father and the Son.
With the Father and the Son he is worshipped and glorified. He has spoken through the Prophets.

The Thirty-nine Articles

V. *Of the Holy Ghost*
The Holy Ghost, proceeding from the Father and the Son, is of one substance, majesty, and glory, with the Father and the Son, very and eternal God.

The Deed of Union

Clause 30.[1]

[1] See pp. 53, 74.

Explanatory Notes upon the New Testament (John Wesley)

Commentary on Acts 1:5
Ye shall be baptized with the Holy Ghost—
And so are all true believers, to the end of the world.

Sermon VIII. The First-fruits of the Spirit (John Wesley)

These are they who indeed 'walk after the Spirit'. Being filled with faith and with the Holy Ghost, they possess in their hearts, and show forth in their lives, in the whole course of their words and actions, the genuine fruits of the Spirit of God, namely, 'love, joy, peace, long-suffering, gentleness, goodness, fidelity, meekness, temperance', and whatsoever else is lovely or praiseworthy. 'They adorn in all things the gospel of God our Saviour'; and give full proof to all mankind, that they are indeed actuated by the same Spirit 'which raised up Jesus from the dead'.

The Senior Catechism of the Methodist Church

17. WHO IS THE HOLY GHOST?
The Holy Ghost is God the Lord and Giver of life, Who continues and fulfils the work of Christ in the life of the Church and of the believer.

The Methodist Service Book

Let us rejoice in the fellowship of the Holy Spirit, the
Lord, the Giver of life.
By him we are born into the family of God, and made
members of the body of Christ;
his witness confirms us;
his wisdom teaches us;
his power enables us;
he will do for us far more than we ask or think.
All praise to you, Holy Spirit

(The Covenant Service p. D4)

213

The Methodist Hymn Book

Creator Spirit
Create all new; our wills control,
Subdue the rebel in our soul;
Make us eternal truths receive,
And practise all that we believe;
Give us Thyself, that we may see
The Father and the Son by Thee.
(293, v. 4) (Anon. *c.* tenth century; tr. John Dryden, 1631–
1700).

Come, Holy Ghost, for moved by Thee
    The prophets wrote and spoke;
Unlock the truth, Thyself the key,
    Unseal the sacred Book.

God, through Himself, we then shall know,
    If Thou within us shine,
And sound, with all Thy saints below,
    The depths of love divine.
                            (305, vv. 2, 4) (Charles Wesley).

B. THE DOCTRINE OF THE HOLY SPIRIT

(1) Old Testament background

The meaning of the Greek word *pneuma* can be guessed from
such English words as pneumatic and pneumonia. There are,
however, no English words derived directly from Hebrew, so
one has to be told that *ruach*, the Hebrew word translated as
pneuma in Greek, is the word for 'wind' and 'breath'. *Ruach*
(in the Old Testament) and *pneuma* (in the New Testament)
are also translated 'spirit', from which it can be deduced that
the images the Biblical writers found most helpful when they
wrote of the spirit of God were those of the hot wind blowing
up from the desert and the breath in the body that is the sign
of life. The spirit of God, then, is the lively, divine energy. A
small 's' is used in this section because, in the Old Testament
Yahweh and his spirit are not equated.

214

The spirit is sometimes thought of simply as a physical force. Obadiah was sure that the spirit could transport Elijah from one place to another (1 Kings 18:12) and the sons of the prophets at Jericho thought that the spirit could propel Elijah up a mountain or down a valley (2 Kings 2:16).

The spirit is active in creation, moving over the face of the waters (Gen: 1:2). The host of heaven was made by the breath (*ruach*) of Yahweh's mouth (Ps. 33:6; see also Ps. 104:30). Elihu declares that the spirit made him (Job 33:4).

Further, the spirit is thought of as working in and through people, enabling them to achieve things beyond their natural capacities. It ('he' cannot yet be used) gives the capacity to interpret dreams (Gen. 41:38), to make priests' vestments (Exod. 28:3), to produce works of craftsmanship (Exod. 31:3-5; 35:30-3), to lead armies in battle (Judg. 6:34) and to tear lions apart with bare hands (Judg. 14:6). When the seventy elders were chosen by Moses (Exod. 11:24-5) Yahweh 'took some of the spirit that was upon him' and put it upon them. The spirit is present also, and prominently so, in the activities of the prophets, from the dervishes (1 Sam. 10:5-6) to the great men who had something to say to their generation (Isa. 61:1, Ezek. 11:5; Micah 3:8, Neh. 9:30).

As, under occupation and oppression, Israel looked forward to the arrival of a New Age, the spirit was thought to be instrumental in the blessings that the Chosen People would then enjoy. Often the spirit had been regarded as a temporary gift, given to an individual for a particular purpose (Judg. 6:34; 14:19), though sometimes it had been thought of as a permanent possession—with the servant of Isaiah 42:1 or the prophet Micah (3:8) for example. But part of the messianic hope was that the spirit would be given to the whole people, not temporarily but permanently (Isa. 44:3-5; Ezek. 36:26-8; 37:14; Joel 2:28-9). The distinctive mark of the Messiah through whom the deliverance would be effected was that 'the spirit of the Lord shall rest upon him' (Isa. 11:2, NEB).

In the Old Testament the gulf fixed between God and man was no small one. The more majestic and exalted God was thought to be, the more remote and inaccessible he became.

215

His name could not even be uttered. Towards the end of the Old Testament period various intermediaries—angels and 'wisdom', for example—were invoked to bridge the gulf. But they were not as effective as 'the spirit' in making it clear that, though God was indeed majestic and exalted, he was also accessible and intensely active in human beings and their affairs (Hag. 2:5). This is so much a reality to the devout man that he cries out that he cannot escape from the spirit (Ps. 139:7).

All the above references from the Old Testament make it clear that though the relationship between Yahweh and the spirit is not precisely defined, it is a very close one. A most significant text is Isaiah 31:3:

The Egyptians are men, and are not God; and their horses are flesh, and not spirit.

The parallels are: men—flesh, God—spirit. It cannot be said from this that God = spirit or spirit = God, but it can be said that spirit is of the nature of God.

(2) How does the New Testament speak of the Holy Spirit?

Before any attempt is made to answer this question a similar point to that made about the titles and attributes of Jesus[2] is relevant here. It is not a matter of assuming that there is a fixed concept (albeit personal) i.e. the Holy Spirit, and then asking what it is that the New Testament has to say about him. Again, the process worked the other way round. It was because of the experiences the first Christians had of God as active in Christ among them that, in the light of their Old Testament background, reference to the Holy Spirit became possible. The doctrine of the Holy Spirit comes out of the New Testament. It is not imposed upon it. *Only if this process has been accepted as basic to all talk about the Holy Spirit in the New Testament, can the titles below, describing what is known of the Holy Spirit, be used.*

Notice that in the title above the small 's' has been raised

2 See p. 149.

216

THE HOLY SPIRIT AND THE TRINITY

to a capital, and that the word 'Holy' has been inserted (also with a capital). This is an indication that the New Testament view is an advance on the Old Testament one.[3] It is not easy to state precisely what 'the New Testament view' is. Thought on the subject was developing all the time—from the impersonal to the personal, for example—and the writers were more concerned that their readers should receive the Spirit than that they should be given an exact and consistent statement about him. We can certainly say that the full Trinitarian doctrine, as it will be described later in this chapter, is not present in the New Testament. It is only foreshadowed. On the other hand —and it is in this area that we have to look for an advance on the Old Testament—the impression is often given that the Spirit is God *himself* in action.

(i) The Holy Spirit is the *Spirit of God*. Paul refers to the Spirit of God in this way. Christians are in the Spirit 'if the Spirit of God really dwells in you' (Rom. 8:9) (see also 1 Cor. 3:16). The Spirit of God 'comprehends the thoughts of God' (1 Cor. 2:11), justifies the saints (1 Cor. 6:11), leads to a right judgement about Jesus (1 Cor. 12:3 where 'Spirit of God' and 'the Holy Spirit' are virtually equated), and is the possession of Paul (1 Cor. 7:40) and of his converts (2 Cor. 3:3).

(ii) But the Holy Spirit is also the *Spirit of Christ*. Romans 8:9 puts the two expressions on the same level. It is 'the Spirit of Jesus Christ' that helps Paul in his imprisonment (Phil. 1:19). The Fourth Gospel relates the Holy Spirit to Jesus: he is sent in the name of Jesus (14:26) or even by Jesus, from the Father (15:26, 16:7). The function of the Spirit is then to continue the work of Jesus, to glorify him, to 'take what is mine and declare it to you' (16:14).

(iii) He is also the *Spirit of truth*. He, who is known only by those who possess him (John 14:17), will teach all things (14:25) and guide into all truth (16:13). It is in this context that we can make sense of the sin against the Holy Ghost,[4]

[3] The expression 'Holy Spirit' is used seven times in the Old Testament and eighty-eight times in the New.
[4] 'Ghost' is the old word for 'spirit'. 'Apparition' is one of its later meanings.

the 'blasphemy against the Spirit' of the Synoptic Gospels (Mark 3:28 f.; Matt. 12:22-32; Luke 12:10). This is not adultery nor perjury nor taking the name of the Lord in vain, as has sometimes been supposed. As the account in Matthew makes clear, it is seeing something you know to be good (the healing of a blind and dumb man) and, because it suits your book, deliberately calling it evil. To call white black when you know perfectly well that it is white is to sin against the Spirit of truth. Such perversity, if persisted in, makes people incapable both of wanting forgiveness and of receiving it.

To refer to the Holy Spirit as 'the Spirit of truth' is again to relate him to God the Father. God is the God of truth, whether we take the word as meaning faithfulness and integrity (this is predominant in the Old Testament) or as 'that which is in fact the case' (John 8:46 and Rom. 9:1 use the word in this sense). It is also to link him to Christ, who is the truth (John 14:6).

(iv) Added to such teaching in the New Testament is the fact that when the first Christians *experienced* the Holy Spirit they were not doing other than experiencing God the Father and Jesus Christ the Son. That was so then, and it is so now. It is God the Father who is himself active in Jesus and in the Holy Spirit. Hence it is impossible to distinguish, in experience, between 'the grace of the Lord Jesus Christ', 'the love of God', and 'the fellowship of the Holy Spirit' (2 Cor. 13:14).

The first Christian theologians were gradually led by this identity of experience to suppose, not unreasonably, that the Holy Spirit *was* God, *was* Christ. It took some time for experience to be translated into theology and there were arguments (still not settled!) about whether the Holy Spirit proceeded from the Father and the Son.[5] It also took time for the experience to find its way through to the liturgy, for the early creeds and hymns do not directly address the Holy Spirit as God, though they do glorify and exalt him. But in due course both of these things happened. What was foreshadowed in the New Testament teaching and implicit in the New Testament experience became definite and explicit in the theology and worship

[5] The Eastern Church accepts the former, the Western the latter.

of the Church. As the Senior Catechism puts it, 'The Holy Ghost is God the Lord and Giver of life'.[6]

(3) What does the Holy Spirit do?

The attempt to define the Holy Spirit has already begun to answer this question, but there is more to be found within the New Testament.

(i) He is at work in Jesus

The first Christians discerned the activity of the Spirit in Jesus. They therefore acclaimed him as Messiah and Lord. In the light of that acclamation the Gospels were written.

The Spirit was active in his birth (Luke 1:35) and descended on him at his baptism (Mark 1:10-11). The Spirit led him into the wilderness to be tempted (Mark 1:12; Matt. 4:1; Luke 4:1). By the Spirit he cast out demons (Matt. 12:28 and Luke 11:20). The ministry of Jesus in its totality was evidence indeed that the New Age of the Spirit had at last arrived (Luke 4:18-21). The Spirit was his permanent possession (John 1:32-3). It has been argued[7] that the alteration in Matthew in the text cited above (12:28) from the 'finger' of God of Luke 11:20 was in the interest of stressing this permanent endowment of the Spirit.

> His consciousness of a spiritual power so real, so effective, so new, so final, was the well-spring of both his proclamation of the presentness of the future kingdom and his authority in deed and word. This consciousness is summed up in the word 'Spirit'. His awareness of being uniquely possessed and used by divine Spirit was the mainspring of his mission and the key to its effectiveness.[8]

It was the Holy Spirit who, according to Paul, was the agent in the Resurrection (Rom. 1:3-4; 8:11) and the hymn of 1 Timothy proclaims it:

[6] See p. 213.
[7] By R. H. Fuller, *The Foundation of New Testament Christology*, (Collins Fontana 1969), p. 193.
[8] James D. G. Dunn, *Jesus and the Spirit* (S.C.M. 1975), p. 54.

He was manifested in the flesh, vindicated in the Spirit (1 Tim. 3:16).

This particular activity of the Holy Spirit has to be seen in the light of God's design for the whole creation, and the end of all things. C. K. Barrett's commentary on Romans 8:11 is:

The resurrection of Christ was an eschatological act, which marked the beginning of the Age to Come. This age was running to its close, and at its end death would be destroyed (1 (Cor. 15:26). The first event was the pledge of the last, and they were connected by the presence and activity of the Holy Spirit.[9]

(ii) He relates people to God and Christ

John V. Taylor has written a justly popular book. Its title is significant: *The Go-Between God.*

We can never be directly aware of the Spirit, since in every experience of meeting and recognition he is always the go-between who creates awareness.[10]

This may overstate the case if one accepts Luke's view of the Spirit as speaking personally to Philip (Acts 8:29), to Peter (Acts 10:19; 11:12) and to the church at Antioch (Acts 13:2), but it is nevertheless a profound insight.

It is the Spirit who brings us to the Father and bears witness with our spirit that we are in fact the children of God (Rom. 8:16). It is the Spirit who relates us to Jesus, indeed by this activity we can recognize him (1 John 4:2–3). No one can acclaim Jesus as Lord without him (1 Cor. 12:13) and through the Spirit believers can see Christ and become like him (2 Cor. 3:17–18). He it is who makes this relationship permanent (1 John 3:24).

For a full exposition of what the Fourth Gospel means by the Paraclete (changing Greek letters to English ones), the Comforter (A.V.),[11] the Counsellor (R.S.V.) or the Advocate

[9] *The Epistle to the Romans* (A. and C. Black 1957), pp. 159–60.
[10] S.C.M., p. 43.
[11] The A.V. translation 'Comforter' is misleading because it was made at a time when 'comfort' could mean 'strengthen' and 'support' as well as 'console'.

(N.E.B.) reference will have to be made to the commentaries, but plainly he is the Spirit and equally plainly he relates believers to God and Christ with the result that they are strengthened for their witness in the world. The Spirit helps people to remember all that Jesus said (14:26). He bears witness to Jesus (15:26), as do believers themselves (15:27). He continues the work of Jesus in judging and acclaims, as believers do, the righteousness of God and Jesus as demonstrated in the cross and Resurrection (16:8–10).

This work of relating continues in the intercessions of the Spirit on our behalf. He intercedes for us with sighs too deep for words (Rom. 8:26). He prays for us according to the will of God (Rom. 8:27).

(iii) He gives birth to the Church

The New Testament contains two accounts of the giving of the Spirit to the first Christian community: John 20:22–3 and the Pentecost narrative of Acts 2. This is no cause for concern, for as C. K. Barrett has said:

> The existence of divergent traditions of the constitutive gift of the Spirit is not surprising; it is probable that to the first Christians the resurrection of Jesus and his appearances to them, his exaltation (however that was understood) and the gift of the Spirit, appeared as one experience, which only later came to be described in separate elements and incidents.[12]

Notice Barrett's use of the word 'constitutive'. It was the gift of the Spirit that caused the Church to be the Church. He gave it birth.

Arts 2 is the fuller account and, many would argue,[13] the one with the stronger historical foundations. The day of Pentecost, when the Holy Spirit was first 'poured out' (Joel 2:28) is therefore celebrated as the birthday of the Church.

What happened on the famous day? On these great festivals in their calendar the Jews really 'went to town', literally as well as metaphorically. They came flocking to Jerusalem from all

[12] The Gospel According to St John (S.P.C.K. 1958), p. 475.
[13] James Dunn, for example, p. 141.

221

those cities in the Mediterranean world to which, in the course of their chequered history, they had been driven. They came 'from every nation under heaven' (Acts 2:5). The official reason for their coming was to give thanks at the Feast of Weeks, when the first-fruits of the corn harvest were presented (Deut. 16:9), but it was much more than that. It was the Jews coming home. And when they came home they celebrated.

This was the lively context in which the one hundred and twenty (Acts 1:15) were 'all together in one place'. Suddenly they heard a sound like a powerful wind blowing. They saw what appeared to be tongues of fire leaping around and resting on their heads. It is profitless arguing whether they literally heard and saw these things or whether this is Luke using traditional Jewish symbols to describe a profound religious experience. We cannot be certain either way. Nor does it matter much—for in both cases this is talk about the arrival of the Spirit.

There are similar problems of interpretation with the other phenomenon of Acts 2, speaking 'in other tongues'. Was this the capacity to speak and understand foreign languages without the necessity of having to learn the grammar and the vocabulary? (Dr Wilbert Howard used to comment with wry humour that if ever this gift were needed by the Church it was when we sent missionaries to China.) Was it gibberish—the mumbo-jumbo of people experiencing a psychological upheaval—which simply meant nothing at all? Was it a confused babbling in which there occurred every now and again odd words of *common* Greek, recognizable because it was the language that travelled along the Roman roads with the soldiers and the pilgrims and across the sea with the traders? Was it a different *sort* of language such as modern Charismatics apparently experience? Was it not history at all but a story, told to justify and continue what was happening in Corinth (1 Cor. 14)? Or was it a symbolic account to reverse the story of the tower of Babel (Gen. 11:1–9) and to make it plain that what was fragmented in fallen man is integrated in Spirit-filled man? These and other interpretations are, and presumably always will be, the subject of fascinating discussion. We must be sure not to miss the main point: that Acts 2,

however interpreted, refers to the Holy Spirit filling the infant
Christian community with his energy and life.

In all this activity of the Holy Spirit, the relationship of
the Church to Jesus must not be forgotten:

> The Church's faith that it was the spirit-inspired community,
> the New Israel created by the Messiah . . . was based upon the
> fact of Jesus, upon his life, death and resurrection regarded as
> decisive events in the eschatological programme.[14]

On this basis the infant Church became the fellowship[15]
(koinonia) of the Holy Spirit, exhibiting a 'togetherness' which,
by the sheer power of the Spirit, transcended racial, economic
and social divisions. Philippians 2:1-2, and particularly the
translation of the New English Bible, enables us to see the
quality of this fellowship through the eyes of Paul:

> If then our common life in Christ yields anything to stir the
> heart, any loving consolation, any sharing of the Spirit, any
> warmth of affection or compassion, fill up my cup of happiness
> by thinking and feeling alike, with the same love for one another,
> the same turn of mind, and a common care for unity.

(iv) He bestows the gifts of the Spirit

These are the 'spiritual gifts' (R.S.V.) or 'gifts of the spirit'
(N.E.B.) to which Paul refers at the beginning of 1 Corinthians
12,[16] though by the end of that chapter he is using the word
charismata, often translated these days as 'grace gifts'.

The gifts are given to individuals, indeed all individual
Christians may expect in one way or another to be 'on the
receiving end' (1 Cor. 12:7). The utterance of wisdom, of
knowledge (12:8), the gift of faith, of healing, of miracles, of
prophecy (12:9-10) and so forth are exercised by individuals,
but in community. The metaphor of the body (12:14-26), a
sustained 'sermon illustration', makes clear that the gifts,
though individually possessed, are corporately exercised. As

[14] C. K. Barrett, The Holy Spirit and the Gospel Tradition (S.P.C.K.
1947), p. 161.
[15] Acts 2:42.
[16] See also Rom. 12:6-8; Eph. 4:11-13.

such they have to work for common good (12:7), for edification (14:26). This accounts for Paul's preferences: his enthusiasm for love (13) and for prophecy (14:1, 3–5, 24–6) and his disapproval of speaking in tongues in church (14:2, 4–11) unless the gift of interpretation into the vernacular is also exercised (14:13, 27–8). It also accounts for his listing with the rest the unsensational gifts like those possessed by helpers and administrators, which have an obvious community value.

This inevitably leads to the question as to whether the gifts of the Spirit are specific and supernatural bestowals or simply the drawing out of natural qualities. It is easier to believe the former about speaking in tongues but the latter about writing up the minutes of the church council. Peter Stephens has, in substance, answered the question in the way the first Christians would have done:

> They may be ordinary gifts that coincide with their natural qualities, or they may be extraordinary gifts that do not coincide with their natural qualities. The critical matter is not their ordinariness or their extraordinariness, but their being gifts of the Spirit. Being gifts of the Spirit stresses the fact that behind them lies in the initiative of God, rather than human initiative.[17]

(v) He gives the fruit of the Spirit

The singular 'fruit' is preferred to the plural because it is thought to express more clearly the single source of these virtues and is what we find in Galatians 5:22–3, the key passage. There is no need to add to what has already been written: love, joy, peace, patience, kindness, goodness, faithfulness, gentleness and self-control are given by the Spirit to individuals but they are constitutive, to use C. K. Barrett's word, of a united, loving community.

(vi) He gives freedom

The key passage here is 2 Corinthians 3:17.

---

[17] 'The Gifts of the Spirit in the Church' in Dow Kirkpatrick (Ed.), *The Holy Spirit*, p. 134.

Now the Lord is the Spirit, and where the Spirit of the Lord is, there is freedom.

As many a preacher has said, freedom is both *from* something and *for* something. The freedom of the Spirit is from legalistic religion (Gal. 4:4) and its slavery to the law (4:7), from sin and from death (Rom. 8:2). It is freedom for sonship (Gal. 4:7), adoption (Rom. 8:14–16), life and peace (8:6).

The freedom the Spirit gives is the freedom exemplified by Jesus. There is a paragraph in *The Go-Between God* that describes it:

What most confused his critics was that he conformed to no pattern. What were they to make of the wandering teacher who typically carried no purse and had nowhere to lay his head and yet appeared to be fond of parties, particularly in disreputable company? How were they to tie him down to a particular breach of the law when his real fault seemed to be a general independence of all the ordinary pressures and claims which both bind and buttress the individual in society? His sense of property was casual and he expected men to lend boat or beast as unhesitatingly as he would have handed over coat and cloak to them. He steadily disobeyed the demands of what we regard as self-interest and self-preservation. He seemed to pass elusive and free as the *ruach* wind through all our interlocking structures of duty and obligation. His whole manner of life, and even more the manner of his dying, was a challenge to necessity.[18]

That is the freedom of the Spirit.

(vii) More to be said
The Bible and traditional theology describe further activities of the Holy Spirit. In the individual Christian he gives new life and brings assurance of salvation; in the Church he inspires worship, prayer and mission and is specially involved in the services of eucharist, baptism, confirmation and ordination. To avoid duplication these matters are not considered here but are left to later chapters.

[18] S.C.M. 1972, p. 98.

C. PRESENT CONSIDERATIONS

(1) The Charismatic Movement

The Pentecostal Movement, in the first part of this century, resulted in the birth and growth of Pentecostal Churches, and the Charismatic Movement, in the latter part of this century, operates within the traditional churches. Both owe their origin[19] (humanly speaking, they would insist on adding) to a dissatisfaction with the state of the Christian Church. Across the world it had become too formal, too institutionalized, too established, too cerebral, too cold, too tired, and altogether too far removed from the dynamic community of the New Testament. So the Spirit broke through. This is no place for a full consideration of the Charismatic Movement (the one of the two that more concerns us). But its main features can be noted and a passing comment or two made.

(i) Baptism in the Spirit
This is not a New Testament expression and charismatics differ in their understanding of the ground it covers. Some use it to describe 'the first filling of the Spirit', others to describe what has been called (as in Methodism years ago) 'The Second Blessing'. In either case the results are the same: a release in praise, a 'blessed assurance' and the receipt of one or more of the gifts of the Spirit.

(ii) The gifts of the Spirit
Many charismatics favour the expression 'grace-gifts' for those donations of the Spirit to which reference has already been made. They believe them to transcend a Christian's natural ability and their purpose is to glorify Christ and to serve the brethren in love. In healing (never to be minimized) and in prophecy (much less formal than preaching and sometimes including elements of prediction) they have revived neglected gifts. Some of them take the risk of exercising the gift of

---

[19] The use of this word does not exclude the possibility that they were resurgences of previous, similar movements.

226

exorcism, though it does not follow that what was an appropriate gift in the first century is necessarily so in the twentieth.

(iii) The gift of tongues

Though not an invariable part of 'baptism in the Spirit', the gift of tongues cannot be ignored, if only because its value is not evident to many modern people.

To take up the point made previously,[20] charismatics maintain that the sounds that come forth are certainly not meaningless gibberish. They form linguistic patterns with phrases, commas, full stops, and when interpreted by one who has the gift of interpretation they make sense. The gift of tongues is essentially a communication between God's Spirit and the spirit of the believer in what a charismatic might call 'a heavenly language'.[21] In personal prayer the gift of tongues is a cleansing process and a release of the spirit. As Simon Tugwell says, 'our souls reach out to glorify God beyond anything we ourselves can comprehend'.[22] Elsewhere he refers to the 'sacrament' of tongues,[23] and in the same book makes this fascinating comment:

> ... the healing of our minds brings us through folly to wisdom, and involves a complete reappraisal of our use of words. In St Ephrem's hymn, the disciples at Pentecost are compared to small birds bursting into song; the words released in us by the Holy Spirit are primordial words, words which spring from our creatureliness as deeply and simply and inexplicably as birdsong. They have a strange power over the minds of those who speak them and those who have ears to hear them.
>
> There is no doubt that people have sometimes experienced speaking in tongues in the same way, as a speaking of words that have a strangely deep power, and that are at one with the 'words' of birds and beasts.[24]

---

[20] See p. 222.

[21] It is claimed by some charismatics that this language is often one spoken somewhere on earth.

[22] *Did you receive the Spirit?* (Darton, Longman and Todd 1972), p. 72.

[23] *New Heaven? New Earth?* (Darton, Longman and Todd 1976), p. 154.

[24] P. 147.

Singing in tongues is not without harmony and beauty, and has its place in the universal hymn of praise.

(iv) Charismatic worship

In reaction to the frigidity and formalism of what they found, and find, in the normal worship of the churches, charismatics turn to more spontaneous worship, more participation 'from the floor', more exercise of the 'grace-gifts', more overt celebration, more open prayer, more vigorous singing. Their services tend not to be planned, but to happen. This does not mean that they are without sequence, as W. J. Hollenweger has shown,[25] but that they are not slaves to the sequence. Now one man's meat is another man's poison, in worship as in most other things but, as a reaction against 'Mattins at 11' and the Methodist Evening Service in which to change a hymn tune is to provoke an ecclesiastical crisis, this style of worship has its place in the Church catholic.

(v) Assessment of the Charismatic Movement

As is by now obvious, there is no space for a full treatment here. That there is liberation and joy in this movement for some is undeniable. That there are dangers, of divisiveness, of sectarianism, of pride, of irrationality, and of escapism, is equally apparent, and some judge that these are more than possibilities.

This section ends with an extract from a recorded conversation[26] between C. K. Barrett and John P. Horner. It took place, before five hundred people, at the Conference Meeting of the Methodist Local Preachers' Department at Newcastle upon Tyne in 1973. Horner had given an address and Barrett had been asked to question him. The dialogue should assist the student in making his own judgement.

C.K.B.: May I put another related query about two phrases that go back to the time of the Reformation. I'm not sure whether they go back further; certainly they were made much of

[25] *Studia Liturgica*, Vol. 8, No. 4.

[26] It was published in full in *Worship and Preaching* (Methodist Publishing House), Vol. 3, No. 5, October 1973.

by Luther. It's about the 'Theology of Glory' and the 'Theology of the Cross'. Luther knew very well and very clearly that it was the latter that was the theology of the New Testament.

Now I wonder (and there's no point in my being here as a questioner if I'm not going to express something of the feelings of the people who look on and wonder a bit about the Charismatic Movement) if there is a danger in all this going in for what could be called the 'Theology of Glory'? It's all Glory Hallelujah and not very much more, one sometimes thinks, of bearing in the body the killing of Jesus. And if Paul knew about the power of the Spirit as he undoubtedly did in his Apostolic life, he also found this—this visible as well as internal bearing of the dying of Jesus. He also found this an inalienable part of his Apostolic experience. Could you comment?

J.P.H.: I want just by way of comment, to say how grateful I am to you for raising it. This is again what I am trying to get at by 'the Christ in the Spirit being under the disciplines of the Christ in the Flesh'. The Christ in the Flesh was Christ in Crucified Flesh, and I'm so glad you've given me the chance to say this, sir.

We fully appreciate that the Spirit was fully poured out because Jesus was glorified. And Jesus was glorified because Jesus died. There are some of us who are very much caught up at the moment in this sort of gathering—in expounding the Charismatic Movement and what it means and what it is, and therefore are having to watch our own lives very closely on this. We are in danger of being caught up in the religion of glory that we have forgotten the religion of the Cross. But I can honestly say with all my heart that it is the Jesus of the Cross that makes all this possible and to whom we go.

C.K.B.: Thank you. The time has come for me to ask my last question, and I want to put it this way.

I may say that there has been no concerting with this, but I hope it's the kind of question you would like to have. I'm taking up words you used yourself at the beginning of your address: Will you please suppose that there is a preacher before you who says to you 'I'm not as conscious as I should like to be of the power of the Holy Spirit. When I preach, my word does not always come to my hearers in power, sometimes it's just talk and it's evaporated two minutes after the benediction has been pronounced. I do not see people converted under my preaching. I do not see the Church being built up in faith and love. I find

229

prayer difficult; I find the Bible dry. I should like to know for myself more about what you've been talking about tonight. Will you please tell me what I do when I get home tonight'?
J.P.H.: That is lecture number two and it takes an hour. Believe that these things are possible; believe that there is a power that works between the transmitting of the word and the heart of the hearer, believe that these things may be.

I think that is the very important beginning, and be honest, brothers and sisters; be honest with yourselves and be honest with God, and be humble. Professor Barrett, I really resisted this whole business of speaking with tongues. I said to the Lord 'Lord, I'm perfectly proficient at A level standard in English language and literature and I do not want this, I do not need it,' and it was precisely at this point that the Lord had to break me before anything else happened.

So often we put these resistances of pride and arrogance in the way of receiving. Believe, be honest, be humble. Go to God and say, 'O Lord, I believe these things really are. Please give me no rest Lord until they really are for me.'

(2) The Holy Spirit in the world

To look for the activity of the Spirit in the world *rather than* in the Church can be the sign of a secularized outlook. To look for the activity of the Spirit in the world *as well as* in the Church can be an appreciation of the *total* biblical view for, if the New Testament is primarily concerned with the work of the Spirit in the Church, the Old Testament sees him at work in the whole created world. It is a large subject for a small section.

(i) In the activities of men
This title covers such an enormous field that one has to particularize immediately. It so happens that I am writing this paragraph early on a Sunday morning. Last night I was at the Royal Albert Hall for one of the Promenade Concerts. Beethoven's Piano Concerto No. 4 and Tchaikovsky's music from Swan Lake formed the main part of the programme. If the Holy Spirit is not to be discerned in the almost excruciating beauty of such sound, then does not the whole theological

THE HOLY SPIRIT AND THE TRINITY

system we are examining stand condemned as artificial, the description of a deeply religious world but, alas, not the real one? Similar acts of discernment can be made in a thousand areas of human activity—from Che Guevara putting his life behind his words: 'The vocation of every lover is to bring about revolution' and so making the cause of social justice the cause of a million youth, to the English lady doctor whose hospice in South London has given its own resounding answer to the ancient question, O death, where is thy sting?

The process of discernment is by no means straightforward. Apart from the fact that many in whose activities we claim to see the Holy Spirit at work fiercely deny it (nothing makes a good humanist so annoyed as to be told he is really a Christian in disguise), the criteria for discerning are often highly subjective. If you transported the crowd from the Kop at Anfield to the Royal Albert Hall would their reaction to the music be the same as the promenaders? Few Christians would question the activity of the Holy Spirit in the work of Dr Cicely Saunders at St Christopher's Hospice, but those who detect the Holy Spirit in the struggle of Che Guevara are not likely to find him in the political activities of Ian Paisley and Enoch Powell. Yet others claim to do so. To be reminded by theologians that the Holy Spirit is the Spirit of Christ does not help so very much, for we are simply presented with the same question in another form—in whom can we see some expression of Jesus, Che Guevara? Ian Paisley? Enoch Powell?

But, however falteringly, the process of discernment must go on, otherwise we are again guilty of excluding the Lord from his own dominions. To which must be added, in these secularized times, that if people simply cannot see the Spirit at work in the Church—and some of them have looked quite hard —then the world is the only other place to look.

(ii) Other religions
Because this is a book on theology, these are entitled to separate treatment, though there is no need to go over again the ground covered in chapter 2.[27] The position there expressed

[27] See pp. 76–81.

is consistent with the view that the Holy Spirit is at work in other faiths. But here too the question of criteria arises. In a paper delivered to the Fifth Oxford Institute on Methodist Theological Studies in 1973, S. J. Samartha asked:

How do Christians clarify to themselves theologically the relationship between the work of the Holy Spirit in the church and the activity of God's Spirit among people of different religious traditions and ideological persuasions? Is it the same Spirit that brooded upon the waters over *all* creation, that spoke through the prophets of the Old Testament, that was with Jesus at the critical points of his life and ministry, that manifested itself in "the outpouring" in Acts which also activated Yajnavalkya, the Buddha, the Prophet Mohammed, and, why not—Mahatma Gandhi, Karl Marx, and Mao Tse-tung? Or is there a qualitative difference? Should we seek a difference? Why? If so, on the basis of what criteria?[28]

If one knows that the Spirit is the Spirit of Jesus, that may help a little. So may obvious criteria, such as the Spirit's predilection for life rather than death, love rather than hate, order rather than chaos, community rather than separation. But, as in the previous case, there seems to be no full and satisfactory answer. Is it possible anyway to assess what is deeply rooted in one culture by criteria that belongs to another, except in the most arbitrary fashion?

It is perhaps more helpful to turn from such a theoretical approach to a more practical one. Can the Holy Spirit be discerned in other faiths through common concerns, common goals, common actions? I recall asking at Taizé how brethren from such widely differing churches could live together in theological amity. The reply I received was: 'When you wash your socks in the same bowl as a brother you come to see into his theology.' S. J. Samartha sees something similar happening with people of other faiths:

Dialogue can take place only between *people*, living persons, sharing the conflicts, ambiguities, tragedies, and hopes of human

28 'The Holy Spirit and People of Various Faiths, Cultures and Ideologies', Dow Kirkpatrick (Ed.), *The Holy Spirit*, p. 23.

life. The co-existence of particular religions might provide the historical context in which such living encounters might take place. When a Christian and a Hindu or a Muslim or a Marxist meet, sharing the mystery of existence, longing for salvation and liberation, groping for meaning and struggling for strength, can one limit the work of the Holy Spirit only to the Christian partner?[29]

If this is the case, then our present multi-racial society in Britain presents us with a heaven-sent opportunity.

(iii) Openness to the world
'Other religions' had to have special treatment as one of the activities of men, but the attitude of openness is necessary in them all if the presence of the Holy Spirit is to be discerned in the modern world. Something similar to the 'indicator experiences' and the 'signals of transcendence' referred to in relation to God[30] may be useful in this field also.

Reference has already been made to John V. Taylor's book, *The Go-Between God*. The first chapter is significantly titled 'Annunciation' and cites experiences that may indicate, or act as signs to, that for which we are looking. He has been writing of his first encounter with music and he continues:

Essentially the same, years later, was my first glimpse of Kilimanjaro serenely shining high above the Tanzanian cloud line, 150 miles away. I knew then that I must climb it: that was a simple matter of fact; and only afterwards did I theatrically recall Mallory's reply when he was asked why he wanted to climb Everest: 'Because it is there'. But that is the point. That is what all such experiences have in common. The fact that something, or someone, is *there* suddenly becomes important. Instead of simply being part of the landscape, part of existence, it presents itself, it becomes present, it commands attention.[31]

Then comes a further illustration:

This happens most vividly when we fall in love. Across the

29 P. 27.   30 See pp. 135–7.
31 P. 8.

crowded ballroom Romeo catches Juliet's eye and one senses the almost electrical current of their mutual attraction. A moment later they are side by side, and the very lightness of their first contact, 'palm to palm' betrays the compulsive force that is drawing them together.[32]

And then this paragraph with its beautiful second sentence:

But these are only the more intense instances of something that is constantly happening to us, and I want to emphasize the ordinariness and frequency of these experiences. In a manner of speaking, we are falling in love at every turn of the road, with a fold in the hills, the mist over the lake, the stars tangled in the bare branches, the yellow chair in the sunlight, an old song at the peasant's fireside, a new thought flashing from the pages of a book, a lined face on a hospital pillow, a hair-ribbon from Ur of fthe Chaldees.[33]

The main thrust of Taylor's argument is that such experiences involve a communication between the subject and the object so that the truth *of* the object (the mountain, the lover and so forth), rather than the truth *about* it, comes home to the subject (you and me), so much so, that there is a certain fusion between the two. Something of this kind does seem to happen in many of our experiences, if we stop to think about them. But whereas in the previous discussion the 'indicators' and the 'signals' pointed us towards God, the concern here is with *what or who is enabling the experience to take place.* Who enables us to see the mountain in a new light? Who makes Romeo aware of Juliet? What made the Beethoven piano concerto come to life for me? Is it not the Holy Spirit who broods over the creation, bringing its separate parts into a mysterious unity? And if so, is not openness to his activity our indispensable need?

If this, or anything like it, is the way in which modern man may perceive the Holy Spirit at work then the mission of the Church will have to be thought out in terms of helping him to do it. To be open to the Spirit, and so to discern him, is the goal, for it is the same Spirit who leads us to Christ.

[32] Pp. 8–9.　　[33] P. 9.

234

II. THE HOLY TRINITY

A. THE FOUNDATION DOCUMENTS

The Creed of St Athanasius[34]

And the Catholick Faith is this: that we worship one God in Trinity, and Trinity in Unity;
Neither confounding the Persons: nor dividing the Substance...
And in this Trinity none is afore, or after other: none is greater, or less than another;
But the whole three Persons are co-eternal together: and co-equal.
So that in all things, as is aforesaid: the Unity in Trinity is to be worshipped.

The Thirty-nine Articles

1. Of faith in the Holy Trinity
...And in the unity of this Godhead there be three Persons, of one substance, power and eternity; the Father, the Son, and the Holy Ghost.

The Deed of Union

Clause 30.[35]

Explanatory Notes upon the New Testament (John Wesley)

Commentary on Hebrews 9:14
The work of redemption being the work of the whole Trinity. Neither is the Second Person alone concerned even in the amazing condescension that was needful to complete it. The Father delivers up the kingdom to the Son; and the Holy

---

[34] This creed was not the work of St Athanasius (c. 296–373) but was written between 381 and 428. It has been widely used in the Western Church.
[35] See pp. 53, 74.

Ghost becomes the gift of the Messiah, being, as it were, sent according to His good pleasure.

Sermon LV. On The Trinity (John Wesley)

But the thing which I here particularly mean is this: The knowledge of the Three-One God is interwoven with all true Christian faith: with all vital religion.

I do not say that every real Christian can say with the Marquis de Renty, 'I bear about with me continually an experimental verity, and a plentitude of the presence of the ever-blessed Trinity'. I apprehend this is not the experience of 'babes', but rather 'fathers in Christ'.

But I know not how any one can be a Christian believer till he 'hath', as St. John speaks, 'the witness in himself'; till 'the Spirit of God witnesses with his spirit, that he is a child of God'; that is, in effect, till God the Holy Ghost witnesses that God the Father has accepted him through the merits of God the Son: And, having this witness, he honours the Son, and the blessed Spirit, 'even as he honours the Father'.

The Senior Catechism of the Methodist Church

18. WHY DO WE SPEAK OF THE HOLY TRINITY?

The Father is God, Jesus Christ is God, the Holy Ghost is God, yet there is one God, not three, and therefore we speak of the Holy Trinity, one God in three Persons, three Persons in one God.

The Methodist Service Book

N., I baptize you in the Name of the Father, and of the Son, and of the Holy Spirit.

(Baptism, p. A11)

We ask this through your Son, Jesus Christ our Lord.
Through him, with him, in him,
in the unity of the Holy Spirit,
all honour and glory be given to you, almighty Father.

(The Sunday Service, p. B14)

236

The Methodist Hymn Book

Hail! holy, holy, holy Lord!
Whom One in Three we know;
By all Thy heavenly host adored,
By all Thy Church below.

One undivided Trinity
With triumph we proclaim;
Thy universe is full of Thee,
And speaks Thy glorious name.

Three Persons equally divine
We magnify and love;
And both the choirs ere long shall join,
To sing Thy praise above.

(37, vv. 1, 2, 4) (Charles Wesley)

B. THE DOCTRINE OF THE TRINITY

The doctrines of God, of the Person of Jesus Christ and of the Holy Spirit have now been considered. It remains to relate them to one another. A first glance at the foundation documents gives the impression that the doctrine of the Trinity is an incomprehensible way of doing it. What can be made of it?

(1) Formulation of the doctrine

The word 'formulation' is appropriate because the doctrine of the Trinity is not to be found in the New Testament but was a subsequent development. What is in the New Testament is a three-fold revelation and experience of God which became the raw material for inescapable theological reflection and expression. There is the Old Testament heritage of the one almighty God, Yahweh, already part of the experience of the first Christians. Then there are passages that give clear enough indications that, when the first Christians reflected on their experience of Jesus and the Holy Spirit, they were starting to think in similar categories. (1 Cor. 6:11; 12:3; 2 Cor. 1:21-2;

237

ROUNDWORK OF THEOLOGY

3:3; Gal. 3:13–14; 1 Cor. 2:10–16; Eph. 2:18 are examples.) Their encounter with Jesus and with the Spirit was for them little, if anything, short of an encounter with God. They met God in Jesus. They met God in the Spirit. It was this three-fold experience that then came to be given the doctrinal treatment.

The delicate nature of the process is easy to see. On the one hand, the essential unity of God could receive such over-whelming emphasis that the three-fold manner in which he was experienced could be thought of in terms of three ways or modes of his activity, rather like an actor wearing different masks and assuming different roles. This was the danger to which the doctrine was exposed in the Western Church, a deviation known as Monarchianism (sometimes referred to as Sabellianism). It stressed the monarchy, the oneness of God at the expense of Jesus and the Holy Spirit.

On the other hand there were those who thought of God, the Father, of Jesus and of the Holy Spirit as each separate and each divine in his own right, so to speak, so that the result was three Gods and not one. This is called 'tritheism' and was as 'off-centre' in one direction as Monarchianism was in the other. It was the prevalent danger in the Eastern Church. The difference between East and West in the matter is that the West assumes God's unity and approaches his trinity as a matter of theorizing, while the East starts with a living experience of the three and then moves to affirm their equal divinity, and therefore, unity. Between these two extremes orthodoxy had to find its way.

(2) Three Persons, one God

The way it found has been set in concrete, as we might say, in the Athanasian Creed. To comment on that part of the Creed quoted in the foundation documents,[36] the Persons are not to be confounded, that is, confused. God the Father, God the Son and God the Holy Spirit are each persons, and each God in his own right. On the other hand the 'Substance' has not to be divided. 'Substance' was the term used by Tertullian (AD 160–220) the North African Father, 'to signify divinity and

36 See p. 235.

238

all that is inherent in it'[37] and if the 'Substance' is not to be divided[38] then plainly we are dealing with one God and not three. This is the one God in Trinity and Trinity in Unity,

Had the Athanasian Creed been quoted in full, the student would have been informed that the Son (the Second Person) was begotten (generated, procreated), but the Holy Ghost (the Third Person) proceeded (came from). Furthermore, the Nicene Creed asserts that the Holy Spirit proceeded from the Father and the Son, a doctrine that rejoices in the name of the Double Procession. The Eastern Church has never accepted it and objects to the *filioque*, ('and the Son'), clause. The temptation to dismiss this as hair-splitting by people who, in those days, had nothing more useful with which to occupy their minds, must be resisted. The point the Eastern Christians were, and are, making is that there must be a single source of divinity in the Godhead, the Father. They go on to argue that the *filioque* clause was craftily inserted years later by some designing theologians in a quiet corner of Spain.

The use of the terms 'Second Person' and 'Third Person' do not imply inferiority. Though the Father is the source of all, the three Persons are 'co-eternal together: and co-equal'.

'Three Persons, one God' may sound arithmetically ridiculous. But theologically it makes sense, for it gives us a way of containing in a single doctrine all that, basically, we are able to say about God. Or rather, to be precise, it enables us to exclude all that we do *not* want to say about God. It makes very clear the kind of God Christians do not believe in. This means that what the doctrine of the Trinity really does is to state the problem rather than to solve it.

Analogies to explain this doctrine (Augustine: the spring, the river and the cup of the substantial water) are of dubious value, sermons notwithstanding. Attempts to justify it by speculating on 'the home life of God' (e.g. he is an eternal fellowship in himself) are not particularly enlightening.

[37] Maldwyn Hughes, *Christian Foundations*, p. 139.
[38] One way of guarding against this was 'interpenetration': that the three Persons penetrate or permeate one another.

C. PRESENT CONSIDERATIONS

(1) Language

Almost every modern book that deals with the doctrine of the Trinity points out that the word 'person' did not mean at the time of the formulation of the doctrine what it means now. If it had done the Fathers would not have used it.[39] They of course used not English but Latin (in the West) and Greek (in the East). There were differences there, for the Greek word *hypostasis* suggests more of an independent being than the Latin *persona*, which was nearer to the mode or role referred to above. When *persona* was translated 'person' and 'person' came to mean an independent, self-conscious being in a fuller sense than *hypostasis* ever did, the muddle was complete. But once the situation is understood, the problem is eased.

Thanks to the attention paid by scholars these days to religious language, there is more to be said. Ian Ramsey points out, in his notable book in this field, that the foundation of the doctrine of the Trinity was not a matter of new discoveries about God 'as though the Early Fathers had some special high-powered telescope by which to inspect the Godhead'.[40] It was a matter of settling 'rules for talking'. The single word 'God' was not adequate on its own, for it did not convey the reality of the threefold experience that the early Christians enjoyed. Father—Son—Holy Spirit did. And what we have in the Athanasian creed is 'a set of logical rules for constructing the Trinitarian formula'.[41] Making sure, that is, that to say 'Father', 'Son' or 'Holy Spirit' is to say 'God', and yet, without compromising that position, to give priority in the structures to the Father. In other words, it ensures that when we say that God is a Trinity of Father, Son and Holy Spirit we are talking sense and not nonsense.

(2) The contribution from the East

One of the most hopeful features of the modern Ecumenical

[39] See also p. 171.   [40] *Religious Language*, p. 173.
[41] Pp. 174–5.

Movement has been an awakening in the minds of Western Christians that the great Orthodox Churches of the East might have something distinctive to contribute to the life of the whole Church. Certainly in theology this is so, and not least in the doctrine of the Trinity.

The Western tradition, as we have seen, has stressed the oneness of God and, if anything, played down the 'threeness'. The Orthodox theologian John Meyendorff proceeds to argue:

There is no doubt that this (the Western) approach to God, popularized by St. Augustine, is, to a degree, responsible for the fact that so many Christians today are practical deists. Venerating God as a single 'Heavenly Father', they tend to view trinitarianism as a mere speculation. In such a context, there is no real place for a theology of the Holy Spirit except in terms of 'gifts', unrelated to the internal life of God.[42]

'Practical deists' suggests a belief in God ('we all believe in a sort of something' as an M.P. put it in a debate in the House), accompanied by a deep respect for Jesus and a monumental ignorance of the Holy Spirit. This combination is not uncommon today. The plea from the East is for an appreciation of the Spirit 'as an active, personal, and guiding presence in the church community and in the personal life of the Christian'.[43] It comes from the historic emphasis on the 'threeness' in the Trinity. If it were answered, it would bring the Spirit-filled life to those many Christians who cannot find it through the Charismatic Movement.

(3) The Trinity as Being

It would be worth re-reading at this point what was said at the beginning of the chapter on 'God' about the difference between Being and a Being.[44] If this is of any help in the use of the word 'God' then that help extends to the doctrine of the Trinity. In *Principles of Christian Theology* John Macquarrie works this out in terms of the Father as primordial Being ('the condition that there should be anything

42 'The Holy Spirit as God' in Dow Kirkpatrick (Ed.), *The Holy Spirit*, p. 80.
43 Meyendorff, p. 81.
44 See pp. 112–13.

241

whatsover'),[45] the Son as 'expressive Being' ('the primordial Being of the Father ... flows out through expressive Being to find its expression in the world of beings',[46] above all in Jesus), the Holy Spirit as 'unitive Being' (restoring the unity of Being with the beings').[47] Once one has an apprehension, however dim, of what is meant by using the word Being in this way, this interpretation is illuminating. It is, of course, grossly unfair to Macquarrie to reduce it to one scrappy sentence, and his book should be studied by those who can, and will, read hard. But even this truncated version is an improvement on the use of the word 'substance' which, as we have seen,[48] now means the opposite of what it once did.

(4) Prayer and worship

God is a mystery.[49] That means the Trinity is a mystery. There is much more that could be revealed but is not. Beyond what is known there is what is not known. But what cannot be penetrated by our thinking may be 'approached' (one is lost for an appropriate word) in our prayers and our worship.

C. S. Lewis, that most imaginative of Christians, gives this account of the Trinity at work:

An ordinary simple Christian kneels down to say his prayers. He is trying to get in touch with God. But if he is a Christian he knows that what is prompting him to pray is also God: God, so to speak, inside him. But he also knows that all his real knowledge of God comes through Christ, the man who was God—that Christ is standing beside him, helping him to pray, praying for him. You see what is happening. God is the thing beyond the universe to which he is praying—the goal he is trying to reach. God is also the thing inside him which is pushing him on, the motive power. God is also the road or bridge along which he is being pushed to that goal. So that the whole threefold life of the three-personal Being is actually going on in that ordinary little bedroom where an ordinary man is saying his prayers.[50]

Worship too can bring us nearer to the Mystery. One of the most ancient hymns that Christians sing, and one of the most

---

[45] P. 183.   [46] P. 183.
[47] P. 184   [48] See p. 171.
[9] See p. 126.   [50] *Mere Christianity* (Collins, Fontana, 1952), p. 138.

moving, is the *Veni Creator Spiritus*. Addressed to the Holy Spirit it is traditionally sung to the ancient plain-song, at ordinations:

> Teach us to know the Father, Son,
> And Thee, of both, to be but One;
> That through the ages all along
> This, this may be our endless song...
>
> All praise to thy eternal merit,
> O Father, Son, and Holy Spirit![51]

[51] MBH 779, v. 4; MSB p. G10.

Chapter 8

Man and his Salvation

A. THE FOUNDATION DOCUMENTS

The Apostles' Creed

I believe in . . . the forgiveness of sins.

The Nicene Creed

For us men and for our salvation
he came down from heaven:

The Thirty-nine Articles

IX Of Original or Birth-sin
Original Sin standeth not in the following of Adam (as
the Pelagians do vainly talk) but it is the fault and corruption of the Nature of every man, that naturally is engen-
dered of the offspring of Adam; whereby man is very far
gone from original righteousness, and is of his own nature
inclined to evil. . . .

XI Of the Justification of Man
We are accounted righteous before God, only for the
merit of our Lord and Saviour Jesus Christ by Faith, and
not for our own works or deservings. . . .

The Deed of Union

Clause 30.[1]

[1] See pp. 53, 74.

244

Explanatory Notes upon the New Testament (John Wesley)

Commentary on Romans 5:21

That as sin had reigned—so grace also might reign—Which could not reign before the Fall; before man had sinned. *Through righteousness to eternal life by Jesus Christ our Lord*—Here is pointed out the source of all our blessings, the rich and free grace of God. The meritorious cause; not any works of righteousness of man, but the alone merits of our Lord Jesus Christ. The effect or end of all; not only pardon, but life; divine life, leading to glory.

Sermon V. Justification by Faith (John Wesley)

In the image of God was man made; holy as He that created him is holy; merciful as the Author of all is merciful; perfect as his Father in heaven is perfect. . . . Such then was the state of man in Paradise. By the free, unmerited love of God, he was holy and happy: he knew, loved, enjoyed God, which is, in substance, life everlasting. And in this life of love he was to continue for ever, if he continued to obey God in all things; but if he disobeyed Him in any, he was to forfeit all. 'In that day', said God, 'thou shalt surely die.'

Man did disobey God. He 'ate of the tree, of which God commanded him, saying, Thou shalt not eat of it'. And in that day he was condemned by the righteous judgement of God. . . . Thus, 'through the offence of one', all are dead, dead to God, dead in sin, dwelling in a corruptible, mortal body, shortly to be dissolved, and under the sentence of death eternal. . . .

In this state we were, even all mankind, when 'God so loved the world, that He gave His only begotten Son, to the end we might not perish, but have everlasting life'.

Sermon I. Salvation by Faith (John Welsey)

This then is the salvation which is through faith, even in the present world: a salvation from sin, and the consequences of sin, both often expressed in the word *justification*; which, taken in the largest sense, implies a deliverance from guilt and punishment, by the atonement of Christ actually applied to the soul of the sinner now believing on Him, and a deliverance from the power of sin, through Christ *formed in his heart*. So that he who is thus justified, or saved by faith, is indeed *born again.*

Sermon X. The Witness of the Spirit (John Wesley)

But what is that testimony of God's Spirit, which is superadded to, and conjoined with, this? How does He 'bear witness with our spirit that we are the children of God'? It is hard to find words in the language of men to explain 'the deep things of God'. Indeed, there are none that will adequately express what the children of God experience. But perhaps one might say (desiring any who are taught of God to correct, to soften, or strengthen the expression), the testimony of the Spirit is an inward impression on the soul, whereby the Spirit of God directly witnesses to my spirit, that I am a child of God; that Jesus Christ hath loved me, and given Himself for me; and that all my sins are blotted out, and I, even I, am reconciled to God.

Sermon VIII. The First-fruits of the Spirit (John Wesley)

Wait in peace, for that hour, when 'the God of peace shall sanctify thee wholly, so that thy whole spirit and soul and body may be preserved blameless unto the coming of our Lord Jesus Christ'!

The Senior Catechism of the Methodist Church

24. WHY DO WE NEED TO BE SAVED?

We need to be saved because we and all mankind are under the destroying power of sin and death, from which we cannot save ourselves.

25. WHAT IS SIN?

Sin is that which corrupts our nature and makes us prefer our own will to God's.

26. WHAT IS SALVATION?

Salvation is deliverance from sin into a new life of righteousness that begins on earth, survives death, and is perfected with God in heaven.

27. HOW DOES GOD SAVE US?

By His grace He freely converts, justifies, regenerates and sanctifies every repentant sinner who has faith in Jesus Christ crucified for us.

28. WHAT IS GRACE?

Grace is the undeserved love of God to all.

29. WHAT IS CONVERSION?

We are converted by God when we respond to His grace in repentance and faith.

30. WHAT IS REPENTANCE?

Repentance is turning to God in sorrow for our sin.

32. WHAT IS JUSTIFICATION?

We are justified when God pardons our sins and accepts us as His children.

33. WHAT IS REGENERATION?

We are born anew when God justifies us and brings us by His Spirit into the new life of righteousness.

34. WHAT IS SANCTIFICATION?

We are made holy as we grow by the power of the Holy Spirit in the new life and in love towards God and our neighbours.

35. WHAT IS ENTIRE SANCTIFICATION?

We are entirely sanctified when the Holy Spirit fulfils His work in our lives and we love God and our neighbour perfectly.

37. HOW DO WE KNOW THAT WE ARE SAVED?

By the sure Word of God, by the inner conviction of the Holy Spirit in our hearts, and by the fruit of the Spirit in our lives we know that we are saved.

The Methodist Service Book

You created all things and made us in your own image.

247

When we had fallen into sin, you gave your only Son to be our Saviour.

(The Sunday Service, p. B12)

We pray that *this child*, now to be baptized in this water, may die to sin and be raised to the new life in Christ. *Amen.*

(Baptism, p. A8)

The Methodist Hymn Book

Plenteous He is in truth and grace;
He wills that all the fallen race
   Should turn, repent, and live;
His pardoning grace for all is free;
Transgression, sin, iniquity,
   He freely doth forgive.

(369, v. 4) (Charles Wesley)

Believe in Him that died for thee,
   And, sure as He hath died,
Thy debt is paid, thy soul is free,
   And thou art justified.

(372, v. 2) (Charles Wesley)

My God, I am Thine;
What a comfort divine,
What a blessing to know that my Jesus is mine!
   In the heavenly Lamb
   Thrice happy I am,
And my heart it doth dance at the sound of His name.

(406, v. 1) (Charles Wesley)

All things are possible to God,
To Christ, the power of God in man,
To me, when I am all renewed,
When I in Christ am formed again,
And witness, from all sin set free,
All things are possible to me.

(548, v. 4) (Charles Wesley)

B. THE DOCTRINE OF MAN

A brief comment is necessary on what some would call the 'sexist' nature of the title. In the foundation documents and in this present section no apology is needed, for over the centuries covered by Scripture and tradition 'man' was the accepted word for the human race. In the third section, Present Considerations, the use of the word in that sense will, as far as possible, be avoided. This is appropriate as it is in our time that the liberation of women has largely taken place.

(1) Created by God

According to the biblical, and therefore the Christian, view, man's chief claim to significance is the fact that he is created by God. 'The Lord God formed man of dust from the ground, and breathed into his nostrils the breath of life' (Gen. 2:7). This is the earlier account. The later one refers to God creating man 'in his own image' (Gen. 1:27), a phrase to be taken up later. In both cases man owes his existence totally to the direct, unilateral action of God. Before the consideration of what has proved to be the contentious question of *how* he created man, it can be asserted that the traditional view is that he did.

The first answer to the 'how' question is: 'male and female he created them' (Gen. 1:27), and this, as far as one knows, has not been contested! Indeed, according to Mark 10:2 ff., Jesus by-passed the laws of Moses to appeal to it as the ground of the indissolubility of marriage. The difficulties lie elsewhere, and only emerged when the theories of evolution were propounded in the last century. Was man created 'at a stroke', complete with an upright stance and a brain capable of solving quadratic equations? Or did his body and his brain slowly evolve from other forms of life? For many years Christians fought a rearguard action on the supposition that if evolution were true the Christian faith could not be. I recall asking, in the brashness of youth, an elderly fundamentalist whether, if I laid a selection of skulls along the Kingston by-pass, beginning with anthropoid apes and finishing with Bertrand Russell and Albert Einstein, he could bring himself to believe in evolution. He replied that he could not, because it was contrary to the Word of God. Happily such arid arguments are becoming rare. And they are doing so as we realize that the Bible is not a textbook on this or that branch of science but the record of a people's faith. Their faith at this point was the affirmation of God's creation. Whatever the method (evolution seems the most likely), it was God's method. Man is his handiwork.

(2) An animal

Man is part of the animal creation. In common with the rest, his body breathes, eats, drinks, sleeps, excretes and procreates. Under the relentless desert sun men and beasts share one need—water. The earth tremor or the flowing lava makes no distinctions. More pleasurably, the fresh mountain stream, the warm sun, the morning air, the filling of an empty stomach and the joys of sex are blessings for the whole animate creation. And as the animals die, so do we.

Of course it will have to be said in a moment that man is more than an animal but, before it is, two results of man being an animal must be noted. They are not logically opposed, but in practice people find it hard to live with both.

One is that if God has seen fit to create us as part of the animal world, then we can enjoy unashamedly our animal pleasures. There is not much difficulty over mountain streams and morning air if we can find the energy to walk; nor over eating and drinking if we first discipline ourselves to be hungry. It is in sex that we encounter the 'hang-ups'. But at least we can say that things are better than they used to be.

The other result is that being an animal means constantly being dragged down to the animal level. To eat four helpings of apple pie is to be 'a greedy pig'; to break the sexual norms is to be 'a filthy beast'. There is truth in this, but it needs no great discernment to see that the worst sins of which we are capable could be committed by the pigs in George Orwell's *Animal Farm*, but not by ordinary pigs.

250

(3) More than animal

The features that distinguish men from animals are variable but most of them have to do with our mental capacities. Memory, for example, seems common among animals but not, even with elephants (!), of the same range and capacity as ours. Logical thought would seem to be a human prerogative. There is a logical inconsistency in the following syllogism:

Good cricketers come from Somerset;
I come from Somerset;
therefore I am a good cricketer;

but it would not be appreciated by the dog from next-door who is wandering over my lawn as I write. Abstract thought is the same. I do not think the sparrows on the telephone wire are reflecting on truth, beauty and goodness. Self-awareness, self-consciousness is another such feature. I know that I am John Stacey, Methodist minister, Secretary for Local Preachers, good at talking but bad at listening, sometimes generous and sometimes mean and so forth. And as such, I persist through time, or some of it. But did the hedgehog run over in the road have the same grasp of his identity?

Such features carry with them freedom and responsibility. Not unlimited freedom, but enough to make us responsible for many of the things we do, or fail to do. Within limits we can choose whether we pollute our rivers or keep them clean, whether we spend our money on photography or theological books, or whether we treat the very animals from whom, in this regard, we differ, with compassion, or whether we hunt them to death across the countryside for fun. Man is unique in the animal creation.

(4) The image of God

Theologians have had a field day with this phrase: One of them, Irenaeus, Bishop of Lyons in the second century, argued on the basis that the Hebrew word for 'image' in the first half of Genesis 1:27 was different from the one in the second

251

half. He decided that the first image was man's reason, with its power of choice; the second was the gift of communion with God. He then worked out an elaborate but artificial scheme to show what the sin of Adam and Eve did to the human race. Other theologians have argued that what the writer of Genesis is saying is that man, in the pristine purity of his creation, is like God. The writer sees him before the Fall, before sin had defaced him, as a visible representation of God. Man is made in the likeness of God. The question then taken up by these theologians is whether, after he had fallen into sin, man retained anything of the divine image.

Another way of understanding man made 'in the image of God' is to notice the close connection between Genesis 1:27 and the preceeding verse. There the basic idea of image is the idea of dominion. Man is allowed to exercise authority, God's authority indeed, over the rest of creation. This is his responsibility, his stewardship. And it could be that Genesis 5:3 is the writer's attempt to say that this exercise of dominion was passed on to succeeding generations even after the Fall. The occupational hazard, so to speak, of being so made in the image of God is that you want to be God. And as you are not, you behave as if you were. This is the great sin against which the book of Genesis makes such a moving protest.

To refer to Jesus as 'the Second Adam' is, among other things, to say that the dominion given to man at the beginning is only properly exercised by him. He bears the authority, of God, and uses it. He is 'the image of the invisible God' (Col. 1:15). Ought not this then to mean that those who are Christ's should have the image restored in them? And be more concerned for the rest of creation as a result?

(5) Soul

There is no immediately obvious connection between the emancipation of the slaves in North America and the discussions of philosophers in ancient Greece. But consider:

John Brown's body lies amouldering in the grave,
But his soul goes marching on.

Clearly there were two parts of John Brown, one that ate and drank and made love and finished up in the grave, the other that engaged in spiritual exercises and went on into eternity. The famous catchphrase from Greece was *soma-sema*, 'the body a tomb'. At death the immortal soul escaped from its tomb and went 'marching on'.

According to the Bible, both Greek philosophers and American song-writers are mistaken. Man cannot be divided up in this arbitrary way. The Hebrew word *nephesh*, often translated 'soul', has a number of meanings. It can mean 'life' as opposed to 'death', (Ex. 4:19); it can mean 'I' (Ps. 6:4 where again RSV has 'life'); it can mean the centre of experience, particularly emotional experience (Gen. 34:3). The New Testament *psyche* which corresponds to *nephesh* has a similar connotation. Neither word can ever be taken to refer to some special part of man concerned with spritual things and immortal in its own right. It is better to speak of man as *being* a soul rather than *having* a soul, and better still not to use the word more than the Bible and the liturgy require. The unsatisfactory nature of the term probably underlay both question and answer in the repartee of Tower Hill: when a materialist asked Lord Soper what was the shape of his soul the reply he received was 'Judging by your face I would say it was oblong'.

(6) Flesh and body

To treat man in sections, as is now being done, may satisfy our Western, analytical minds but it is largely foreign to the Biblical understanding of man. Man is a living creature, living because God has 'breathed into his nostrils the breath of life', and the unity of man's nature that that implies is basic to the Hebrew view. Within that unity, when the Hebrew wanted to refer to the physical substances of which he was composed he said 'flesh' (*basar*) and he certainly did not mean that 'flesh' was evil.

The New Testament makes the following distinction between 'flesh' (*sarx*) and 'body' (*soma*).

'Flesh' appears to be something of a 'bogey' word in the writings of Paul (e.g. Rom. 7:5, 18). That is because it is the word used in association with sin as it attempts to take over our physical nature. Paul does *not* say that our physical nature is evil in itself. It is worth reminding our congregations sometimes that enmity, strife, jealousy, anger, selfishness, dissension, party spirit and envy (Gal. 5:20) are sins of *the flesh*. The reason for this is that 'flesh' was used by Paul to represent man in his worldliness and vulnerability, whether given physical, or what we would call spiritual, expression.

'Body' is the New Testament word for a person in his totality— all that he is. Indeed 'person' is the word that best conveys its most significant meaning.

253

(7) Spirit

According to Paul every man has a spirit (1 Cor. 2:11):

> There is a personal *pneuma*, the natural possession of every man, which, of itself, is neither good nor bad, and is not easily distinguished from *psyche*.[2]

When the natural man becomes a Christian it is his spirit which is recreated by the Holy Spirit, and this of course is Paul's chief interest. But even in unregenerate man, the spirit is man at his highest:

> Spirit was the controlling, directing, and reflective element in the whole man.[3]

(8) A social animal

If we say in our context that man is a social animal we mean that individual people are part of a larger whole. If we say in the biblical context that man is a social animal we mean that the larger whole is comprised of individual people. The thinking starts at opposite ends. Take, for example, the covenant. At the heart of our Covenant Service the words run:

> I am no longer my own, but yours. Put me to what you will, rank me whom you will; put me to doing, put me to suffering ... And now, glorious and blessed God, Father, Son, and Holy Spirit, you are mine and I am yours. ...[4]

Compare this with Exodus 24:7–8:

> Then he took the book of the covenant, and read it in the hearing of the people; and they said, 'all that the Lord has spoken we will do, and we will be obedient.' And Moses took the blood and threw it upon the people, and said, 'Behold the

[2] W. David Stacey, *The Pauline View of Man* (Macmillan 1956), p. 129.
[3] W. David Stacey, p. 135.
[4] MSB, p. D10.

254

blood of the covenant which the Lord has made with you in accordance with all these words.'

The difference is not only that we do not now throw basins of blood over our congregations. It is also that for our individualism they had what is known as 'corporate personality'. No absolute distinction between these two can be made. Our Covenant Service speaks of 'this Covenant which God has made *with his people*'[5] and on the other hand, in the Old Testament, there is the individualism of Jeremiah 31 and Ezekiel 18. But the priorities are different.

(9) Man is a sinner

This section is sub-divided for the sake of clarity.

(i) What is sin?

The Bible uses many words to describe it. They have the sense of 'missing the mark' (the commonest in the New Testament), 'distortion', 'rebellion', 'unfaithfulness', 'folly', 'law-breaking', and so on. When they are all examined in their context, two assertions can be made. One is that sin, as the Bible understands it, is rooted in the self, in self-interest, selfishness, self-seeking, self-indulgence and the rest. We make ourselves the centre of the universe. This leads to the second assertion. God is the centre of the universe and the essence of sin is that in some way or another we are always trying to take his place. This is not to say, of course, that we want to run the whole show. We do not care who rolls the stars along or who makes it rain in Singapore. But we want to run *our* show. And God help God if he tries to interfere.

It is obvious, then, that sin is a religious term. If you do not believe in God then, strictly speaking, you can call yourself a criminal or a cad, but not a sinner. Sin is I against God.

Against thee, thee only, have I sinned, and done that which is evil in thy sight. (Ps. 51: 4)

[5] MSB, p. D9.

255

It is precisely for this reason that pride is the worst of all sins. As C. S. Lewis says in one of his brilliant essays on Christian morals:

> According to Christian teachers, the essential vice, the utmost evil, is Pride. Unchastity, anger, greed, drunkenness, and all that, are mere flea-bites in comparison: it was through Pride that the devil became the devil: Pride leads to every other vice: it is the complete anti-God state of mind.[6]

Lewis then explains why:

> In God you come up against something which is in every respect immeasurably superior to yourself. Unless you know God as that—and therefore know yourself as nothing in comparison— you can't know God at all. As long as you are proud you can't know God at all. A proud man is always looking down on things and people: and, of course, as long as you're looking down, you can't see something that's above you.[7]

In short, you are God. That is the root of sin.

(ii)   Original sin

This is not sin that nobody has so far thought of (there isn't any). It is an attempt to account for the fact that we cannot help being sinners. We seem somehow to have been born into the wretched business. Our fathers before us and our children after us are just the same. We all find it easier to do wrong than to do right. It is not that we deliberately choose when we are young that we want to be God of our own little show. It is that it is our nature to be like that. Cut-throat capitalism starts in the play-pen. Rowdy self-assertion begins at the breast.

If sin is 'original' in this sense, then it is necessary to look at what is claimed to be its origin.

(iii)   The Fall

Augustine (AD 354–430) argued that, because the whole human race existed potentially in Adam, all men have a corrupt nature

6 *Christian Behaviour* (Geoffrey Bles 1943), p. 42.
7 P. 44.

as the result of Adam's sin.[8] What happened in the garden of Eden was the cause of all the trouble. It is known as the 'Fall', and is described in Genesis chapter 3.

The notion that we are sinners as a direct consequence of Adam having sinned is rejected by many theologians as a misinterpretation of Genesis 3. This is no place for a full-blooded commentary on that chapter. It can only be said that it contains a myth in the sense referred to earlier.[9] As David Jenkins says:

> The story of the Fall is the way of moving from the opening powerful assertions of the splendour and goodness of creation to the actual history and experience of the human race.[10]

That history and experience included the pain of childbirth, the sweat of work in the fields, the embarrassment of the genitals, the revulsion at creatures that slithered along without legs, the fact of death. In the mind of the writer of the tenth century BC these disruptions of what was intended are due to the sin of Adam and Eve. What he considered that sin to be precisely is a matter for exegesis.[11] As we read his story we see it to be pride. It was the desire to 'be like God' (v. 5).

It is understandable that some theologians link the universality of sin (Rom. 3:23) to the sin of Adam, the father of the race (Rom. 5:12 ff.; 1 Cor. 15:22), but the link is not one of cause and effect. The Fall tells us the way things are.

C. THE DOCTRINE OF SALVATION

(1) Salvation the work of God

The conflict between Jesus and the leaders of Jewish religion, central in his life and ministry, raises the initial questions. Was a relationship with the living God something man was able

---

[8] He maintained that the guilt of Adam was passed on by 'concupiscence', i.e. through sexual intercourse.
[9] See pp. 17–19.
[10] *What is Man?* (S.C.M. 1970), p. 81.
[11] Exegesis is the process of drawing the writer's meaning from the text.

257

to establish by his own righteousness? Did God welcome only those who had kept the Law? Was salvation by works? The Jewish leaders referred to in the Gospels[12] in effect were saying 'yes'. Jesus said 'no'. He spoke and lived on the huge assumption that God accepted men as they were, in their sin.[13] The tax-gatherers and the harlots—the dregs—might well enter the kingdom before the godly who had never broken the Law. One can understand how this infuriated 'the Jews' and, in the end, brought Jesus to the cross.

Christian theologians however took the point, and Paul was the first of them. He saw clearly the essential point of what Jesus said and did. A reading of the first eight chapters of Romans allows only one conclusion; God accepts sinners, therefore salvation of man is not man's own achievement. It lies in the saving action of God, and all man can do is to respond.

Whenever this basic position has been threatened theologians have fought to preserve it. In the early part of the fifth century a British (possibly Irish) lay monk named Pelagius (his followers are referred to in Article IX)[14] taught that man took the initial and fundamental steps towards salvation by his own efforts. The sin of Adam, argued Pelagius, has nothing to do with it. Men are responsible for their own good or evil deeds and they are free to accept God or reject him. Pelagius was resisted by Augustine, who in the strongest terms and in the most comprehensive fashion, argued that man can do nothing whatever to save himself. God had done everything that needed to be done. Salvation was entirely of God. As far as the Church was concerned Augustine won the argument.

One of the many factors involved in the Reformation was the belief that the medieval Church had been unfaithful to the basic Biblical position in this matter. If man could earn his salvation by the accumulation of merit, whether by giving his wealth to the Church when he was alive or having masses

[12] Not all Jewish teachers in the time of Jesus took this view. Some, for example, set much store on the text 'I will be gracious to whom I will be gracious' (Exod. 33:19).
[13] Repentance was the result of this acceptance, not its condition.
[14] See p. 244.

said for him when he was dead, the position of Paul and Augustine was being violated. The Reformers put a stop to that.

It is easy to give a balanced statement if you are not in the heat of a battle for what you believe to be the truth of the Gospel, as Augustine and the Reformers were. We are in a position to conclude that our salvation lies in the saving action of God and not in our own achievements, nevertheless the response we make must be made in freedom.

(2) Grace

At this point it is essential to introduce into the discussion the key theological word. It has a range of meanings in our normal usage. Consider:

> We only say grace when Grandma comes to tea.
> She danced the waltz with poise and grace.
> If he is not elected President of the Conference, we hope he will accept it with a good grace.

It is necessary, therefore, to be very precise about the use of such a word. What exactly is meant by 'the grace of God'?

It is an error to suppose that grace is a kind of spiritual fluid that flows from God to man, particularly in the formal services of the Church. There have been people (and perhaps there still are) who have believed that, when a bishop ordains a man, 'grace' somehow travels down the episcopal arm and out through the episcopal fingers, a travesty of course, of Catholic doctrine. Some have believed that 'it' comes with the water of baptism or the bread and wine of the eucharist.

There is no such spiritual fluid. The two realities with which we are dealing are God, Father, Son and Holy Spirit on the one hand, and man on the other. Both are personal. To speak of the grace of God, then, means not a hose-pipe theology, but what John Oman in *Grace and Personality* described as 'a gracious relationship':

> We have a gracious relationship which has its whole quality and distinction from being personal on both sides. With that

259

GROUNDWORK OF THEOLOGY

beginning, the task of salvation is manifestly to display God's mind towards us and elicit our minds towards Him, and not merely to cleanse our souls by a grace acting as impersonally as bleaching powder whitening cotton.[15]

But what, on God's side, makes the relationship gracious? What is the grace of God? According to Paul it is the act of free forgiveness performed by God. We are 'justified by his grace as a gift, through the redemption which is in Christ Jesus'. (Rom. 3:24)

God's action is gracious because in it he is taking the initiative. He does not wait until we are 'acceptable', until we repent or keep the law or otherwise qualify. He acts first because it is his nature so to act. He *is* gracious, that is why he does not wait for anything. Theologians have sometimes called this 'prevenient' grace. The meaning is that he comes to us before we come to him.

But God shows his love for us in that while we were yet sinners Christ died for us. (Rom. 5:8)

In so expounding the grace of God, Paul is expanding theologically what we find in Jesus. As Oman says of 'the gracious relationship', 'the answer of the Gospels is that God deals with us as with children'.[16] He is the Father who acts with grace. And the parables of the Prodigal Son and the Labourers in the Vineyard show that the qualifications we can boast are not in the same league, so to speak, as the Father's love and care.

Finally, in this 'gracious relationship' we can find a working answer, if not an intellectual one, to the chief theological problem in the field of grace. It is the question as to whether or not grace is irresistible. Or, to put it another way, are we predestined or are we free? Why should God save A rather than B?[17] Attention has already been drawn to the differing views of Pelagius and Augustine on this matter. Augustine believed that God's grace could not be resisted and that God

[15] *Grace and Personality* (C.U.P. 1917), p. 66.
[16] P. 66.   [17] See p. 270.

260

had predestined some people for salvation and the rest for damnation. In this he was followed—with moderation—by the English theologian John Wyclif and—with typical vigour—by the French Reformer, John Calvin, and indeed by Martin Luther. These men had massive minds. Yet their theology at this point seems to us to be open to obvious and powerful objections. If God predestinates some people to damnation before they have a chance, then he is a tyrant. If God predetermines all we do then we are not free at all, and therefore not responsible. Why then did they opt for a doctrine of predestination? A quick answer to this question is impossible. All we can say is that it lies along two lines. First, they were convinced that their convictions were grounded in the Scriptures, though we can now see that they interpreted Paul outside the context of his particular problem. Secondly, their own Christian experience persuaded them that salvation was *entirely* of God. They were convinced that they had not chosen him. He had chosen them. And so it went on. They were what they were by his grace alone. This was the experience which lay behind the grim intellectual systems they constructed.

In 'the gracious relationship' we come to know that Pelagius, uncorrected by Augustine, Wyclif, Calvin and Luther, will not do. We cannot, on our own, achieve, and still less earn, our salvation. We also know that Augustine and the others, unmodified by Pelagius, will not do either. We are not God's pawns. The grace of God is offered constantly to all men in Christ, and without it there could be no salvation. But we have to respond, and keep responding, from a freedom which, if limited, is real.

(3) The pattern of salvation

Within the framework of the operation of grace and freewill just described there is a traditional pattern of salvation. It results from the study of the New Testament, from the tradition of the Church and from personal Christian experience. But it is not a rigid, fixed pattern in the sense that every Christian has to have all these things happen to him in precisely this

261

way and in exactly this order. Life is larger than tidy schemes in theological books. The value of the pattern is that it clarifies the elements that, in some fashion or another, are present in the classical Christian experience of salvation.

(i) Conviction of sin

The traditional view is that little progress can be made in the matter of a man's salvation until he realizes that he is a sinner, helpless and undone. Once he is convicted of his sin and knows he is indeed a lost soul the first essential condition (on the human side) has been met. He is ready to be saved.

The conviction of sin has frequently been a disturbing emotional experience. Religious revivals yield many examples, like the following from the *Journal of John Wesley*. It is one of the less dramatic:

> I then designed going to the Cross (at Grimsby), but the rain prevented; so that we were a little at a loss, till we were offered a very convenient place by a 'woman which was a sinner'. I there declared 'Him' (about one o'clock) whom 'God hath exalted, to give repentance and remission of sins'. And God so confirmed the word of His grace that I marvelled any one could withstand Him.
>
> However, the prodigal held out till the evening, when I enlarged upon *her* sins and faith who 'washed our Lord's feet with tears, and wiped them with the hairs of her head'. She was then utterly broken in pieces (as, indeed, was wellnigh the whole congregation) and came after me to my lodging, crying out, 'Oh, sir! what must I do to be saved?'[18]

In the experience of being 'utterly broken in pieces' lies the conviction of sin.

The conviction can be brought about, as with the prostitute at Grimsby, by the preaching of the Gospel. To 'offer Christ' is to make people aware of their own sinful state. To expose the love of God is to expose the sin of man. But it can also be brought about by the operation of the Law. It is given a capital letter simply to distinguish it from the law of the land. It is

[18] *The Journal of John Wesley* (Epworth 1938), Vol. III, p. 105.

the theological word for a moral code. What a strict moral code does is to reduce people to despair because they know they must keep it but soon discover that they cannot. Part of this despair is the conviction of sin. This is the predicament about which Paul writes in Romans (see particularly 7:7–25) where the moral code is the Jewish law.

(ii) Repentance
The Senior Catechism says that repentance is 'turning to God in sorrow for our sin'.[19] The use of the word in the Bible has more to do with the turning than the sorrow. The Hebrew word usually translated 'repent' is the ordinary word for 'turn'. As somebody has said, if you shouted the Greek word 'Repent!' at a company of soldiers (presumably Greek ones) on the march they would not fall down on their knees and begin to cry. They would about turn and march off in the opposite direction.

It is this element of 'turning' that distinguishes repentance from remorse. In remorse a man simply sits down and wrings his hands in despair. The past imprisons him. In repentance he sorrows for his sin and he takes a new direction. The future welcomes him. Repentance is full of hope. It is significant that when, on the day of Pentecost, Peter and the rest of the apostles were asked, 'Brethren what shall we do?' (Acts 2:37), the first word of their reply was 'Repent'.

(iii) Faith
This heading must appear for the completeness of the pattern being described, but there is no point in repeating what was said in chapter 3. The student is recommended to re-read the section of that chapter on 'Faith'.

The only addition needed is a comment on the relationship between faith and good works. It comes from A. Raymond George:

> We are justified through faith, not by works (cf. Gal. 2:16), that is, not by our own good conduct. It is not inconsistent with this

[19] See p. 247.

to say 'Faith apart from works is dead' (Jas 2:26); a trust in
Christ which does not result in good conduct is no true trust;
yet we are not saved by our good conduct, but by the trust which
is its source.[20]

(iv) Forgiveness

This section must now move on from those aspects of salvation
in which man would appear to have a significant role ('appear'
because of what has already been said about prevenient grace)
to those in which God's action is obviously primary. It is God
who forgives man.

The meaning of the word gives no difficulty. It is to treat
the sinner as if he had not committed sin at all. Of course he
has, and nothing can alter that. But the crucial words are 'as
if'. To forgive really is to forget.

The answer of the Senior Catechism to the question 'How
are our sins forgiven?' is 'We are forgiven by the grace of God,
through faith in Jesus Christ, Who died for our sins'. The
great theological words of that statement have been considered
in previous sections. God's forgiveness is rooted in his love.
Our forgiveness of each other (without which, according to
the Lord's Prayer, we cannot have the forgiveness of God)
must have the same root. We cannot hate and forgive at the
same time.

The way in which God's forgiveness is brought home to
believers in the Church opens up some interesting questions. Is
it enough to proclaim it in the preaching? Is the Sacrament
of Penance in which the priest says 'I absolve thee in the name
of the Father and of the Son and of the Holy Spirit' a case
of man usurping the function of God? And what of our own:

> Hear then the word of grace:
> Your sins are forgiven?[21]

(v) Conversion

This is a word that could be inserted at almost any point in
this section. It is certainly the work of God, as the answer to

20 'The Holy Spirit', *An Approach to Christian Doctrine*, p. 120.
21 The Sunday Service, MSB, p. B6.

question 29 in the Senior Catechism makes clear. The word means a 'turning' and so, in derivation at least, is close to repentance. But, as Raymond George says:

It has come to mean that whole change in a man's character and outlook which salvation produces.[22]

That some conversions happen more quickly than others, and some very quickly, is evident from the long experience of the Church. But grace seems to choose its own speed.

(vi) Justification

The idea of justification is best seen against a legal background. Man is accused of sin by God's law or by the voice of conscience, but God the judge dismisses the case if the man has faith in him and is repentant.

Some argue that 'to justify' means 'to declare righteous', 'to treat as righteous'. But C. K. Barrett has a stronger case: that 'to justify' means 'to *make* righteous' but

'righteous' does not mean 'virtuous', but 'right', 'clear', 'acquitted' in God's court.[23]

Justification is obviously very near to forgiveness. The word occurs in the assertion of Martin Luther that became a cornerstone of Protestant theology: justification is by faith alone. Luther is saying that good works cannot obtain it for us, but faith can. And faith of course in the God who actually does the justifying (Rom. 4:5). This was the theology preached by John Wesley, as is shown by the quotation from his sermon Salvation by Faith.[24]

(vii) Redemption

Here is yet another word to describe what God does to save man. It has its roots in the Old Testament. A slave could be

[22] *An Approach to Christian Doctrine*, p. 116.
[23] C. K. Barrett *The Epistle to the Romans* (A. and C. Black 1957), pp. 75–6.
[24] See p. 245.

'redeemed': he could be set free if a price were paid for him. But often the reference is to deliverance in a more general sense, like the deliverance of the Hebrews from Egypt, and the question of price did not arise. If some of the early Christian theologians had realized that, we might have been spared some of those speculative questions about who paid what ransom to whom. In traditional Christian theology, however, the word 'redemption' does carry this reference to the price paid. It also includes the freedom with which Christ has set us free (Gal. 5:1).

(viii) Adoption

The key texts here are Romans 8:15 and Galatians 4:4–7. Adoption was widespread in the Roman world and an adopted child was reckoned a member of the family. So Paul had an illustration at hand, and he used it. Dying and rising with Christ mean adoption as sons of God. And it is the sons of God who have 'the Spirit of his Son' in their hearts and are able to cry, 'Abba! Father!' (Gal. 4:6).

(ix) Regeneration

> So that he who is thus justified, or saved by faith, is indeed born again.[25]

Regeneration means being born again and such a concept is used in the New Testament to describe the birth in the believer of the new life in Christ through the inward working of the Holy Spirit. It is found in the Johannine writings (John 3:3 ff.; 1 John 2:29; 3:9) as well as in 1 Peter 1:23. It is another way of speaking of dying and rising with Christ (Rom. 6:4), to which reference has already been made.

John Wesley has a sermon *The New Birth*, and here is part of his definition:

> It is that great change which God works in the soul when He brings it to life; when He raises it from the death of sin to the life of righteousness. It is the change wrought in the whole soul

[25] John Wesley, 'Salvation by Faith', see p. 246.

by the almighty Spirit of God when it is 'created anew in Christ Jesus'.[26]

The situation has been confused by the distinction between 'once-born' and 'twice-born' Christians, popularized by William James in his influential book *Varieties of Religious Experience*. But if the new birth means the beginning of the new life in Christ through the work of the Holy Spirit, then every repenting and believing Christian is born again. To assert that this is the prerogative of those who experience an emotional and dramatic form of repenting and believing is virtually to tell the Holy Spirit what he can and what he cannot do. The evidence is that he does not seem to pay much attention.

(x) Reconciliation
The forgiven, converted, justified, redeemed, adopted, regenerated person is also reconciled to God. As 2 Corinthians 5:19 puts it:

God was in Christ reconciling the world to himself, not counting their trespasses against them.

Paul makes this the ground of evangelism (see below):

We beseech you on behalf of Christ, be reconciled to God. (v. 20)

(xi) Assurance
It will not have escaped the reader that in this section there are more references than previously to specifically Methodist sources. This is no accident. The Methodist Revival centred on the preaching of salvation through Christ to sinful men. The processes by which salvation was appropriated were therefore of immediate concern. The sermons of John Wesley deal with them at length; so do the hymns of Charles.

Assurance was no exception. It is, simply, the certain knowledge that we are saved. Sometimes it is called the 'Witness of the Spirit' after Romans 8:16 and the sermon of John Wesley on the subject.

[26] Sermon XXXIX, *Wesley's Standard Sermons* (Epworth 1921), Vol. II, p. 234.

The assurance hymns of Charles Wesley, still singable, are a more effective way of communicating the emphasis than the printed sermons of John, hardly preachable. So the Methodist sings to the Holy Spirit:

> My peace, my life, my comfort Thou,
>   My treasure and my all Thou art;
> True witness of my sonship, now
>   Engraving pardon on my heart,
> Seal of my sins in Christ forgiven,
> Earnest of love, and pledge of heaven.[27]

That such certainty, and the joy that flows from it, is the work of the Holy Spirit, few would deny. The problem is, however, that not all Christians are always assured—from the saints who experienced the Dark Night of the Soul to many a Methodist on a wet Monday morning. But if assurance is given by the Spirit only to some of the people for some of the time—and this characteristic it would share with some of his other gifts—it is not to be written off on that account. It must rather be treated as a privilege. Wesley himself recognized this in his later years. He wrote:

When fifty years ago my brother Charles and I, in the simplicity of our hearts, told the good people of England that, unless they *knew* (Wesley's italics) their sins were forgiven, they were under the wrath and curse of God, I marvel they did not stone us! The Methodists, I hope, know better now; we preach assurance as we always did, as a common privilege of the children of God; but we do not enforce it, under the pain of damnation, denounced on all who enjoy it not![28]

As with all privileges, those who have them should be grateful.

(xii) Sanctification and Christian perfection
Sanctification means being made holy. It is traditionally

[27] MHB 299, v. 3.
[28] Letter to Melville Home in Robert Southey, *Life of John Wesley*, Vol. 1, p. 295.

thought of, not in terms of moral struggle, though that is not absent, but in relation to the continuing work of the Holy Spirit in the believer. Thus the resulting holiness is best seen as 'the fruit of the Spirit' of Galatians 5.

Another emphasis of the Wesleys was that the process of sanctification could reach a goal in the life-time of the believer, the goal of perfection. What are we to make of this? The question is asked because initially the doctrine seems to be quite out of touch with reality. We have probably met some very good people in our time. But a *perfect* one? And if we look inward instead of outward any suggestion of perfection is laughable.

It all depends, of course, on what you mean by perfection. Sometimes the doctrine is called Perfect Love and this gives us an indication. Love concerns the basic direction of the will, the fundamental attitude and stance of a person towards God and his fellows. A loving person can, and does, make mistakes. He can, and does, sin. Perfect Love then, is not infallibility and sinlessness. It is the perfection of the will always directed in love, the perfection of *attitude* to God and man.

John Wesley taught that this was possible, though he did not claim that it had happened to him. It was, again, the work of the Spirit and not the believer's own achievement. As such it was a statement of faith: it is impossible to set limits to what the Spirit can do. He can, incredibly, remove the *root* of inward sin. As Charles Wesley said, with an almost swash-buckling faith:

The thing impossible *shall be*.[29]

We must be satisfied with nothing less (Phil. 4:13).

The doctrine has a social connotation. John Wesley contended that the Gospel of Christ knew 'no holiness but social holiness'. It really is impossible to live in perfect love on your own. It also, like every other doctrine of the Christian faith, has an eschatological connotation. Perfection is, in the minds of most Christians, part of what one day, by the grace of God,

---

[29] MHB 548, v. 3.

we shall be. This doctrine of Wesley expresses the truth that the last things are 'now' as well as 'then'.

(4) Evangelism

To return to the issue discussed at the beginning of this section: is the conclusion that the pattern of salvation as now described is in the inscrutable wisdom of God and that he will save those he wills to save and no one else? Or is it that this salvation, and all that goes into it, is, by the grace of God, on offer to all mankind? This was an issue of some size in Wesley's day. In theology it was the choice between Calvinism and Arminianism, Arminius being a Dutch theologian who resisted the hard line taken by Calvin on predestination. The Wesleys, and Methodism after them, were Arminians, and their Arminianism made them evangelicals,[30] not in the party sense in which the word has subsequently been used, but in the sense that salvation was 'for every soul of man'. All the work of grace, from conviction of sin to Christian Perfection, was for 'whosoever will'. Methodism's answer to hard predestination was clear enough:

> Thy undistinguishing regard
> Was cast on Adam's fallen race;
> For all thou hast in Christ prepared
> Sufficient, sovereign, saving grace.[31]

This *had* to be followed by:

> Come, sinners, to the gospel feast,
> Let every soul be Jesu's guest.[32]

D. PRESENT CONSIDERATIONS

The evidence of our half-empty churches suggests that modern people are not exactly falling over one another to accept the

[30] Not all Arminians were Evangelicals in practice; see Geoffrey F. Nuttall, *The Puritan Spirit* (Epworth 1967), p. 78.
[31] Charles Wesley, MHB 75, v. 3.
[32] Charles Wesley, MHB 323, v. 1.

salvation that is offered to them. The themes of this chapter so far: that man is a sinner, and that he is saved by grace through faith, seem to have very little appeal. What we are saying in the name of God is not heard and we suspect that, even if it were, it would be thought of little significance. People accepted the words of John Wesley as the words of life. But when we say more or less the same things, they do not even bother to listen.

This situation raises an important question. Are modern people *basically* different from, say, eighteenth century people, so that the categories of sin and salvation ought not to be used about them at all? Or are modern people only *superficially* different from their predecessors, so that the old pattern of salvation is still the pattern for them, with only the proviso that it be put into modern language? In other words, is there a secular salvation for secular people? Or must they have the old religious one brought up to date? In accordance with the general mood of these sections on present considerations, no dogmatic answers will be given to these questions. Students will find their own answers as they consider the following material.

(1) Secular people

Students should at this point re-read the short section on secularization.[33] Secularization has produced secular people. The Renaissance not only gave an importance to secular pursuits—those listed by John Baillie for example—but also it encouraged some people to see themselves in a different light. They reacted from the notion that they were miserable sinners in perpetuity, ever under the awful judgement of God, and deprived of their higher powers through the sin of Adam. Instead, in the opportunities of discovery and creation that lay open in so many fields, they began to see something of the glory of the human being. Inevitably their attention shifted from the other world to this one, from the divine to the human.

Leonardo da Vinci and Erasmus of Rotterdam are examples

[33] See pp. 128–30.

of men who were more interested in human beings than in God. They were not atheists; they were sons of the Church. But this world appealed more to them than the next and they revelled in all it meant to be human. They were, in fact, humanists.

(2) Humanism

The word 'humanist' is virtually an alternative these days for 'a secular person' so the drift of the argument does not change, even if the terms do. The humanism of Leonardo and Erasmus was not without its dignity and certainly the use of the word 'humanist' in the derogatory sense found in some religious circles is entirely out of place. The truth of the matter is that having entered into new and exciting worlds, all man-centred, they began all their thinking from that point. Thus, as one of the greatest of modern theologians puts it:

> Leonardo da Vinci is more concerned to prove that the mathematical method, which unlocks nature's mysteries and discloses her regularities and dependable recurrences, is a fruit and symbol of the greatness of the human mind, than that it is a tool of nature's mastery.[34]

Just as secularization gave rise to the exaggeration of secularism, so the Christian humanism of Leonardo and Erasmus opened the way for the eventual emergence of the kind of humanism which takes a positive joy in declaring its emancipation from religion. As H. J. Blackham, at one time chairman of the British Humanist Association pointed out, humanism proceeds from two main assumptions: 'that man is on his own, and that this life is all'. It should of course be added that many humanists treat this belief, not as the excuse for a life of self-centredness, but as a reason for working for the betterment of mankind. But there is no denying that your modern humanist, your truly secular person, unlike Leonardo and Erasmus, does not see himself as within the Christian fold.

[34] Reinhold Niebuhr, *The Nature and Destiny of Man* (Nisbet 1949), p. 20.

This does indeed mean that the doctrines of this chapter are, to secular people, part of a culture that has had its day. As for the doctrine of sin, we listen again to Reinhold Niebuhr:

Modern man has an essentially easy conscience; and nothing gives the diverse and discordant notes of modern culture so much harmony as the unanimous opposition of modern man to Christian conceptions of the sinfulness of man. The idea that man is sinful at the very centre of his personality, that is in his will, is universally rejected. It is this rejection which has seemed to make the Christian gospel simply irrelevant to modern man, a fact which is of more importance than any conviction about its incredibility.[35]

And as for the doctrine of salvation, if people are convinced that there is nothing from which they need to be saved, it would seem to be a waste of words.

(3) Contradiction and alienation

It does not follow that because modern man, as Niebuhr says, rejects the notion that he is essentially sinful he therefore resorts to the opposite view that he is basically good. This may indeed have been the thinking of a handful of liberal humanists before the First World War. A rather moderate poet, William Ernest Henley (1849–1903), always seems to draw to himself the fire from those anxious to attack the view that human beings are noble creatures in charge of their own destiny. Poor Henley, after thanking 'whatever gods may be' for his 'unconquerable soul' went on to write:

> It matters not how strait the gate,
> How charged with punishments the scroll,
> I am the master of my fate:
> I am the captain of my soul.[36]

For this verse he has certainly suffered at the hands of the

[35] P. 24.
[36] 'Unconquerable', *An Anthology of Modern Verse* (Methuen 1921), p. 109.

Christian orthodox. But perhaps the criticism has been a little harsh. Within the limitations, often painful and severe, of our circumstances we are free to respond one way or the other. We can face the specialist's report with courage, or without it. Modern humanists who have done their thinking may look to the resources of man rather than to those of God (a too simplistic distinction?) as Henley did, but they would not deny the human predicament. And they would not, because they recognize the presence of what the title of this section refers to as 'contradiction and alienation'. This recognition, we have to admit, does not come because they have conceded that the Christians are right after all, and that the doctrine of original sin is true. It comes because massive minds and bitter experience have piled up evidence that is irrefutable.

(i) Freud

It is derisory to give one short paragraph to the 'massive mind' of the great psychologist, but it has to be so. Freud, who was not a Christian, has had an immense influence on people's thinking about themselves. He pointed to a deep, inner contradiction in human nature. Down in the unconscious mind there is a system of stresses and conflicts between the various drives that go to make up our natures. If these conflicts are held in balance, with no one basic drive obtaining the mastery, then a person may be said to be normal. Otherwise, there is trouble. Hence human beings are basically a mass of contradictions. Alas, they live under the delusion that the choices and decisions they make are the result of conscious rational thought. If I choose to spend Saturday afternoon gardening instead of cleaning the car I think this is because I have made a cool, dispassionate choice. If, more importantly, a person who has just finished training for a career decides not to live at home any more but in a flat with three other friends, he or she may well believe that the decision is the result of weighing up carefully all the pros and cons, and then deciding. It was Freud who first put forward the view that the unconscious factors involved in human decisions and actions are the determining ones. We do not usually know the real reasons why we do things, at least not at the time we do them. They have to do with the conflict that is going on down there in the unconscious mind. This baldly stated, and without space for the proper qualifications, is the Freudian account of human nature. One does not have to be a psychologist to see that it is not compatible with the view that human beings are basically balanced and good people, quite capable of choosing and controlling their own destiny.

(ii) Marx

Another short paragraph for a 'massive mind'! Marx saw the contradictions of the human condition not in the unconscious mind but in the economic development of society.

> The contradictions which man experiences and which he embodies are part of the dialectic of history which evolves itself by the conflicts of opposites (thesis and antithesis) producing resolutions (synthesis) which form stages in the evolutionary process and the basis of the next set of conflicts.[37]

Thus the serf class conflict with the baron class and out of the conflict emerges the middle class who conflict with the working class and so on. Conflict is everywhere, but particularly in capitalist society. As Marx himself wrote in the Preface to the Second German edition of Das Kapital:

> The contradictions inherent in the movement of capitalist society are most conspicuous to the practical bourgeois in the vicissitudes of the periodic cycles to which modern industry is subject, and in the culminating point of these cycles, a universal crisis. Such a crisis is once more approaching, although as yet in its preliminary stages. By its universality and its intensity, it will drum dialectics into the heads even of the upstarts of the New, Holy, Prussian-German Empire.[38]

When at last the classless society arrives all will be perfect peace. Meanwhile it is the business of human beings to participate actively in the conflicts, and indeed to promote them, making sure that they are on the right side, the side of history.

At this juncture the second word, 'alienation', has to be considered. In the Marxist view human beings are alienated, estranged, from themselves by being alienated from the control of their own labour and the wealth it produces. The revolution, establishing the proletariate as the ruling class, will put an end to that. But for the present, alienation, like contradiction, prevails.

One thing that the Marxist analysis and the Christian doctrine of

[37] David Jenkins, What is Man?, p. 58.
[38] Karl Marx, Capital, trans. E. and C. Paul (Dent 1933), p. 874.

275

original sin have in common is that human beings define the good, and seek it, in terms of their own interest. But whereas Christianity sees this as a defect in human nature, at any rate since the Fall, Marxism uses it as a tool of class conflict, screening it, so to speak, behind the onward march to the classless society. The question is: what happens to the self-interest when the revolution comes? Christianity and Marxism give different answers to that. But as things are now, neither would give much credence to the view that human beings should be content to remain as they are.

(iii) Bitter experience

We turn from what the 'massive minds' have told us to what we have experienced ourselves. The First World War, that most hideous of wars, with all its senseless slaughter, killed, along with 'the seed of Europe', the facile notion that human beings are basically good and that, left to themselves, they could produce the Utopia of their dreams within the life-time of their children. Then, twenty years on, the Nazi tyranny and the horrors of the concentration camps made an easy-going humanism seem for ever impossible. But perhaps each generation has to learn the lesson again, and the Vietnam war took this role to itself.

This leads to a further point. In Vietnam it was not only human beings that were killed. The land was killed as well. Trees and plants, as well as men, were massacred. Our human experience in this century is not only of alienation between people. It is also of alienation between people and the rest of creation. The battery hen is a pathetic symbol of our time. Pollution tells the same story. We have poured our sewers into the sea. We have made our clear air dark with diesel fumes. Those who fall into our lakes need anti-tetanus injections, if not stomach pumps. Worst of all we have used the atomic power of creation for the prosecution and the threat of war.

The story of our contradictions and our alienation is a depressing one indeed. We shall pursue it no further.

(4) Wholeness

Modern secular people, living in a culture in which both Freud and Marx have written, and in a world in which the Somme,

Belsen, Mi Lai and Hiroshima have all occurred, have not simply resigned themselves to being creatures divided within themselves and at odds with the rest of creation. The search for wholeness is an indication that people are not content to let the last word be with the unconscious mind, the class war, the machine gun and the hydrogen bomb. Two examples of this search can be given.

(i) Shālōm

The first is an interest in this Jewish word, and the idea it expresses, that extends well beyond the Jewish community. Perhaps the place Israel is assuming in the modern world has facilitated this interest. The word with which one Jew greets another, *shālōm* (the a as in 'far', the o as in 'home'), can be translated 'peace', but that is only part of its meaning. It means, indeed, wholeness, the wholeness, for example, of Solomon's completed Temple; the wholeness of a person at peace with himself, unconscious mind or not. *Shālōm* is all that any man or nation could desire.

Although *shālōm* is often translated 'peace' it is not just the opposite of war. It is rather the wholeness that consists of harmony between friends and victory over enemies. Everything then is as it should be. In Old Testament times this meant that when the enemies of Yahweh were defeated and the Israelite came home from the wars carrying his booty in his arms, to celebrate with his wife and family and to take up life again on the field and in the town in health, happiness and prosperity, then everything was as it was meant to be. Long life put the seal upon it, which is why Abraham was reckoned to be 175 years old when he died.

To be able to rest in the acceptance that everything is, for you, as it was meant to be may sound facile. But perhaps it is not always so. It is not mere romanticism to say that when a mechanic starts up an engine that he has built, or rebuilt, when a gardener finishes his planting or when a builder and his men 'top off' a soaring building, then everything is as it should be. Such people are, in those moments at least, whole and complete. They have *shālōm*. Not surprisingly, the world is interested in it.

277

(ii) Yoga

Not even French conversation classes for holidays abroad or car servicing classes to offset the ever-rising garage bills can compete with the phenomenal increase in demand for evening classes in *yoga*. Why should this be? One suspects it is because modern people have begun to realize that the sense of relaxation, peace and well-being which they both want and need, cannot be theirs until they have found that harmony of mind and body which *yoga* reckons to provide. It is the quest for wholeness again.

The methods of *yoga* are well enough known. There are the postures (*asanas*), the control of breathing (*pranayana*) leading to the meditation. Trevor Rowe, in a short chapter, has this to say:

> The aim of yoga is spiritual. It is not an ancient discipline directed to health and beauty. All exercises in posture and breathing are directed towards meditation—what I have called the entry into silence. The Christian using the techniques should do so in order that God's grace may come to him—through meditation prepared for by the exercises.[39]

Those who are not religious would not think in terms of God's grace, but they seek and, we may fairly say find, a harmony of body, mind and spirit.

(5) Freedom

The assumption under which modern people pursue this quest for wholeness is that they can do so in freedom. The choices they make must be real choices. The way out of contradiction and alienation may be wholeness, but you cannot be whole if you are not free. Hence an aversion to forces that reckon to determine your future for you. The old predestination systems are not as much an issue now, but their modern successors are. Under condemnation here must come schools of psychology that see human conduct following the rigid laws of animal life, explicable in terms of stimulus and response so that we all

---

[39] *Wholeness* (Epworth 1976), p. 58.

behave like Pavlov's dogs.[40] The dictatorship of the environment must also be resisted so that a child born in a bad year in Bangladesh need not necessarily die nor a person's morality be determined by the circumstances of his life.

> A farmer in the land of Uz will find it on the whole easier to obey the ten commandments than a waiter in one of the nightclubs of Sodom.[41]

That is one thing, but to have one's ethics decided by the fact that one's parents were Jehovah's Witnesses is quite another. Again, the repudiation of Marxism by so many who are engaged in the quest for freedom is not only a question of politics, though that has its story to tell of the loss of freedom. It is also a question, as Niebuhr says, that Marxist psychology reduces rational processes to biological dimensions.[42] That is to say, mind is the product of matter, and about that you can do nothing at all. You are not free. The revulsion of all liberal men and women from the determinism of race—that if you are black you cannot govern nor stay in the best hotels nor keep wicket for your country—is a further expression of this concern. Human beings must be free, and Martin Luther King's great climactic words, 'Free! Free at last!' express in a phrase what modern people must have if they are to be truly human.

(6) The enjoyment of life

The search for wholeness, exemplified in the interest in *shālōm* and *yoga* and requiring freedom as its basic condition, goes on. But search is not all, so secular people would contend. There is achievement too. The full-blooded enjoyment of this present earthly life is not merely sought, it is found. There is a secular heaven, already here. Consider this letter written by the poet, Dylan Thomas to his friends, the McAlpines:

[40] Dogs whose mouths watered at the sound of a buzzer on its own, following a period in which the buzzer sounded when the dogs had dinner.
[41] S. Körner, 'A Humanist's Reflections on Morality, Religion and the Churches', *Epworth Review*, Vol. 3, No. 1, Jan. 1976, p. 74.
[42] *The Nature and Destiny of Man*, p. 49.

Villa del Beccaro,
Mosciano,
Scandicci,
Florence
May 20th 1947

My dear Helen and Bill,
I'd have written much, much sooner—did you get a postcard?
—but waited until we had a house of our own to write from. Up
to now, we've been staying in hotels and pensions: expensive
and unsatisfactory. And the Riviera sea was too tidy. Now, on
the hills above Florence, some five miles from the centre, we
have found a lovely villa in the pinewoods: beautiful, night-
ingaled gardens, cypresses, pillared terraces, olive trees, deep
wild woods, our own vineyard and swimming pool, very tasty.
There is a big room waiting for you. The cellar is full of wine.
We live on asparagus, artichokes, oranges, gorgonzola, olive oil,
strawberries, and more red wine. We have the villa until the last
day of July. Can you come? We'd love it so much. Write at
once, and forgive this delay. Best love from Cat and me.

Yours ever,
Dylan.[43]

Here, in the joys of beautiful surroundings, food, drink and
the company of other human beings, the secular man is entering into his kingdom. Life is to be enjoyed, and Dylan is
enjoying it.

Another example of this revelling in the joys of the secular
is the more open and obvious enjoyment of sex. It is no longer,
as my grandmother once furtively whispered to my mother,
'something we only do in the dark and never talk about'. The
work of Alex Comfort illustrates the point. In his preface to
The Joy of Sex, he writes:

Sex in man is only about one-tenth reproduction—nine-tenths
are play, the affectionate bond between long-term concerned
lovers, through which we express relationship, explore ourselves and one another, and exorcize basic and mammalian
worries through tender but unscared playfulness. Religion and

[43] Constantine Fitzgibbon, *Selected Letters of Dylan Thomas* (Dent 1966),
p. 306.

psychiatry have unfortunately misread this play-function, as often as not, and set about converting what nature programmed as turn-ons and resources into hangups. Playfulness, like tenderness, is something our culture has undersold.[44]

Comfort's book certainly does its best to set the matter right. The factors that have made this secular enjoyment possible are many and varied. The turning away from the supernatural to the natural—the process of secularization itself—is one. The release from a sense of guilt if you are enjoying yourself is another (a perversion of the Christian religion if ever there was one). Then there is scientific, and particularly medical, progress. Pain can be killed, handicaps overcome and death eased, making possible more enjoyment for more people. The increase in living standards is another factor. Golf courses are now covered with factory workers, and those who as children took their holidays at Southend-on-Sea or Blackpool now take them in the Austrian Tyrol or on the Costa Brava. So one could go on. The time is ripe for secular people.

Of course, there is the other side, and the religious reader will not be slow to seize upon it. A line of John Newton's hymn says it for him:

Fading is the worldling's pleasure.[45]

Even Dylan Thomas tired of his villa and on 11th July 1947 we find him writing to T. W. Earp:

I am awfully sick of it here, on the beautiful hills above Florence, drinking chianti in our marble shanty, sick of vini and contadini and bambini, and sicker still when I go, bumby with mosquito bites, to Florence itself, which is a gruelling museum.[46]

And doubtless the end of the Welsh poet will be quoted in support. Not all sex is liberated nor all pain killed nor all death eased. There are the deprived in our inner cities who have

44 Quartet Books 1974, p. 1.
45 MHB 706, v. 3.
46 P. 315.

hardly ever seen a golf course, let alone the Costa Brava. To this must be added the evidence considered under 'Contradiction and alienation'.

But when all this has been said, there is no denying the existence of the secular joys nor the experience of the secular people who enjoy them. Does such experience constitute a secular salvation that can now take over from the religious one? Or is it an integral part of the religious one, as seen through twentieth century eyes? And if this is the case, how can such a salvation be proclaimed to twentieth century people?

Chapter 9

The Kingdom of God

A. THE FOUNDATION DOCUMENTS

The Apostles' Creed

He will come again to judge the living and the dead.

The Nicene Creed

He will come again in glory
to judge the living and the dead,
and his kingdom will have no end.

The Deed of Union

Clause 30.[1]

Explanatory Notes upon the New Testament (John Wesley)

Commentary on Mark 1:15
The time is fulfilled—The time of My kingdom, foretold
by Daniel, expected by you, is fully come.

Commentary on Matthew 6:10
Thy kingdom come—May Thy kingdom of grace come
quickly, and swallow up all the kingdoms of the earth! May
all mankind, receiving Thee, O Christ, for their King, truly
believing in Thy name, be filled with righteousness and

[1] See pp. 53, 74.

peace and joy, with holiness and happiness, till they are removed hence into Thy kingdom of glory, to reign with Thee for ever and ever.

Sermon VII. The Way to the Kingdom (John Wesley)

It is termed, 'the kingdom of God', because it is the immediate fruit of God's reigning in the soul. So as soon as ever He takes unto Himself His mighty power, and sets up His throne in our hearts, they are instantly filled with this 'righteousness, and peace, and joy in the Holy Ghost'. It is called 'the kingdom of heaven', because it is (in a degree) heaven opened in the soul.... And this 'kingdom of God', or of heaven, 'is at hand'. As these words were originally spoken, they implied that 'the time' was then fulfilled, God being 'made manifest in the flesh', when He would set up His kingdom among men, and reign in the hearts of His people. And is not the time now fulfilled? ... Wheresoever, therefore, the gospel of Christ is preached, this His 'kingdom is nigh at hand'. It is not far from every one of you. Ye may this hour enter thereinto, if so be ye hearken to His voice, 'Repent ye, and believe the gospel.'

Sermon IV. Scriptural Christianity (John Wesley)

But shall we not see greater things than these? Yea greater than have been yet from the beginning of the world. Can Satan cause the truth of God to fail, or His promises to be of none effect? If not, the time will come when Christianity will prevail over all, and cover the earth.

The Senior Catechism of the Methodist Church

66. WHAT IS THE KINGDOM OF GOD?

The Kingdom of God is His rightful rule over our lives, offered to us in Jesus Christ, and one day to be established for ever through the same Jesus Christ, Who shall come to judge both the living and the dead.

16. WHAT DO WE BELIEVE ABOUT THE SECOND COMING OF CHRIST AND THE LAST JUDGEMENT?

In His own way and in His own time God will finally judge the world through Christ, sum up all things in Him, and establish His Kingdom for ever.

23. WHAT DO WE MEAN BY THE RESURRECTION OF THE BODY AND THE LIFE EVERLASTING?

Those who have the life which Christ came to give will overcome death and with a body suited to the life of heaven will rise to eternal fellowship with God.

38. WHAT IS THE STATE OF THOSE WHO FINALLY REFUSE TO REPENT AND TURN TO GOD?

They are separated from God in hell.

The Methodist Service Book

Christ has died.
Christ is risen.
Christ will come again.

Accept us as we offer ourselves to be a living sacrifice,
and bring us with the whole creation to your
heavenly kingdom.

(The Sunday Service, pp. B13–14)

The Methodist Hymn Book

Hail to the Lord's Anointed;
 Great David's greater Son!
Hail, in the time appointed,
 His reign on earth begun!

(245, v. 1) (James Montgomery)

Jesus shall reign where'er the sun
Doth his successive journeys run;
His kingdom stretch from shore to shore,
Till suns shall rise and set no more.

(272, v. 1) (Isaac Watts)

285

His kingdom cannot fail,
  He rules o'er earth and heaven;
The keys of death and hell
  Are to our Jesus given:

Rejoice in glorious hope;
Jesus the Judge shall come,
And take His servants up
To their eternal home.

(247, vv. 3, 6) (Charles Wesley)

B. THE DOCTRINE OF THE KINGDOM OF GOD

(1) Definition

The good news of Jesus Christ in Mark 1:1 is interpreted, in verse 2, in terms of Isaiah 40:3. That profound chapter of Isaiah asserts the sovereignty of God:

Behold the Lord God comes with might, and his arm rules for him. (v. 10)

He is the one

who brings princes to nought, and makes the rulers of the earth as nothing. (v. 23)

God reigns and God rules. There is no doubt about that. Furthermore, in Isaiah 52:7 the fact that God reigns is treated as good tidings to be proclaimed. When Mark begins by quoting Isaiah and goes on to speak of Jesus preaching the good news of God (v. 14) it is not unreasonable to assume that this is a reference to God's kingly rule. This is what the word in the next verse, translated 'kingdom', means in both Hebrew and Greek.

The term 'kingdom' is in English somewhat ambiguous, but it naturally suggests a territory or a community governed by a king. The Greek term *basileia* which it translates is also ambiguous. But there

286

can be no doubt that the expression before us represents an Aramaic phrase well-established in Jewish usage, 'The *malkuth* of Heaven'. *Malkuth*, like other substantives of the same formation, is properly an abstract noun, meaning 'kingship', 'kingly rule', 'reign', or 'sovereignty'. The expression 'the *malkuth* of God' connotes the fact that God reigns as King.[2]

(i) If *malkuth* can legitimately be rendered 'kingdom' then the first inference is that this is primarily a reference to a *community*. God can indeed rule over individuals, but if he is to have a kingdom then his kingly rule must relate to a people. This is in fact what happened. He exercised his kingly rule first over his people Israel (one of the arguments against having a king in Israel was that this would usurp the prerogative of God, 1 Sam. 10:19) and then over those who responded to the proclamation of his rule by Jesus. The kingdom as we meet it in the Bible is not first a matter of private piety. It is a matter of community.

(ii) One of the things a king inevitably does is to *confer* the blessings, or otherwise, of his rule upon his people. King Solomon conferred forced labour, King Arthur (if there was one) the deeds of chivalry, Caesar the *pax Romana*. What does the kingly rule of God confer? When John Wesley stood on his father's tomb in the churchyard at Epworth in 1742 and started to preach on 'The Way to the Kingdom' he thought it right to begin by answering this question:

I stood near the east end of the church, upon my father's tomb-stone, and cried, 'The kingdom of heaven is not meat and drink; but righteousness, and peace, and joy in the Holy Ghost'.[3]

This text (Rom. 14:17) he proceeded to expound.

Those three words still define the kingdom. 'Righteousness' refers to the saving activity of God, God in action vindicating the right. Such action constitutes his kingly rule. As for 'peace' and 'joy', in chapter 14, Paul is concerned with the relationships between the Christians at Rome. Some had been judgemental and had despised their brethren (v. 10), producing injury

[2] C. H. Dodd, *The Parables of the Kingdom* (Nisbet 1935), p. 34.
[3] *Wesley's Standard Sermons* (Epworth 1921), Vol. I, p. 147.

(v. 15). He asks for the opposite: peace and joy in the Holy Spirit. In these, he argues, the kingdom of God consists. These are the benefits conferred by the kingly rule.

(iii) The only other point to be made in preliminary definition is to take note of the alternative *kingdom of heaven* for *kingdom of God*. Heaven is 'an evasive reference to God, characteristic of later Judaism'.[4] As far as we are concerned the two expressions are synonymous.

(2) Jesus and the kingdom

For Jesus as Messiah, Son of Man and inaugurator of the kingdom, see pages 149–51.

(3) The kingdom in the teaching of Jesus

The field for study is primarily the parables of the kingdom. In these parables the nature of the kingdom is described, though the word 'kingdom' is not necessarily used. There is no space here for exposition, only for a list, and that by no means an exhaustive one. The student is referred to the text of the Bible and one or more of the books in the bibliography.

The sower: Mark 4:1–9; Matt. 13:1–9; Luke 8:4–8.

The seed growing secretly: Mark 4:26–9.

The mustard seed: Mark 4:30–2; Matt. 13:31–2; Luke 13:18–19.

The leaven: Matt. 13:33; Luke 13:20–1.

The fig tree: Mark 13:28–9; Mark 24:32–3; Luke 21:29–31.

The foolish and wise virgins: Matt. 25:1–13.

The wicked husbandmen: Mark 12:1–9; Matt. 21:33–41; Luke 20:9–16a.

The children at play: Matt. 11:16–19; Luke 7:31–5.

The unjust steward: Luke 16:1–8.

The treasure in the field and the pearl of great value: Matt. 13:44–6.

---

[4] G. Abbott-Smith, *A Manual Greek Lexicon of the New Testament* (T. and T. Clark 1921), pp. 328–9.

The talents and the pounds: Matt. 25:14–30; Luke 19:11–27.

The tares and the drag-net: Matt. 13:24–30, 36–43, 47–50.

The labourers in the vineyard: Matt. 20:1–16.

The lost sheep: Matt. 18:10–14; Luke 15:3–7.

The lost coin: Luke 15:8–10.

The unforgiving servant: Matt. 18:23–35.

By the time one has read through these passages one has a fair idea of what Jesus had in mind when he spoke of the 'kingdom of God' or the 'kingdom of heaven'. A number of points need to be stressed.

(i) The kingdom is a gift

When Jesus arrived upon the scene the gates of the kingdom were, so to say, flung open and tax collectors and prostitutes, and everybody else for that matter, could troop through in their thousands. The way in which Jesus fraternized with those whom some would doubtless call the lowest of the low is highly significant. It was not simply a matter of food and wine and conviviality, though clearly they were not despised. The action was symbolic. Jesus was doing what he saw God doing: welcoming sinners into his kingdom because he loved them. Their place in his kingdom was his gift to them. (Luke 12:32). They did not deserve it, but who does?

(ii) The kingdom is a demand

There are those, and they were not lacking in Jesus's time as they are not lacking in ours, who say that if you make things easy for the undeserving, giving that which is precious to those who have no entitlement to it, you are asking for trouble. They will simply take what is going and give nothing in return. Your kingdom will then be full of wasters and vagabonds. The answer to such arguments is not to assert that entering the kingdom demands devotion and obedience, but rather to make it clear that the gift *is* the demand. If obedience is a hard and fast condition then most of us had better give up now, for we shall never make it. But if obedience is evoked by the gift, indeed is almost part of it, then we are in with a chance.

289

(iii) The kingdom is good news

It is the gift and the demand together that make up the good news. The demand alone will not do. One is reminded of the shop steward who returned from his talks with the management to say to the men, 'I've got good news for you. You've got to work harder.' The gift alone will not do either, though it needs a little perception to understand the reason. But taken together, they make up the good news of the kingdom.

Good news has to *be* good news. That is to say, it cannot be an abstraction. It has to be something that people are actually glad to hear. This raises difficult questions as to why some people receive it as such and others do not.

(iv) The kingdom is a mystery

Why, if the kingdom is all it is made out to be, do people treat it with such indifference? Why do they not accept what God is giving with such open-handed generosity? This was a problem as early as the time when the Gospel of Mark was written. Just why Jesus was not widely recognized as the inaugurator of God's kingdom, and membership in that kingdom universally embraced, raises all kinds of questions, then and now. Did Jesus deliberately restrict his offer? Was it God's intention that some people should never see what it was all about (Mark 4:10-2)? Is the kingdom meant to be a 'godly remnant'? Or are we dealing here with that intractable part of human nature that just will not be shifted from its rut of self-interest and self-centredness? Or is it all to do with the position of Jesus himself? Did he keep his Messiahship secret? Or was this an invention of the first Christians? If he was to be a Messiah *incognito*,[5] why was he?

No certain answers are available to these questions. The kingdom is a mystery. We therefore enter it by faith.

(v) The kingdom is to be preached

This takes us back to Isaiah 52:7 and the proclamation that God reigns. Jesus came into Galilee 'preaching the gospel of God' (Mark 1:14). The first Christian preachers proclaimed

[5] Unknown.

290

'good news about the kingdom of God' (Acts 8:12; 20:25). It is the task still laid upon Christian preachers, and it is no accident that the Old Testament Lesson prescribed in the Recognition and Commissioning Service for Local Preachers in the Methodist Church is Isaiah 52:7–12.

(4) The kingdom in the ministry of Jesus

(i) Miracles

The first Christians held the biblical view of the nature of God. God was for them the personal, active, living Lord. As such he was the source of all power, including the power that caused miracles to happen. Thus miracles presented no difficulties for the makers of the Gospel tradition. In them the power of God was breaking through on the human scene. The first Christian preachers were quick to see this. Indeed it was precisely because they recognized that God was at work in Jesus in this way that they responded to him as they did (Acts 2:22).

Furthermore, this power of God, expressing itself through the miracles of Jesus, is the means by which the kingdom breaks in. The mighty works of Jesus are the miracles of the kingdom of God. That is to say, they are evidence that God's kingly rule has actually begun, and begun, as we might say, in a big way. This is made very clear in the Beezebul controversy recorded in Mark 3:22–30, Matthew 12:25–37 and Luke 11:17–23. It was not by the power of the prince of demons that Jesus cast the demons out but by the power of God. Matthew and Luke then add the significant statement that if this is in fact being done by the Spirit, or the 'finger' (Luke) of God, 'then the kingdom of God has come upon you'.

(ii) Healings and exorcisms

These two types of miracle best demonstrate the breaking-in of God's power, and of his kingdom. In reply to John the Baptist's question to Jesus 'Are you he who is to come, or shall we look for another?' Jesus referred to his works of healing (Matt. 11:2–6; Luke 7:18–23). When he healed it was because 'the power of the Lord was with him to heal' (Luke 5:17).

291

This was exactly how the apostolic preachers saw it too. Peter rehearses:

How God anointed Jesus of Nazareth with the Holy Spirit and with power; how he went about doing good and healing all that were oppressed by the devil, for God was with him. (Acts 10:38)

This was also the case with the casting out of demons. Jesus interprets his exorcisms as the arrival of the kingdom of God (Matt. 12:28; Luke 11:20). This interpretation implied that the exorcisms were not the performances of a wonder-worker, but rather that in them the power of God was active.

(5) The kingdom as the breaking-in of the New Age

C. H. Dodd's book *The Parables of the Kingdom* was a landmark in this field of scholarship and following his previously quoted remarks about 'the *malkuth* of God'[6] he points out how Jews thought of the kingdom of God. First, they accepted it as a present fact, with God's kingly rule effective insofar as Israel was obedient to his will as revealed in the Law. Dodd then continues:

But in another sense 'The Kingdom of God' is something yet to be revealed. God is more than King of Israel; He is King of all the world. But the world does not recognize Him as King. His own people is in fact subject to secular powers, which in the present age are permitted to exercise *malkuth*. Israel, however, looks forward to the day when 'The saints of the Most High shall take the kingdom,' (Dan. 7:18), and so the kingship of God will become effective over the whole world. It is with this intention that pious Jews in the first century prayed (as they still pray), 'May He establish His Kingdom during your life and during your days, and during the life of all the house of Israel.' In this sense 'The Kingdom of God' is a hope for the future. It is itself the *eschaton*, or 'ultimate', with which 'eschatology' is concerned.[7]

When this, God's kingdom shall have come, then there will be a judgement on all the evil in the world, then there will be victory over all the powers of evil, then the meaning of the entire human story will be made plain. This is the Messianic Age, the kingdom in all its fullness. It cannot be brought about by man's efforts, however well-intentioned. It will not simply evolve. It is the decisive intervention of God, determined by him alone. So far every good Jew would say

6 See p. 287.
7 C. H. Dodd, p. 36.

'Amen'. But then comes the break: the Christian assertion that in the teaching and ministry of Jesus, this intervention had taken place. The kingdom had come.

This is the 'realized eschatology' which C. H. Dodd made famous. That which had been consigned to the future has arrived in the present.

It is in the light of the breaking-in of the New Age that writers of the Gospels see the miracles, the healings and the exorcisms. The recorded reply of Jesus to the question from John is not a mere list of the healings. It is a description of them in the terms of Isaiah's prophecy of the Age to Come. And to say 'lepers are cleansed' (Matt. 11:5, Luke 7:22) rather than 'I am cleansing lepers' indicates that this is not a matter of a wonder-worker 'doing his thing' but a God acting as he was expected to do in the day of the kingdom.

Thus the miracles are signs that in Jesus the kingdom has come, the Last Days have now begun. This, it would seem, is how Jesus understood them himself. Though he refused to give a sign to the unbelieving Pharisees, he reproved the disciples for not appreciating that the miracle of the loaves and fishes was such a sign (Mark 8:14–21). It was certainly how the first Christians understood them. Peter's sermon on the day of Pentecost says exactly that.

(6) The kingdom has still to come

If the Last Days began with Jesus, they did not end with him. If the kingdom arrived with Jesus it did not proceed to 'cover the earth', to use John Wesley's phrase.[8] If the Messianic Age had dawned it did not move on to its zenith. Why not? Believing Christians, whether in the first century or the twentieth, have no obvious answer to this question, or at any rate no answer acceptable to their belief. It could be said, of course, that it was simply a matter of rebellious human beings asserting themselves as they always had done. But this can hardly be squared with the belief that the kingdom is the decisive act of God. Why, then, had God stayed his hand? That is the question with no obvious answer. But its very unanswerability

[8] See p. 284.

served only to strengthen two great assertions of faith. One was that in Jesus the kingdom *had* come. The other was that though, for whatever reason, God had, so to speak, put off the Great Day, there would still be a Great Day. It was a postponement, not a cancellation. As noted above,[9] the Jews already looked forward to the Messianic Age. For Christians, the belief that it had actually begun with Jesus made its final appearing all the more certain.

Hence Christians are told to pray for the coming of the kingdom. The Lord's Prayer, in both Matthew and Luke, contains the petition 'Thy kingdom come' (Matt. 6:10; Luke 11:2). Joachim Jeremias has this to say about it:

> Those who pray in these words as disciples of Jesus ask for the coming of the consummation as people who know that the great turning-point of the ages has already taken place. God has already begun his saving work. It is only the full accomplishment which is lacking.[10]

How do Christians understand the kingdom for the coming of which they pray? How do they see the consummation? What will it be like on the Great Day?

(i) There will be an End
Consider these sentences:

> At the end of the film they sailed away into the sunset.
> The end of my doing two hundred skips before breakfast is to avoid having a coronary thrombosis.

The first 'end' has to do with time, the second with purpose. Both meanings of the word are involved in talk about the End which is the consummation of the kingdom, but it is necessary to have them clearly distinguished.

As for time, human thinking soon comes to a full stop. We can of course conceive of the End if by that we mean the kingdom 'covering the earth'. The Old Testament looks forward to such a time, variously described. Sometimes it is a time of

9 See p. 292.
10 'The Lord's Prayer in Modern Research' in R. Batey (Ed.), *New Testament Issues* (S.C.M. 1970), p. 96.

triumph for Israel (Isa. 61:1–9); sometimes a time when the whole creation is at peace with itself (Isa. 11:1–10); sometimes a time when, through the suffering of Israel all people will come to the knowledge of God and so find their salvation (Isa. 52:13–53:12). But it is *a time* and because it is we can understand what is being said. The same is true of those New Testament passages like Luke 4:18 and perhaps Romans 8:21 where the reference is to creation as we now know it. But once we get outside of the space-time structure for which at least physically we appear to have been made, we are in trouble. The mind simply cannot grasp what it is like to be outside of time, nor to be independent of space. So when the End is thought of in those terms, as it is for example in Matthew 24, Colossians 3:4, 1 Thessalonians 4:13–18 and Revelation 11:15, we do not have the mental and linguistic equipment to cope with it. We can say that in that Day the past, present and future will all be experienced together in an eternal now, but we have no idea what the experience will be like.

As for purpose, here we shall probably, in understanding at least, feel more at home. We have seen something of the purpose of God in Jesus, and we Christians are committed to what we have seen. From our point of view to speak of the End in this way is to give an ultimate and final importance to that to which we are committed.[11] As Henry McKeating puts it:

> Eschatological language is useful because it is a convenient way of indicating what *in the last resort* matters most to us; what *in the final analysis* we are prepared to stand or fall by; what *at the end of the day* we set most store by.[12]

The New Testament expresses this in terms of the triumph of Christ. The Son of man will come on the clouds of heaven with power and great glory (Matt. 24:30); it is the Lamb who receives the acclamation of the angels and every creature in creation (Rev. 5:9–14). In other words, what God has done in Christ is the whole purpose of creation.

---

[11] This use of eschatological language is complementary and not opposed to, the traditional one.

[12] *God and the Future*, p. 96 (Author's italics).

To sum up the doctrine of the End:

History must reach its climax, time and space must come to an end, the universe must achieve its God-given destiny. From our point of view that must mean a consummation and a Last Day. The triumph of God is not complete while there is a time and a place where man can still deny Him. The final stroke must, then, be universal. There must come a moment when all things are subject to His glory, when all that is must either be raised to dwell in the light unapproachable, or else cease to be.[13]

(ii) There will be a Final Coming of Jesus

The word for this often found in theological books is the word 'Parousia'. It means 'a presence', 'a being there' as well as 'a coming'. The first coming of Jesus, the Incarnation, was a 'parousia'. But normally the word is reserved for the Final Coming and is given capital letters because it is one of the significant features of the End.

That the New Testament looks forward to the return of Jesus is undeniable. His first coming was in humiliation; his final coming will be in glory (Mark 13:26; 14:62). There will be angels and trumpets (Matt. 24:31) and a cry of command from the descending conqueror (1 Thess. 4:16). For this coming the faithful are patiently waiting (Phil. 3:20); it will come like lightning (Matt. 24:27), like a thief in the night (1 Thess. 5:2), which can hardly mean other than that the first Christians expected it soon. The command therefore is to watch, to be ready, for 'the Son of man is coming at an hour you do not expect' (Matt. 24:44). The Parousia will be preceded by fearful signs: sacrilege (Matt. 24:15), lawlessless and rebellion (2 Thess. 2:3 f.), cosmic disruption (Matt. 24:29). (It could well be that at this point the New Testament writers use some of the imagery and language found in Jewish literature dealing with the Messianic Age and the End of all things, but this is not inconsistent with their habit of seeing Jewish hopes fulfilled in Christ.) When Jesus came the first time, people could choose whether they responded to him or not, but when he comes for the final time there will be no choice. Every eye

13 W. David Stacey, *Is That Good Doctrine?* (Epworth 1960), p. 139.

will see him (Rev. 1:7), and immediately one will be taken and another left (Matt. 24:40-1).

Unhappily this magnificent conception of the involvement of Jesus in the End of all things has been trivialized by litera-lism. If a personal reference may be permitted, the first girl I ever asked to come with me to the pictures (that is the lan-guage of the 1930s) said that she was sorry, but if Jesus were to come again she would not like him to find her in the pic-tures. The thought of Jesus appearing behind the girl selling ice-creams was altogether too much for my Christology, so the beautiful friendship ended on theological grounds. It is a pity that the Final Coming has been talked about in such trivial terms, for it is one of the finest and most moving of the New Testament images of Jesus, and at the same time a great asser-tion of the sovereignty of God.

To take the second first, the Final Coming expresses the Biblical, and therefore the Christian view, that the consumma-tion of history comes from outside of history. If you see the End in terms of the triumphant descent of the Son of man you do not see it in terms of a steady progress towards Utopia by clever human beings. The doctrine of the Second Advent ('Advent' is another word for 'coming') is rooted in the doctrine of God. It is his creation, and he decides when the last trumpet shall sound.

The fact that God sends his Son a second and final time, as the protagonist in the great drama of the End, is one of the ways the New Testament has of saying that, to use a modern phrase, Jesus had 'ultimate significance'. What Christians saw in him was the meaning of life, and indeed of the whole of creation. He really was the Lord. This is, of course, the heart of the Christian faith. Hence the doctrine of the Final Coming may need demythologizing[14] but it should never be trivialized.

(iii) There will be a Resurrection

The Hebrew name for the place of the dead was Sheol. In much of the Old Testament it is described as a dark, silent cavern beneath the earth where the dead continue a witless and feeble existence. Once in Sheol there was no return (Job 7:9)

[14] See p. 20.

and no hope (Job 7:21). Nothing good could be remembered there (Ps. 88:12) and, worst of all, there could be no knowledge of God (Ps. 6:5). Isaiah 38:16–20 is a contrast between a glowing account of life here and an exceedingly miserable one of life in Sheol.

But as the Old Testament moves on, things change. Psalm 139:7–12 is the key passage. Here the logic of belief in the one, omnipotent God is beginning to work itself out: he must be the Lord of Sheol, as of every other place. Once it was accepted that the dead were not beyond the control of God, the way was open for the further belief that one day God would raise them from their condition. Late passages in the Old Testament (Isa. 26:19; Dan. 12:2) express this hope, which is developed in the literature in the period between the two Testaments. For example, there is a gruesome story in 2 Maccabees of seven brothers who were mutilated and then fried over a fire. They express their faith in a resurrection as they die and their mother sums it up:

> But doubtless the Creator of the world, who formed the generation of man, and found out the beginning of all things, will also of his own mercy give you breath and life again, as ye now regard not your own selves for his laws' sake. (2 Macc. 7:23)

It is important to be clear that this passage is not dealing with the question of what happens to individuals when they die. The concern is with a *day* of Resurrection on which the dead would be raised. There is, however, a distinction in this story between the righteous who would be raised, and the unrighteous who would not. The Daniel 12:2 text, on the other hand, says that all will be raised, 'some to everlasting life, and some to shame and everlasting contempt'.

In the New Testament the day of Resurrection comes into its own. Jesus is clearly not on the side of the Sadducees 'who say there is no resurrection' (Mark 12:18), and his own resurrection demonstrates that what must now be a hope can indeed become a reality. He is the first resurrected man. But what God has done for him he will do for his people. Easter makes the day of Resurrection a certainty:

298

But in fact Christ has been raised from the dead, the first fruits of those who have fallen asleep. (1 Cor. 15:20)

So the dead sleep on, until God, through the returning Jesus, raises them to be always with the Lord (1 Thess. 4:13–18). On that day 'the trumpet will sound, and the dead will be raised imperishable, and we shall be changed' (1 Cor. 15:52). The day of Resurrection is clearly part of the End.

Who will share in it? On this the New Testament has its uncertainties. 1 Corinthians 15 is positive, saying what will happen to those who are in Christ, but remaining silent about what will happen to those who are not. How widely are we to interpret 'the dead' in this chapter? In Romans, Paul first says that on the great day some will be given 'eternal life' but others 'wrath and fury' (2:7–8), in 6:23 he asserts that the wages of sin is death as distinct from 'eternal life in Christ Jesus our Lord', but in 11:25–32 he turns towards universalism:

For God has consigned all men to disobedience, that he may have mercy upon all. (v. 32)

2 Thessalonians chapter 1 is savage in the fate it metes out to the unbeliever. It rather looks as if we shall not know whom we shall meet on the Great Day until it arrives.

What will it be like? It will be, as part of the End, beyond space ('meeting the Lord in the air': 1 Thess. 4:17) and beyond time ('eternal life'). It will be unhindered fellowship with God. And on that day death will be swallowed up in victory.

(iv) There will be a Judgement
To draw up a time-table for the Last Day would be altogether inappropriate. The order of Parousia, Resurrection and Judgement has been followed on the grounds that people cannot be judged while they are still asleep and they cannot be raised from their sleep until the Lord comes. Significance lies however, not in their order, but in the fact that in each of them God is acting through his Son. As for the day of Judgement, Anglican Christians have been singing cheerfully to Christ in

the *Te Deum* every Sunday morning for over three hundred years:

> We believe that thou shalt come to be our Judge;

and they quite properly hurry on to the next verse:

> We therefore pray thee, help thy servants.

The association of judgement with the Great Day goes back to the Old Testament. The day of the Lord in Amos is a day of darkness, not light (5:18). After listing the sins of Israel, Amos announces that the Lord 'will never forget any of their deeds' (8:7), and one of the verses describing the subsequent day of Judgement ends with the words:

> I will make it like the mourning for an only son, and the end of it like a bitter day. (8:10)

Other passages in the Old Testament, though equally adamant that God will come in judgement, are nothing like so gloomy. Psalm 96:11–13 rejoices in the prospect. The reason for this is that judgement is seen in a much more positive fashion than the mere condemnation and punishment of wrongdoers. It is envisaged that God will put things right, give every man his due, right any wrongs and see that there is fair play all round. It was all part of his being a reliable, trustworthy, faithful God.

Again, an Old Testament image has been 'baptized into Christ.' He is the coming Judge. One of the reasons Paul gives for Christian behaviour is:

> For we must all appear before the judgement seat of Christ, so that each one may receive good or evil, according to what he has done in the body. (2 Cor. 5:10)

The day envisaged by Matthew 25:31–46, when the Son of man will come in his glory, will be a bad day for the goats. Paul speaks of 'the day of Christ' (Phil. 1:10), the day that is at hand (Rom. 13:12). Other parts of the New Testament

300

say the same thing in similar words: Jesus is 'the one ordained by God to be judge of the living and the dead' (Acts 10:42; 2 Tim. 4:1), and to him an account will have to be given (1 Pet. 4:5). In symbolic language, it is the Lamb who is worthy to 'take the scroll and to open its seals' (Rev. 5:9).

How will things go on the day of Judgement? The answer the New Testament provides is that they will go then as they go now, when people encounter Jesus. It is in the Gospel of John that this theme is emphasized. There is a present judgement and the day of Judgement is today:

> He who believes in him is not condemned; he who does not believe is condemned already, because he has not believed in the name of the only Son of God. And this is the judgement, that the light has come into the world, and men loved darkness rather than light, because their deeds were evil. (3:18-19)

One other thing has to be said in answering the question 'how will things go?' It is that the Judge is also the Saviour. If the man of the Old Testament could look forward to God acting righteously in the sense of Psalm 96, the Christian can anticipate, not the whitewashing of his sins, for that is the last thing that could ever happen, but their judgement by Jesus, whom God sent into the world because he loved it (John 3:16). The one thing that makes the day of Judgement even tolerable to think about is that the central figure is on record as having said 'him who comes to me I will not cast out' (John 6:37).

(7) The individual Christian and the Last Things

Many Protestants place much emphasis upon those parts of the Christian faith that are individualistic and subjective.[15] This is understandable. From the Reformation onwards, in their eagerness to turn away from what they believed to be the tyranny of the medieval Church and the corruption of its practices, they have stressed the importance of personal faith. The crux of the Christian faith, Protestants have said, is to know the Lord Jesus Christ as your own personal Saviour. No community, no institution, no doctrine, can be a substitute for that.

[15] Concerned with the inward life of the individual.

301

The nineteenth century in the West, with its ideal of the true man as a free, independent, enterprising individual, weakened still further the importance placed upon the corporate nature of Christianity. At the same time the Romantic Movement, the work of a most influential theologian named Schleiermacher (1768–1834), and the Methodist 'religion of the warmed heart', gave more weight to the subjective side than to the objective. The result is that many Christians, including many Methodists, can work up little enthusiasm for doctrines with a strong corporate and objective element such as the Kingdom, the Church, the Sacraments, and the End.

It is easy to be misunderstood, at this point, particularly by those to whom this approach is new. There is, of course, a large place in Christianity for personal religion, subjective piety and devotion, personal commitment and individual experience of the Lord Jesus Christ as one's own personal Saviour. Without these things the Christian religion can be a cold and formal thing. But though it does not ignore the individual, the Biblical revelation gives pride of place to God's dealings with his people (this will be substantiated in the next chapter), and to those mighty objective acts of deliverance and redemption which have happened and will happen, whatever we may feel about them personally. In this chapter the same pride of place is being given.

It is for this reason that the individual Christian's position with regard to the Last Things is being allocated to this secondary place in the chapter. To many a modern Protestant, still under the influence of the trends described so sketchily above, the nub of the whole matter is not the End nor the Parousia nor the day of Resurrection nor the day of Judgement, the great objective events that affect the whole people of God, indeed the whole creation. He is primarily concerned with life after death for the individual Christian and precisely what is meant by heaven and hell, as the likelihood is that he will be going to one or the other. These subjects must now be considered.

(i) Immortality
Though some scholars have protested that it has been over-

done,[16] the distinction between the Greek and Hebrew approach to this matter is a valid one. It can be stated briefly. The Greek view was that man consisted of a soul imprisoned within a body. At death the body fell away and the soul went to wherever souls go. It was an *immortal* soul. The Hebrew view was that there was no such distinction. Man was created whole, lived whole, sinned whole, died whole. To take up the refrain quoted earlier,[17] if John Brown's body lay a-mouldering in the grave, so did John Brown.

This goes down very badly with most modern congregations. They are Greeks virtually to a man. They believe that souls go marching on just because they are souls. They believe that man is immortal. They cherish the belief that their loved ones who are deceased are living in another and, they always suppose, happier world. They speak of death as passing from one room into another. And if, in the name of Biblical truth, a preacher sets out to change their beliefs, he has to proceed with care and understanding.

In a situation of some delicacy we need to be very clear about the precise difficulty. The stumbling-block for Christian doctrine is not so much immortality. It is the belief that man is immortal in his own right, and by his own nature. It is the immortal soul that causes the trouble, though, as Maurice Wiles argues,[18] too much must not be made of this, for if man did have an immortal soul, it would be God who had given it to him. There is nothing, however, in the Bible about immortal souls. What can be found there is the Hebrew view of man as described above and a strong belief that whatever happens to man after death, is due not to his nature, but to the sovereign activity of the ever-living God. This may, for all we know, include the giving of immortality to everybody, willy-nilly, though the Bible does not say so. It uses another category altogether, the category of the resurrection of the body.

(ii) The resurrection of the body
In death everything dies; not bodies without souls, but every-

[16] C. K. Barrett, for example, in 'Immortality and Resurrection', *The London Quarterly and Holborn Review*, April 1965.
[17] See p. 252.
[18] *The Re-making of Christian Doctrine*, pp. 128–9.

thing. That is why death has to be treated so seriously, as indeed, the last enemy. That is why, up to this point, one can have some sympathy with Lenin the Marxist who said that if he could see a man still alive after the top of his head had been chopped off he would believe in life after death.

Where the Bible and the Christian faith part company with Lenin is in their profound belief that what God created once he can create again. If he could create a man for this world he can create a man for the next. In the context of death this re-creation is called resurrection. That God will in fact do this for us is the Christian hope. And what we see in the resurrected Jesus is the demonstration that it can actually be done. The soul of Jesus did not go marching on. *He* was raised from the dead. We rest in the hope that he who raised the Lord Jesus will raise us also with Jesus (2 Cor. 4:14).

As for the mechanics, 1 Corinthians 15 gives us our only intimations. When this earthly life is over, this body of flesh and blood has completed its work; it cannot inherit the kingdom of God (v. 50). The resurrection life involves the creation by God of a resurrection body to be the vehicle of the re-created person. Although it is true that we do not know what the resurrection body will be like, at least it offers more possibilities of activity and recognition than disembodied souls which defy all imagining. Paul does not take us further than saying that the relationship between the flesh and blood body and the resurrection, or spiritual, body is akin to the relationship between the seed sown in the ground and the full corn (vv. 36–7).

On the vexed question of when the resurrection will take place there are three New Testament traditions:

(a) There will be a general resurrection on the Last Day.[19] This is how Paul sees it in 1 Corinthians 15. It is when the last trumpet sounds that the dead will be raised imperishable (vv. 51–2).

(b) Each individual is resurrected at death. The reference in 1 Peter to Christ preaching to the dead (3:19; 4:6) would seem to preclude the belief that they were all asleep waiting for the

[19] See pp. 297–9.

day of Resurrection. In 1 Philippains 1:23 Paul speaks of departing and being with Christ, a statement which sounds like a reference to what happens at death, as does 2 Corinthians 5:1–10.

(c) The resurrection has already begun. This will be considered later.

No dogmatic answer can be given as between the first and second options. They are different images, struggling to relate the immediate to the distant. The third is compatible with either of the others.

Will a resurrection body be given to everybody or only to those who are 'in Christ'? The answer is problematical, whether one thinks of resurrection at death or of a day of Resurrection. What needs to be stressed, however, is that though there are many uncertainties, *there will be a resurrection.* That is a sure and certain Christian hope, for it has already happened to Christ (1 Cor. 15:12–19).

(iii) Heaven

Here too there are problems. Just when will the pearly gates be flung open? And who precisely will be allowed to pass through? It is best to concentrate upon the positive things the Bible has to say.

In the Old Testament the word 'heaven' has both a physical meaning and a theological one. It is both the sky and the home of God. He rules from heaven. To heaven prayers ascend (1 Kings 8:30) and from heaven all blessings come (Gen. 49:25). The New Testament accepts this and relates it to Christ. His birth is announced by the heavenly host (Luke 2:13–14); at his baptism a voice speaks from heaven (Mark 1:11); his prayer confirms the sovereignty of God in heaven (Matt. 5:10); in the symbolic and magnificent descriptions of heaven in Revelation, the Lamb is there (5:8 ff; 21:22; 22:1). Some of the imagery of Revelation—white robes, thrones, crowns, harps and endless Hallelujahs—has become the familiar way in which Christians have written and sung about heaven. The meaning is clear enough. In heaven God reigns, and the ceaseless activity of his redeemed people is to praise him. In that is their blessedness.

305

(iv) Hell

The Old Testament does not sort out the good from the bad in Sheol, but in the period between the Testaments there are indications of Sheol being subdivided into Gehenna for the bad and Paradise for the good. As this doctrine develops there emerges the unquenchable fire of the New Testament (Mark 9:43; Matt. 13:41–2), subsequently used by Christian theologians and preachers as an encouragement to belief, to put it charitably.

As with heaven, the concern is with what is ultimate and outside of space and time. Geography cannot cope with this, so it is pointless to talk about 'up there' or 'down there'. If heaven means being with God, hell means being without him; if heaven means praise, then hell means the opposite: total preoccupation with self; if heaven means blessedness, hell means misery. If this is how it is to be understood, then people can hardly be sent by anyone, least of all God, to hell. Hell would appear to be something which people bring upon themselves in spite of the efforts of God to prevent them. In which case sermons using hell as an encouragement to belief might still have their uses.

Whether hell is full or empty (the words apply to places and are therefore inappropriate, but they are all we have) is unknown. But the possibility of there being room must always be there. The way must be open for us to say a final 'no' to God, even if no one ever says it.

C. PRESENT CONSIDERATIONS

(1) The middle term

The title 'Present Considerations' makes for concentration upon the here and now. In this case the doctrine lends itself readily to such treatment, for the main themes of this chapter refer to what happened, to what will happen and to what is happening now. The present is the middle term between the past and the future. This can be followed through in four cases.

(i) The present kingdom

Jesus was the inaugurator of the kingdom. It arrived with him. But the kingdom in its fullness is still to come. It has therefore a past and it has a future. Does it have a present? And if so what is it?

The immediate answer to the first of those questions emerges from the definition of the kingdom.[20] If the kingdom is the kingly rule of God, then the kingdom now exists wherever God reigns as king. It is a present kingdom. The second question is the one that takes longer to answer. Where does God reign as king? Where precisely can we discern the presence of the kingdom?

It can be argued that as God is king of the entire creation, the kingdom itself is present where his kingship is acknowledged. There is a large oil painting in the Australia Room of the Royal Commonwealth Society in London of the first Englishmen to land at Botany Bay. As they stand on that beach, so many miles from home, a small ship's company of twenty or so, watching the hoisting of the Union Jack, it is not difficult to think their thoughts. Among them, and over this place which they now claimed in his name, their king ruled. This was now his empire. The flag, hoisted and saluted, said it all. Where the king's rule is acknowledged, there is the kingdom. It is in the area of personal discipleship that this finds its clearest expression. A Christian is indeed a person who, through Christ, acknowledges God as king, places himself under his authority and resolves to obey his commands. On this showing the kingdom of God is the company of Christian believers, for it is, as we say, in their hearts that he reigns.

Furthermore, the kingdom was inaugurated and expressed in the words and deeds of Jesus. It was when the blind received their sight, the lame walked, the lepers were cleansed, the deaf heard, the dead were raised up and the poor had the good news preached to them that the kingdom became a present kingdom. Can it not then fairly be said that we may look for the kingly rule of God wherever the words and deeds of Jesus are being repeated and re-enacted in our own day? That where a preacher 'offers Christ' so that people repent and believe; that

[20] See p. 286.

where a surgeon works in the theatre to bring healing and health to a diseased or broken body; that where a marriage guidance counsellor listens and listens and then tries to help people to find solutions to the problems that have brought them to despair; that where an Oxfam worker teaches the unskilled to drive a tractor in a land where people starve— that there is the kingly rule of God? The name that is above every name may not always be named, but when it is not perhaps Jesus will take the deed for the word?

There is one delicate issue that cannot be evaded at this point. When a large statue of Dr Nkrumah was erected in Ghana at the time of its inception as an independent state there were carved on the base the words 'Seek ye first the political kingdom'. Some Christians were irritated, some even outraged, by what they regarded as a distortion of Scripture. Be that as it may, we are forced to recognize the close relationship that there has to be between the kingdom of God and the political kingdom.

'Politics in the pulpit' is, more often than not, used not to commend a sermon but to condemn it. And if by this is meant that the preacher spent his twenty minutes urging his congregation to vote Conservative or Labour in the next election, then the stricture is deserved. But the matter cannot be disposed of so easily. Politics is the way things happen. It is through politics that we decide how much we shall pay our senior citizens, whether we shall hang people or imprison them, whether we shall build houses or office blocks, whether we shall teach the Christian faith in schools, and all the thousand and one issues that make up life as we know it. If we are silent on such matters are we not creating a 'religious' world quite separate from the real one in which people have to live? And is not this again to exclude God from his own dominions? Of course one has to proceed with care and grace: it may be necessary to state more than one view. Certainly it is always necessary to try to distinguish between the prophetic word of the Lord and the latest bee buzzing around in the preacher's bonnet. To equate the gospel with a specific political programme is to exclude that programme from the judgement of God. But it is hard to see that we must always be silent about the political kingdom. And the reason? Not a mere desire to 'stir things up', for that would be reprehensible. The reason is that in the arena where things happen, Christians may be enabled to continue the deeds of Jesus. In some areas of politics this may be more obviously possible than in others: housing seems a more likely field than weights and measures, abortion than a flood dam across the Thames. But that is a difference of degree, not of kind. In which case seeking the political kingdom may not be far from seeking the kingdom of God.

(ii) The present Lord

The notion of the middle term operates here also. If Jesus inaugurated the kingdom and will bring it to its glorious consummation at the Last Day, then in between he is the Lord of the present, interim kingdom. Because of who he is, Jesus belongs not only to the past and the future but also to the present. As *The Sunday Service* puts it:

> Christ has died.
> Christ is risen.
> Christ will come again.[21]

The middle term is in the present tense. The Lord of the kingdom is in the here and now.

The devotional life of Christians is centred in this fact. The classic 'Jesus prayer', said over and over again—'Lord Jesus Christ, Son of God, have mercy on me a sinner'—assumes the present Lord. The liturgy of the Church invokes the Lord who is now with his people, as in Charles Wesley's hymn:

> Yet come, Thou heavenly Guest,
> And purify my breast;
>   Come, thou great and glorious King,
>   While before Thy Cross I bow;
>   With Thyself salvation bring,
>   Cleanse the house by entering now.[22]

[21] MSB, p. B13.
[22] MHB 760, v. 3.

The danger is that the present Lord, who is at the heart of Christian devotion, should be separated in the lives of Christians from the Lord of the present kingdom, so close to the political kingdom. Prayer and politics belong together in the kingdom. Both are subject to the king.

(iii) The present judgement

Judgement came with Jesus. 'Now is the judgment of this world', records the Fourth Gospel (12:31). There is also to be a day of final judgement when the sheep will be separated from the goats. Between these two lies the present judgement, the middle term. This instance of 'the last things now' can be used to relate to this present life what was said about heaven and hell.

I once had the privilege, during the war, of being present in an R.A.F. officers' mess when C. S. Lewis, the Anglican lay theologian, was invited to answer questions about the Christian religion. The fact that he was the author of *The Screwtape Letters* quickly led to questions about Satan and his affairs. The adjutant asked him, perhaps with an eye to his own future, what hell was like. After a delicious story about the seance in the Albert Hall immediately following the death of the spiritualist Arthur Conan Doyle, where the message came through to the medium: 'I have had a very *warm* reception on the other side', Lewis expatiated on hell. He said, I remember, that the worst state you can get into in this life is one of complete self-pity and misery: the condition in which you keep saying to yourself, 'They might have told me', 'I might have been consulted', 'Very well, they can have my resignation', and so forth. You wallow in your own wretchedness. But happily in this mortal life there are things to take your mind off your misery. You can go to the theatre or watch a county cricket match or go out for a drink with your friends, and as a result the black mood passes. But in hell, said Lewis, there are no theatres, no county cricket matches and (with a chuckle) no public houses—worse still, no friends. You are just left alone through all eternity, saying to yourself, 'They might have told me', 'I might have been consulted', 'Very well, they can have my resignation'. It was brilliantly done, and expressed in

310

terms that the officers' mess could understand the truth that hell is just to be apart from God and from everybody else for ever.

They did not ask Lewis about heaven but, if they had, on the basis of what he had said about hell, his answer would have been predictable. Heaven is to be joyful in company with God and with everybody else. That presumably is why we draw on the imagery of feasts and banquets to say what we want to say about heaven. For if you go out to a dinner you are so lost in the joy of the occasion, the pleasures of food and drink and the company of friends, that you are taken out of your misery. You can hardly sit at the dinner table, where everybody is laughing, muttering away 'I might have been consulted'. Heaven is to be taken out of oneself and caught up with others and with God.

It is almost superfluous to add that hell and heaven, so conceived, begin here and now. They are with us every day, and as the years go by the chances are that we shall be drawn to one rather than the other. This is the present judgement. It would be a mistake to think that, because this account of the matter has not mentioned Jesus, he is therefore excluded. On the contrary, he exemplifies it and sums it all up (John 3:17–21; 5:12–17). To be with him and his friends at a feast is heaven indeed. And the opposite follows.

(iv) The present resurrection

Between the Resurrection of Jesus from the dead and the day of Resurrection, whether that is thought of as the Last Day or as the day the individual Christian dies, there is the middle term, the present resurrection. Jesus *is* the resurrection and the life (John 11:25), and because this is so the believer may know the power of the resurrection (Phil. 3:10). He has been 'raised with Christ' (Col. 3:1). In the New Testament such raising has a very close connection with baptism, and that has a section to itself in the next chapter. The point to be made here is that the resurrection life, the life that is undefeated by both physical death and the death of sin, is enjoyed by the Christian here and now, because he is already 'with Christ'. The text 'And this is eternal life, that they know thee the only true God, and Jesus Christ whom thou hast sent' (John 17:3) is in the present tense.

Chapter 6 contained references to the 'liberated zones' in which modern people actually experienced resurrection, and examples were quoted from *True Resurrection* by H. A. Williams. As he comes to his last chapter, 'Resurrection and Death', Williams summarizes what has gone before. The book has been full of illustrations of resurrection experiences:

So far our concern has been with those death-dealing properties of human life which are occasions in the present of our resurrection. The deadness of the body as a slave-machine can be raised up to the glory of its own life. The final frustration of the mind as no more than an observing and calculating instrument can lead it to receive its capacity for communion with what it surveys, and thus come into life-giving riches. The past, in so far as it squeezes the life out of us by imposing upon us its calculated necessities, can be transformed by the freedom of a goodness which is creative and which therefore actually changes the situation. And the sheer destructiveness of suffering, by being taken on by the person and assimilated, can be the means whereby we pass beyond that strait-jacket of a self which is all we have been aware of so far, to the discovery of a self which is unlimited because it finds its identity in the Eternal Word. In these various ways we can come to a knowledge of life where death was throned and experience resurrection as a present reality.[23]

Williams goes on to write of death in similar terms of transformation:

If we are ready for life in the sense of being open to its power and possibilities, then we are also ready for death.[24]

It is for the reader to ponder this long paragraph and to fill it out with the experiences that have come to him in his encounters with other people, but most of all in his encounters with himself. Sometimes such experiences are mediated through literature or art or drama or music or other human activities that become sacramental for the occasion. But often they are the things that happen to us directly. They terrify us by their power over us. Sin and death go very near to destroying us. The present resurrection means that in the here and now they can themselves be defeated. Not finally, but sufficiently to make us aware that we are on the winning side.

(2) Eschatology for modern people

Secular people do not evidence much interest in eschatology

[23] P. 171.   [24] P. 180.

as Christians have traditionally understood it. Most of our contemporaries do not take the Final Coming of Christ, the day of Judgement and the day of Resurrection into their calculations at all. Some of them hope that their deceased relatives are in a pleasant place, but maybe even that hope takes away their right to the title 'secular'. Even the sentimental pieces about the One Great Scorer and the pearly gates being flung wide open for Mum have gone out of fashion. People nowadays do not have their ears cocked for the last trumpet.

If they have any eschatology at all, any passing interest in what the end of all things may be, it will relate to this 'terrestrial ball' rather than what happens beyond space and time. Oddly enough there are links here with Isaiah's vision of a world at total peace (11:1-10) (though he attributed it to the rule of God) and with John Wesley's point about 'covering the earth' (though he was referring to Christianity). Eschatology then means 'what is going to happen on earth in the future?'

The first subject to raise is the future of the planet earth, for if it ceases to exist nobody will be around to ask any more questions. What are the chances then? Will the earth cool down so that we cannot live here any more? Or shall we blow it up with our hydrogen bombs? Or shall we poison it with our pollution and our filth? Or shall we overpopulate it so that it can no longer feed us? These are a layman's questions as any scientist will discern. Any cooling down will presumably take so long as not to notice that it is happening. Any blowing up cannot be predicted but it is clearly a possibility (speaking politically not scientifically). It looks as if the large and powerful nations at present possessing hydrogen bombs intend to exercise restraint, but situations may arise that are too much for them. And what can one say about smaller and less stable countries that suddenly decide to assert themselves? If secular people see a future through such uncertainty they need as much faith as the religious do to believe in God.

As for destroying our environment and eating ourselves out of existence, there are optimists and pessimists. A pessimist will tell you that, if we go on as we are, in a while there will

313

be neither air to breathe, nor food to eat, nor fuel to keep us warm. An optimist will speak differently, as Edward Rogers does in the matter of food and population:

The resources of the world, and the technical skill available, can cope with the high, probably exaggerated, estimate of six thousand million living human beings by AD 2000. After that we can look forward with some confidence to a stabilization. So yet once more a spine-chilling melodrama of imminent disaster turns on calm consideration into a complicated but soluble problem.[25]

If Rogers is correct in his optimistic view, the question then to be asked is whether, now it is not too late, human beings are going to prove themselves capable of ensuring that they have a future. In this context much attention has been given in recent years to the writings of Teilhard de Chardin. Teilhard took evolution seriously. It is 'a light illuminating all facts, a curve that all lines must follow'.[26] He argued that all matter contains a certain element of consciousness. As it evolves it becomes both more complex and more conscious, emerging at last into man. But it does not stop there. With man, so to speak, put in charge, evolution proceeds. And it proceeds precisely in the direction that Isaiah and John Wesley and our secular contemporaries would all think desirable—towards that point (Teilhard called it the Omega Point) where all human beings will live together in peace and love and will then go on doing so for ever. Whether Teilhard was right or wrong only time will tell. Certainly he would say that the evolution of which he wrote was not conceivable without Jesus Christ who is its goal (Col. 1:15–20), and in this he parts company with those wholly committed to a secular interpretation.

There is some common ground between Christians and secular people as they ask the big questions about the future. Both hope that there will be one, for man and for the planet that is his home. Both concede (though the final list of reasons

[25] *Plundered Planet* (Denholm House 1973), p. 62.
[26] *The Phenomenon of Man* (Collins 1959), p. 219.

would be different) that the possibility of the opposite has to be taken seriously. Both would agree, to be sure, that what people are looking for in the future helps to determine what they do in the present. And with both, the kingdom that is to come is the full and consummate expression of the kingdom that is already here.

Chapter 10

The Church

A. THE FOUNDATION DOCUMENTS

The Apostles' Creed

I believe in ...
the holy catholic Church,
the communion of saints.

The Nicene Creed

We believe in one holy catholic and apostolic Church.

The Thirty-nine Articles

XIX. Of the Church
The Visible Church of Christ is a congregation of faithful
men, in which the pure Word of God is preached, and the
Sacraments be duly administered according to Christ's
ordinance in all those things that of necessity are requisite
to the same.

The Deed of Union

Clause 30.[1]

Explanatory Notes upon the New Testament (John Wesley)

Commentary on Colossians 1:18
He is the head of the church—Universal; the supreme and

[1] See pp 53, 74, 347-8.

316

only head both of influence and of government to the whole body of believers.

Commentary on Romans 6:3

As many as have been baptized into Jesus Christ have been baptized into his death—In baptism we, through faith, are ingrafted into Christ.

Commentary on 1 Corinthians 11:24

This is my body, which is broken for you—That is, this broken bread is the sign of My body . . . Take then, and eat of, this bread, in a humble, thankful, obediental remembrance of My dying love.

Commentary on Acts 20:28

To the flock, over which the Holy Ghost hath made you overseers—For no man or number of men upon earth can constitute an overseer bishop, or any other Christian minister. To do this is the peculiar work of the Holy Ghost.

Sermon XXXIV. Catholic Spirit (John Wesley)

'If it be, give me thy hand.' I do not mean, 'Be of my opinion'. You need not: I do not expect or desire it. Neither do I mean, 'I will be of your opinion'. I cannot: it does not depend on my choice: I can no more think, than I can see or hear, as I will. Keep you your opinion; I mine; and that as steadily as ever. You need not even endeavour to come over to me, or bring me over to you. I do not desire you to dispute those points, or hear or speak one word concerning them. Let all opinions alone on one side and the other: only 'give me thine hand'.

I do not mean, 'Embrace my modes of worship'; or, 'I will embrace yours'. This also is a thing which does not depend either on your choice or mine. We must both act as each is fully persuaded in his own mind. Hold fast that which you believe is most acceptable to God, and I will do the same. I believe the Episcopal form of church government to be scriptural and apostolical. If you think the

317

Presbyterian or Independent is better, think so still and act accordingly. I believe infants ought to be baptized; and this may be done either by dipping or sprinkling. If you are otherwise persuaded, be so still, and follow your own persuasion. It appears to me, that forms of prayer are of excellent use, particularly in the great congregation. If you judge extemporary prayer to be of more use, act suitably to your own judgment ... I have no desire to dispute with you one moment upon any of the preceding heads. Let all these smaller points stand aside. Let them never come into sight. 'If thine heart is as my heart', if thou lovest God and all mankind, I ask no more: 'give me thine hand'.

The Senior Catechism of the Methodist Church

19. WHAT IS THE CHURCH?

The Church is the whole company of those who trust in Christ as Lord and Saviour and are united in the fellowship of the Holy Spirit.

20. HOW IS THE CHURCH HOLY AND CATHOLIC?

It is holy because it belongs to God who has set it apart to do His work, and catholic because it offers the whole Gospel of Christ to all men everywhere.

21. WHAT IS THE COMMUNION OF SAINTS?

It is the fellowship of all who belong to the Church in heaven and on earth.

40. WHERE IS THE CHURCH?

Wherever Christ is, there is the Church, and His presence is shown by the preaching of His Word, the administration of the Sacraments, and the living of the Christian life.

41. WHAT ARE THE PROTESTANT CHURCHES?

Those Churches are called protestant which have been raised up by God to revive the witness to the supreme authority of the Scriptures, Salvation by Faith, the Priesthood of All Believers, and the Ministry of the Whole Church.

42. WHAT IS THE METHODIST CHURCH?

Within the one holy, catholic, and apostolic Church

the Methodist Church is the communion which was brought into being by the Holy Spirit, chiefly through the work of John Wesley, and continues as a witness to the universal grace of God, to the gift of assurance by the Holy Spirit, and to the power of the Holy Spirit to make us perfect in love.

43. WHO ARE THE MEMBERS OF THE METHODIST CHURCH?

All those who confess Jesus Christ as Lord and Saviour and accept the obligation to serve Him in the life of the Church and the world are welcome as full members of the Methodist Church. If not already baptized those seeking membership will be baptized before being received as full members.

44. WHAT IS THE PRIESTHOOD OF ALL BELIEVERS?

All members of the Church share the privilege and responsibility of direct access to God, of bringing others into personal relationship with Him, and of interceding for them.

45. WHAT IS THE MINISTRY OF THE CHURCH?

The ministry of the Church is the continuance of Christ's own ministry through the whole membership of the Church.

46. HOW IS THE MINISTRY EXERCISED?

The ministry of the Church is exercised by all those ordained to the care of souls, the preaching of the Word, and the administration of the Sacraments, by those fulfilling particular functions in the ordered life of the Church, and by all members in their worship and service.

47. WHAT IS THE WORSHIP OF GOD?

Worship is giving God the glory due to His Name.

48. HOW DO WE WORSHIP GOD?

We worship God whenever we offer Him our praise and thanksgiving, confess to Him our sins, ask His blessing for others and for ourselves, and hear and obey His word.

49. WHAT ARE THE SACRAMENTS?

The Lord Jesus appointed two Sacraments of the Gospel, Baptism and the Lord's Supper.

50. WHAT IS THE SACRAMENT OF BAPTISM?

By Baptism we are received by Christ into the congregation of His flock and share the heritage of grace and truth which He has bestowed upon it.

51. WHAT IS THE LORD'S SUPPER?

In the Lord's Supper, which is the Sacrament of Holy Communion, Jesus Christ gives Himself to us as our Lord and Saviour, and we give thanks with the whole Church for His sacrifice of Himself once offered, proclaim His passion and death, offer ourselves anew to Him, and anticipate by faith the perfect fellowship of the Heavenly Feast.

52. WHAT IS PRAYER?

Prayer is the whole converse of the soul with God.

54. WHAT ARE THE CHIEF FORMS OF PRAYER?

The chief forms of prayer are adoration, confession, thanksgiving, intercession and petition.

The Methodist Service Book

Through him you have sent your holy and life-giving Spirit and made us your people, a royal priesthood, to stand before you to proclaim your glory and celebrate your mighty acts.

And so with all the company of heaven we join in the unending hymn of praise.

(The Sunday Service, p. B13)

We pray for the Church throughout the world and for this church and all its members that in faith and unity we may be constantly renewed by your Holy Spirit for mission and service.

(The Sunday Service, p. B7)

By Baptism we receive this child into the congregation of Christ's flock, and pray that *he* may not be ashamed to hold fast the faith of Christ crucified, to fight against evil, and to persevere as Christ's faithful soldier and servant to *his* life's end.

(The Baptism of Infants, p. A11)

Lord, confirm your servant *N.* by your Holy Spirit that *he* may continue to be yours for ever.

(Public Reception into Full Membership
or Confirmation, p. A23)

Grant that by the power of the Holy Spirit we who receive
your gifts of bread and wine may share in the body and
blood of Christ.

(The Sunday Service, p. B14)

Father, send the Holy Spirit upon N., for the office and
work of a Minister in the Church of Christ.

(The Ordination of Ministers also called Presbyters, p. G11)

Hymns and Songs (A Supplement to the Methodist Hymn Book)

Thy hand, O God, has guided
Thy flock, from age to age;
The wondrous tale is written,
Full clear, on every page;
Our fathers owned thy goodness,
And we their deeds record;
And both of this bear witness:
One Church, one Faith, one Lord.

(71, v. 1) (E. H. Plumptre)

The Methodist Hymn Book

Christ, from whom all blessings flow,
Perfecting the saints below,
Hear us, who Thy nature share,
Who Thy mystic body are.

(720, v. 1) (Charles Wesley)

Come, Holy Ghost, Thine influence shed,
And realize the sign;
Thy life infuse into the bread,
Thy power into the wine.

(767, v. 1) (Charles Wesley)

Come, Holy Ghost, our souls inspire,
And lighten with celestial fire;
Thou the anointing Spirit art,
Who dost The sevenfold gifts impart.

(779, v. 1) (Anon.)

321

So shall we pray, and never cease,
So shall we thankfully confess
　　Thy wisdom, truth, and power, and love;
With joy unspeakable adore,
And bless and praise Thee evermore,
　　And serve Thee as Thy hosts above:

Till, added to that heavenly choir,
We raise our songs of triumph higher,
　　And praise Thee in a bolder strain,
Out-soar the first-born seraph's flight,
And sing, with all our friends in light,
Thy everlasting love to man.

(730, vv. 3–4) Charles Wesley)

B. THE DOCTRINE OF THE CHURCH, THE SACRAMENTS AND THE MINISTRY

(1) The People of God

Biblical revelation gives pride of place to God's dealings with his people.[2] This is the assertion in the last chapter that has to be substantiated in this one. It needs such substantiating because the concern of so many Protestants with personal religion has tended to weaken the doctrine of the Church. One would not have to look far to find Methodists who think of the Church as the coming together for worship and fellowship of people with the same religious convictions, and nothing more than that. It is still possible to find people in the dark corners of the Protestant underworld who regard a sermon on the Church as a waste of twenty minutes that could have been spent preaching the Gospel. Why are these people wrong?

Not, of course, in their insistence on the necessity for personal faith, but in their failure to see that that is only half the story. From the beginning God has worked through communities. His dealings were first and foremost with his people:

And I will dwell among the people of Israel, and will be their

2 See p. 302.

322

God. (Exod. 29:45; see also Lev. 26:12, Ezek. 38:23, 27, Zech. 8:8, etc.)

His covenants were made with groups rather than with individuals: with Noah, his descendants and his quaint little community in the ark (Gen. 9:9 ff.); with Abraham, the chosen, and his descendants (Gen. 15:18; 17:7); with Moses and the people (Exod. 24:8), not just with Noah, Abraham and Moses. It is true that in Jeremiah the responsibility of the individual within the covenant is stressed, and properly so, but the new covenant itself is to be made 'with the house of Israel and the house of Judah' (31:31). When Jesus came he proceeded in this matter, as in others, not to destroy the Old Testament ways but to fulfil them. He gathered his own community around him (Mark 3:14). They were his 'little flock' (Luke 12:32); and to them he gave, not separately but together, the new covenant in his blood (Mark 14:24). The followers of Jesus, the Church, became, with the old Israel, the Israel of God (Gal. 6:16), the new chosen race (1 Pet. 2:9) with whom God had a covenant relation.

The Church therefore is primary for the Christian. It is not a question of putting an institution (a 'man-made organization', according to some) before the one-to-one encounter with God of personal faith. It is rather to say that without the Christian community there could not have been any record of Jesus, any New Testament, any tradition of worship, any creeds and therefore any twentieth century Christians or any personal faith. It was probably thoughts of that kind that made Augustine (AD 354–430) write *Salus extra ecclesiam non est*, 'Outside the Church there is no salvation', and Cyprian (d. AD 258) say that he cannot have God for his father who does not have the Church for his mother.

(2) The New Testament beginnings

Jesus then, gathered his community about him. He did not use the word 'church' very much (the Greek word is *ecclesia* and it means an assembly of people called together for some purpose); but one of the two occasions in which it occurs in the

323

Gospels is significant for the origin of the Church. In Matthew 16:18 Jesus is recorded as saying to Peter:

> And I tell you, you are Peter, and on this rock I will build my church.

There has been some odd exegesis of this sentence. Roman Catholics have used it to prove that Peter was the first Pope and John Wesley, like John Wyclif before him, thought that when he said 'this rock' Jesus might well have pointed to himself. Others argue that the rock is Peter's faith. But the main clause is 'I will build my church'. It refers to the fact that this community began when Jesus called men to be with him, taught them and sent them out on mission. As the hymn says, in echo of 1 Corinthians 3:11:

> The Church's one foundation
> Is Jesus Christ her Lord:
> She is His new creation. . . .

The very close relation between Jesus and the Church is brought out in the metaphors that the New Testament uses. He is the vine, we are the branches (John 15:1–6); the Church is the bride of Christ (Rev. 21:2, 9); the Church is like a body (Rom. 12:4–5; 1 Cor. 12:12–26), indeed it is the body of Christ (1 Cor. 12:27; Col. 1:24; Eph. 4:12; 5:30—for this is Pauline thought even if he did not put the letter together); Christ is the head of the body (Eph. 1:22–3; 4:15–16; 5:23; Col. 1:18; 2:19). The Church then, is no man-made organization begun, like rugby clubs and allotment holders' associations and branches of the British Legion, by human votes under human chairmen. There was no meeting in an upper room with Peter in the chair debating a motion 'That we begin the Church' (with perhaps an amendment moved by James that it be for Jews only!). It had its origin in the person, life, death and resurrection of Jesus of Nazareth.

And in something else. The 'birthday of the Church' is celebrated at Pentecost. The community had indeed begun with Jesus but at Pentecost it received its baptism of power. As we might say, it found its identity. The student should re-read at this point what was said in chapter 7[3] about the work of the Spirit in giving birth to the Church. This puts entirely out of court, as far as the New Testament is concerned, any idea that the Church was anything other than the creation of God through Jesus and through the Holy Spirit.

(3) What is the Church for?

If God so created the Church, why did he do it? This is not an attempt to probe the divine intentions, which would be impertinent, but simply to ask what is the purpose, then and now, of this particular creation. Answers to the question have emerged as the Church has lived through the centuries and, if the promise of the Holy Spirit to lead into all truth is taken seriously, those answers must have some validity. What then is the Church for?

(i) The Church is for worship
The Church exists primarily for God, to worship and glorify him for ever. The liturgy of the Church tries to put this into words, and not without success. What more can language provide than 'the unending hymn of praise'?

> Holy, holy, holy Lord,
> God of power and might,
> heaven and earth are full of your glory.[4]

As so often in religion, we have succeeded in standing the thing on its head, and we talk and behave as if the Church existed primarily for us. We assess services of worship on the basis of whether they helped or inspired or comforted or stimulated us. Not that these things are reprehensible in themselves; they are not. It is giving them pride of place that is wrong. But, if they are treated as by-products of the main purpose of giving praise to God, not only shall we have our priorities right, we shall be more likely to end up with these other blessings added unto us.

[3] See pp. 221–3.
[4] MSB, The Sunday Service, p. B13.

Sometimes what is right theologically is easy to practise. On a glorious spring Sunday morning, when life is treating us well, we can throw back our heads and sing the *Te Deum* or some other great hymn of praise and mean every word. But on a wet November night, when life is treating us very badly indeed, we do not feel like praising anybody or anything and it is as much as we can do just to be there. No one can presume to speak for God, but one likes to think that he accepts both the lusty *Te Deum* and the weary body that can hardly drag itself to the pew, for both are worshipping, and that is what the Church is for.

The Christian view of the matter does not end there. Since the days of the Apostles, Christians who have worshipped God in their lifetimes have died. The Church, guided by Scripture (e.g. Rev. 5) and tradition, came to believe that in the Communion of Saints, in the Church Triumphant as it is sometimes called, their praise continued. So the hymns of a small, shabby chapel in a back street of an inner city, sung by four or five creaking voices to a bronchial harmonium, are caught up with the praises of the angels and archangels and all the company of heaven. That is why even the most hardened Methodist minister is not unmoved when at the Conference Memorial Service every year the names are read out and the hymn sung:

> Let all the saints terrestrial sing
> With those to glory gone;
> For all the servants of our King,
> In earth and heaven, are one.[5]

The climax of the Thanksgiving in the eucharist has it right:

> ... all honour and glory to be given to you, almighty Father, from all who dwell on earth and in heaven throughout all ages. Amen.[6]

(ii) The Church is for prayer

Prayer was obviously part of the corporate life of the early Church. As with worship, the forms they used were in the first

[5] MHB 824, v. 1.
[6] MSB, p. B14.

instance Jewish, and 'the prayers' of Acts 2:42 were probably the prayers of the Jewish liturgy. But their prayer life extended beyond the formal. The Spirit gave the first Christians the capacity to pray. In their most traumatic experiences they prayed (4:23 ff.; 12:5, 12), and they commissioned men by prayer (13:3).

So too Paul's epistles frequently begin with a reference to his thanksgivings and intercessions for the Christians to whom he writes (e.g. Rom. 1:9; Phil. 1:3–4). Prayer was a strong bond between those early Christian communities. Epaphras, for example, 'greets you, always remembering you earnestly in his prayers, that you may stand mature and fully assured in all the will of God' (Col. 4:12).

It is not surprising then that when the Church began to settle down, so to say, the forms of worship that took shape should include places for prayer. In *The Shape of the Liturgy*, Dom Gregory Dix gives the 'original unchanging outline' of Christian worship:

> Opening greeting by the officiant and reply of the church
> Lesson
> Psalmody
> Lesson
> Sermon
> Dismissal of those who did not belong to the church
> Prayers
> Dismissal of the church.[7]

Notice that prayer was reckoned to be the privilege of those who had 'put on Christ' and received the Spirit. Dix has this interesting account of what happened when the Church 'fell to prayer':

> First a subject was announced, either by the officiant (in the West) or the chief deacon (in the East), and the congregation was bidden to pray. All prayed silently on their knees for a while; then, on the signal being given, they rose from their knees, and the officiant summed up the petitions of all in a brief collect. They knelt to pray as individuals, but the corporate prayer of

[7] *The Shape of the Liturgy* (A. and C. Black 1945), p. 38.

327

the church is a priestly act, to be done in the priestly posture for prayer, standing.[8]

As the liturgies of the Church evolved, what the Methodist Catechism calls 'the chief forms of prayer'[9]—adoration, confession, thanksgiving, intercession and petition—all find their place, and the *Methodist Service Book* carries on this tradition.

But, as the quotation from Dix reveals, there is a close relationship between corporate and individual prayer; and that not only 'in church' (put in inverted commas because originally there were no church buildings). The Church is 'for prayer' in the sense that its members carry on a private life of prayer which is gathered up into the corporate prayers of the liturgy. The word often used of both the believer's private prayers and the corporate prayer of the Church is the word 'spirituality'. It is, as Henry Rack says:

> the whole Christian enterprise of pursuing, achieving and culti-
> vating communion with God, which includes both public worship
> and private devotion, and the results of these in actual Christian
> life.[10]

Without such a spirituality at its heart the Church loses its identity. To put it another way, we could more easily dispense with theologians, administrators or even preachers than we could with saints.

(iii) The Church is for preaching and teaching
In 1936 the New Testament scholar C. H. Dodd published *The Apostolic Preaching and its Development*[11] and it raised the question as to the content of the proclamation, the preaching, that was done by the first Christians. The New Testament word for proclamation is *Kerygma* (pronounced kay-rug-ma), and Dodd first gave an outline of it as he gleaned it from the Pauline epistles:

8 P. 42.
9 See p. 320.
10 *Twentieth-century Spirituality* (Epworth 1969), p. 2.
11 Hodder and Stoughton 1936.

The prophecies are fulfilled, and the new Age is inaugurated by the coming of Christ.

He was born of the seed of David.

He died according to the Scriptures, to deliver us out of the present evil age.

He was buried.

He rose on the third day according to the Scriptures

He is exalted at the right hand of God, as Son of God and Lord of quick and dead.

He will come again as Judge and Saviour of men.[12]

Turning then to the Acts, and particularly to the first four speeches of Peter, Dodd reconstructed what he called the Jerusalem *Kerygma*. This is similar to the Pauline version, though 'Son of God' does not appear, nor does the explicit connection of the death of Jesus with our deliverance. The Jerusalem *Kerygma* refers more specifically to the ministry of Jesus, his miracles and teaching (the later speech of Peter in Acts 10: 34–43 is important here), and to the Holy Spirit in the Church as the sign that the new age had begun.

Since Dodd wrote further work has suggested that he, having seized on a truth, pressed it too far. Interest now centres on the variety of *kerygmata* (the plural) and the possibility that the amount of common material was not as large as Dodd suggested.

Whatever the truth of the matter may be, there is no doubt but that the early Church was a preaching Church. The first Christians were heralds of Christ.

The *Kerygma*, the proclamation, was followed by the *Didache* (pronounced did-a-kay), the teaching. This was basically instruction in what it meant to be a Christian and a large proportion of Paul's letters is taken up with instruction of this kind. Such teaching for the edification of the faithful was an indispensable part of the life of the Church. Strictly speaking the preacher was the herald, announcing the *Kerygma*, giving the good news, and leaving the *Didache* to others, but obviously it was not possible to maintain a rigid division of function. It is not possible to do so today, and often the preacher has to do it all.

[12] *The Apostolic Preaching and its Development*, p. 17.

329

The Protestant Reformation saw the preaching task as one of the marks of the true Church. As Article XIX of the Thirty-nine Articles puts it:

The Visible Church of Christ is a congregation of faithful men in which the pure Word of God is preached. . . .

The preacher is a preacher of the Word. What precisely does this mean? In commenting upon John 1:1 C. K. Barrett says that the writer begins with:

the fundamental conviction that Christ himself is the Gospel, the Word which God has spoken.[13]

Christ is the Word, and to preach the Word is to preach Christ. It is a little confusing that we use 'Word' about the Bible (the written word) and the preaching itself (the proclaimed word), but no great harm is done if we do not depart from the conviction of the writer of the Fourth Gospel. That is why John Wesley's phrase 'offering Christ' was such a good description of preaching.

For the sake of order in its institutional life, and the promulgation of sound doctrine, the Church exercises control over preachers. It recognizes that people are 'called to preach' by God, but has the responsibility of deciding whether or not to confirm that call.

As far as Methodist Local Preachers are concerned this theology of preaching finds liturgical expression in the *Recognition and Commissioning Service*.[14] First comes the statement that the candidates have been 'tested and approved' and then the question:

Do you trust that you are truly called by God to the office and work of a Local Preacher in his Church?
Answer : I do so trust.

Later, after the commissioning prayer invoking the Holy Spirit, the service continues:

13 *The Gospel According to St John*, p. 129.
14 Methodist Publishing House 1975.

330

May they exercise the ministry of your Word to the good of your Church and to the glory of your holy Name, through Jesus Christ our Lord. *Amen.*

And then, with the Bible:

Take now this Bible, and may he who gave the Word give you grace, wisdom and power to proclaim the truth which is in Jesus.

(iv) The Church is for celebrating the sacraments
Consider the following:

1. The Queen launches a new ship. She says: 'May God bless her and all who sail in her' and then she smashes (electronically these days) a bottle of champagne against the bow.

2. Liverpool score a goal at Anfield. Their fervent supporters on the Kop cheer their heads off. At the same time they wave scarves, jump up and down, and throw their own or their neighbours' hats into the air.

3. In Jeremiah 13 the Lord tells Jeremiah to buy a linen waist-cloth, to wear it and then to take it and hide it in a cleft of the rock by the river Euphrates. This Jeremiah obediently does. Then some time later the Lord tells him to collect it, and when he does: 'Behold, the waist-cloth was spoiled; it was good for nothing.' The text continues:

Thus says the Lord: Even so will I spoil the pride of Judah and the great pride of Jerusalem. (v. 9)

What is common to these three occasions? It is that in each of them there is a combination of word and action, of speaking and doing. And the two together produce a stronger effect than either would on its own.

It is therefore necessary to keep the two together. Sometimes an unhappy polarization has come about in the Church between prophets or preachers, in the speaking tradition, and priests, in the acting tradition. This is quite unbiblical. It is true that the Old Testament prophets had no time for corrupt priests, but that was because they were corrupt, not because they were priests. The prophets themselves, as Jeremiah demonstrates, held together the speaking and the acting. Conversely, the

331

priests, especially in the early days, had a significant teaching role. The reason for avoiding tension between the two is obvious enough: both are expressions of what the Lord has to say to his people.

This means, in the present context, that a consideration of the sacraments of the Church should begin by recognizing that there should be no opposition between what is said and what is done in the name of the Lord. We do not want the Christian world divided into churches that stress the sacraments and churches that stress preaching. The two belong together.[15]

Sacraments themselves are illustrations of this general truth that words go with actions, that speaking goes with doing. For example:

> The Minister, taking each child into *his* arms, says to the parents or guardians: Name this child; and, naming *him* accordingly, pours or sprinkles water upon *him*, or dips *him* in water, saying: N., I baptize you in the Name of the Father, and of the Son, and of the Holy Spirit.[16]

The two sacraments of the Protestant churches must now be considered. These two are recognized because the Gospels record a close association of Jesus with them. Our Roman brethren, expanding a little more on the biblical records, recognize another five.[17]

(a) Baptism
1. Baptism in the New Testament
The first chapter of the earliest Gospel has only run three verses before its first reference to baptism is encountered. John came 'preaching a baptism of repentance for the forgiveness of sins' (Mark 1:4). The meaning that John gave to his baptism arrested people. A terrifying judgement was about to happen and he offered the chance to repent while there was still

15 For a Roman Catholic statement of this truth see Louis Bouyer, *Life and Liturgy* (Sheed and Ward 1956), p. 29, and for a Protestant see Article XIX on p. 316.
16 MSB, p. A11.
17 Confirmation, Penance, Marriage, Ordination and Extreme Unction.

time. It seems a far cry from these fiery affairs on the banks of the Jordan to a pink baby lying in the vicar's arms on a Sunday afternoon in a quiet parish church, but in fact, as this section should show, there is a direct line between them.

Jesus himself submitted to John's baptism (Mark 1:9). Contentions that he did not need to because he had no sins of which to repent nor any need to fear the coming judgement miss the main point. That point is that, by submitting to John's baptism, Jesus aligned himself with the 'remnant', the faithful minority in Israel, of which John was the representative.

Jesus did not then proceed to baptize others.[18] Why not? An American Methodist scholar gives a likely answer:

> I venture the proposition that Jesus did not baptise because all that baptism really signified was in the process of being summed up, literally epitomised, in his ministry as the Elect One, the true Israel of God, and that until his ministry was perfected in total submission to the Father, further baptisms, like those of John, were neither appropriate nor possible.[19]

But by the time of Pentecost, when through the cross and resurrection the ministry of Jesus was in fact 'perfected in total submission to the Father', baptisms became both appropriate and possible, and they started right away. According to Acts there were three thousand on the first day (Acts 2:41), and the book continues to record the practice of baptism as the way of entry into the Christian community, linking it with belief in Jesus as the Christ and with the gift of the Spirit, though not with complete consistency.

What did Christian baptism mean in the life of the early Church? It meant, first, entry. It was the way in. And as the Church was living in the Last Days baptism was eschatological in its reference. 'Get in quick before the balloon goes up' would be a slang way of putting it.

If this were all that baptism meant, then it would simply have been a rite of entry, paying one's money at the ecclesiastical turnstile, so to speak. But it was not all. John 3:5 refers

18 See John 3:22; 4:1–2.
19 Robert E. Cushman, 'Baptism and the Family of God' in Dow Kirkpatrick (Ed.), *The Doctrine of the Church* (Epworth 1964), p. 91.

333

to being born of the Spirit as well as of water, thus confirming the practice of Acts. Furthermore consider Romans 6:1–12 and particularly verse 4:

> We were buried therefore with him by baptism into death, so that as Christ was raised from the dead by the glory of the Father, we too might walk in newness of life.

Colossians 2:12 says the same thing. Dying to the old life of sin happened in baptism. The believer then had to share in the sufferings of Christ (Rom. 8:17; Phil. 3:10; 2 Tim. 2:11). But he shared in the Resurrection too, as he 'walked in newness of life'. In other words baptism, far from being only an entry ticket, was a personal revolution.

2. Infant baptism

All that has been said so far applies so obviously, both in theory and in New Testament practice, to believing adults, that infant baptism seems at first sight an incongruity. The Baptists, indeed, maintain that this is just what it is, and they are not without their sympathizers in other churches. If salvation is by faith, ought not entry into the community of faith to be restricted to those who are able to give evidence that they believe? Furthermore, the total immersion often associated with the rite of believers' baptism is thought to be a more suitable sign of dying and rising with Christ. A number of considerations, however, have to be reckoned with that have led most of Christendom to the opposite conclusion in the matter.

Christians, like most other people, lived in households, and if baptism meant entering the Church and so being saved from the unbelieving world, then it was imperative that the entire household should be baptized. Who wanted to leave their children to share the fate of unbelievers? That could well have been why Paul baptized the household of Stephanas (1 Cor. 1:16). If it is argued that the hope of an early Parousia and Last Day receded, and therefore children could have waited until they grew up, it has to be remembered that in the history of the Church the doctrine of original sin took the place of the Last Day as the fate worse than death from which all

334

Christian children should be delivered. This, it was believed, was effected by their being baptized.

Not surprisingly, in the course of time the theology of being 'born again' through the operation of the Holy Spirit was transferred to infant baptism. This view, known as 'baptismal regeneration', was held by John Wesley, though he appeared to believe that the grace of baptism could be lost. The view is unambiguously stated in the *Book of Common Prayer*:

> Seeing now, dearly beloved brethren, that this child is regenerate and grafted into the body of Christ's Church let us give thanks....[20]

Methodism by and large rejects this view, and simply has an invocation:

> Father, be present with us in the power of your Spirit.[21]

and a final prayer that the Church, into which the child has been received, may be strengthened by the Holy Spirit.

Apart from regeneration, the infant baptism position has a strong theological base. The Gospel, the good news of what God has done for man in Christ, is rooted in the sovereign love of God. He acts before we respond. We love, because he first loved us (1 John 4:19). The Gospel is a Gospel of prevenient[22] grace, of God coming to us before we ever come to him. This is the deep theological truth expressed in the sacrament of infant baptism. As the Methodist Conference Statement puts it:

> The practice of Infant Baptism is in itself an impressive witness to the truth that the Grace of God comes before our response, and is wholly apart from our deserts.[23]

Babies cannot repent, cannot believe, cannot decide for Christ,

[20] Public Baptism of Infants.
[21] MSB, p. A8.
[22] 'Coming before'.
[23] *Statement on Holy Baptism*, p. 4.

cannot love God, in any active sense. They just lie in the minister's arms, noisy or silent. What happens therefore in infant baptism is *entirely* the action of God. It is the sacrament of sovereign grace.[24] Furthermore, 'what happens' has to be thought of in precisely the terms that the New Testament uses: entering the Church, the visible community that is the sign of the kingdom; being grafted into the body of Christ and so having a share in the dying and rising with Christ which is the lot of all the baptized.

Of course there are other things to be said. The sacrament must take place in the context of faith, though it is the faith of the Church, not of the baby. There are other secondary features that are important: the baptismal promises and the prayers for the child. And certainly a supplementary rite, normally 'Public Reception into Full Membership or Confirmation', is necessary (see below). But these factors must not be allowed to detract from the sovereign love of God at work in this sacrament. Nothing makes the nature of the Gospel more clear than baptism given to a helpless child.

In the diversity of theology and practice in the universal Church, believers' baptism and infant baptism both have their place. What is entirely unacceptable is that people who are baptized already should be 'baptized' again. This is to substitute personal experience for the grace of God, and virtually to tell the good Lord that his first attempt was not good enough.

(b) Confirmation

This service, usually known in the Methodist Church by its longer title, 'Public Reception into Full Membership', is not a sacrament in Protestant churches, but as part of the process of Entry into the Church it can properly be mentioned at this point.

Confirmation has its antecedents in the New Testament, particularly in Acts,[25] where the laying on of hands and the gift

24 Some theologians do not find the 'prevenient grace' argument entirely convincing. They would rather say that in infant baptism the element of *sign* is at its maximum and its instrumentality at its minimum. What is indicated is of more significance than what is done.

25 See 8:15–17; 15:3, 8; 16:15, 33; 19:1–6.

of the Holy Spirit were associated with baptism though, as has been said, with no consistent pattern. For various reasons the churches of the East and the West have diverged in their practice of confirmation. In the East it takes place at the same time as baptism, though the word 'confirmation' is not used. In the West it has been separated in time from baptism, and as a result the individual concerned has the opportunity, by his personal commitment and profession of faith in Christ, of sharing in the confirmation of that which was done for him at his baptism. But the major work in confirmation is that of the Holy Spirit, as the Methodist service makes clear:

Lord, confirm your servant N. by your Holy Spirit that *he* may continue to be yours for ever.[26]

(c) The eucharist[27]

The central rite of the Church has its origin in the action of Jesus and in the Jewish faith and practice behind that action. A specific Jewish feast lies immediately behind the eucharist. There is some debate among liturgical scholars as to which it was.

The traditional view is that it was the Passover, the Jewish family festival when the passage telling of the exodus from Egypt was read, the paschal lamb was offered, unleavened bread was eaten, cups of wine were drunk and prayers of thanks for the mighty acts of God were said. The Gospels on the whole give support to this view (Mark 14:14; Matt. 26:17; Luke 22:8).

The institution by Jesus

There has been so much argument in the Church about the meaning of the eucharist that all kinds of questions have been asked. Would it be a eucharist at all if the words of Jesus, 'This is my body', 'This is my blood' were left out? Suppose there were no bread or wine and rice-cakes and China tea were used instead? One cannot tie the God down so that he is imprisoned by the form (the precise words said) or the matter

[26] MSB, p. A23.
[27] For the sense in which this word is used see footnote 4 on p. 48.

337

(the precise elements used) of his own sacraments. But normally one would suppose that for a eucharist to be a eucharist, and to stand in the tradition that goes back to the upper room in Jerusalem, it is necessary at least to repeat the words and actions of Jesus.

As for the words, they should be carefully read in the Gospel records (Mark 14:22–25; Matt. 26:26–9; Luke 22:14–23) and in the earlier account given by Paul in 1 Corinthians 11:23–6, for there are some variations. Liturgies always include a form of them, and the Methodist form is as good an example as any:

We praise you, Lord God, King of the universe,
through our Lord Jesus Christ,
who, on the night in which he was betrayed,
took bread, gave thanks, broke it, and gave it to his disciples,
   saying,
'Take this and eat it. This is my body given for you.
Do this in remembrance of me.'
In the same way, after supper,
he took the cup, gave thanks, and gave it to them, saying,
'Drink from it all of you.
This is my blood of the new covenant,
poured out for you and for many, for the forgiveness of sins.
Do this, whenever you drink it, in remembrance of me.'

As for the actions, they are the fourfold ones of taking, giving thanks, breaking and giving. A good liturgy allows these to stand out as the service proceeds: 'taking' in The Setting of the Table,[28] or The Offertory (*not* another word for 'collection') as it is sometimes called; 'giving thanks' in The Thanksgiving;[29] 'breaking' in The Breaking of the Bread;[30] 'giving' in The Sharing of the Bread and Wine,[31] or Communion.

Eucharists have been celebrated in all sorts of ways in all kinds of places. In the early Church they were often associated with another, and sometimes a much larger, meal. But always

28 MSB, p. B12.
29 P. B12.
30 P. B14.
31 P. B15.

338

they should have this close association with the institution of the rite by Jesus.

The theology of the eucharist

Theology is concerned with the meaning of what is said and done. This can be explored under five headings. Each of these theological approaches to the eucharist is associated with one of the names given to the rite.

1. The eucharist is a memorial

'Do this in remembrance of me' (1 Cor. 11:24). There are some Christians who believe that the eucharist is primarily a matter of remembering. When the bread is broken and the wine poured out, their *memories* become active and they go back, mentally and spiritually, to the upper room in Jerusalem. They recall what happened there and, even more, what happened on the cross outside the city wall soon afterwards. They are happy to refer to the rite as The Lord's Supper:

> In memory of the Saviour's love
> We keep the sacred feast.[32]

This act of remembering is an authentic part of the theology of the eucharist, and we have the reformer Zwingli (1484–1531) to thank that when the Church in the West was being renewed this aspect was not overlooked. (This is not to say that Zwingli thought of the eucharist *only* in that way.)

The crucial question is whether the word 'remembrance' in the sentence 'Do this in remembrance of me' means 'remembering' in our sense of simply thinking about the past. Many scholars think that the word *anamnésis* (pronounced 'anamnaysis') is a good deal richer in its meaning than that, and carries the sense of re-calling or re-presenting before God an event in the past so that it becomes operative in the present.[33] This view does not quite justify such renderings as 'Do this to call me back',[34] but it is in line with the Old Testament tradi-

---

[32] MHB 762, v. 1.
[33] See p. 20 for 'Be born in us today'.
[34] J. Jeremias has suggested 'This do to remind God of me'.

339

tion of the Passover which did not merely look back to the Exodus, but brought it into the present, so to speak, so that God could be thanked for a past, a present and indeed a future deliverance.

2. The eucharist is a thanksgiving

The word 'eucharist' means 'thanksgiving'. In the Methodist version, as in others, the central prayer of the service is called 'The Thanksgiving', and in it are rehearsed the mighty acts of God in Christ. It begins:

Father, all-powerful and ever-living God,
it is indeed right, it is our joy and our salvation,
always and everywhere to give you thanks and praise
through Jesus Christ your Son our Lord.[35]

The life, death, resurrection and ascension of Jesus and the gift of the Holy Spirit to the people of God are then not simply remembered, but celebrated.

It is this theological approach that has made the most of the word 'feast'. The eucharist is a feast and its keynote must be joy.

Thy presence makes the feast;
Now let our spirits feel
The glory not to be expressed,
The joy unspeakable.[36]

3. The eucharist is a communion

It is a communion with Jesus. Just how Jesus is present at the eucharist has, unhappily, been the source not only of millions of words of theological argument and indeed, abuse, but also of imprisonment, torture and death at the stake. There are those who are content to say that Jesus is the president or host at the feast and in that capacity he enters into communion with believers who come to receive the bread and wine in faith. There are others who experience the presence of the Lord in a manner much more closely related to the bread and

[35] MSB, p. B12.
[36] MHB 761, v. 3.

wine of the feast. Protestants tend to take fright at the word
'transubstantiation' but there is no need, for it is but one way
of expressing what is called the 'Real Presence' of Christ in the
eucharist. The main objection to it is not that it is too crude
(eating the 'actual' body of Jesus) but that it is too subtle,
depending on a refined distinction[37] in medieval philosophy.
Not all Roman Catholic theologians now regard themselves as
tied to that particular—even if official—interpretation of the
Real Presence.

It is a pity that the matter has been polarized in this way,
for there is truth in both ways of enjoying communion with
the Lord. He is there, no believer denies that. But cannot one
go on to say that he is there under the sign of bread and wine?
It all depends on what 'under the sign of' means. Here we
come to the critical sentences 'This is my body', 'This is my
blood'. Letting the first do duty for both, can it not be said
that just as my body in a room is the sign that I, in my totality,
am present, so the bread which is the body of Christ is, in
similar sense, the sign under which he is present to those who
come to his table in faith?

His body, broken in our stead,
Is here in this memorial bread.

In the service we ask that the Holy Spirit may enable such
communion (hence the title, Holy Communion) to take place.
The Sunday Service expresses this one way:

Grant that by the power of the Holy Spirit we who receive your

[37] The difference is between substance and accidents. Bread possesses
'breadness', the essential 'substance' which is common to all bread everywhere. It also possesses colour, weight, taste, smell and so forth, the properties that make it bread. These are the 'accidents'. Transubstantiation is
the doctrine that while the accidents of the bread (and the wine) on the
altar remain those of bread, the substance is changed into the body (and
the blood) of Christ.

On the ways in which Roman Catholics and Methodists agree, and
disagree, in their approaches to the eucharist, see *Growth in Understanding*
(Catholic Information Services and Methodist Ecumenical Committee), the
Report of the Joint Roman Catholic Church-World Methodist Council
Commission, pp. 12–19.

gifts of bread and wine may share in the body and blood of Christ.[38]

Charles Wesley expresses it another:

> Come, Holy Ghost, Thine influence shed,
>   And realize the sign;
> Thy life infuse into the bread,
> Thy power into the wine.[39]

Communion is not only between believers and the Lord. A feast is a 'get-together' in which people are happy in one another's company. More than that, unity with the Lord means, at one and the same time, unity with other believers. As *The Sunday Service* has it:

> Though we are many, we are one body because we all share in the one loaf.[40]

4. The eucharist is a sacrifice

'The Mass' is the title that comes immediately to mind when we speak of sacrifice, though the word itself has nothing to do with sacrifice. It seems to have come from the phrase at the end of the Latin service *Ite missa est* which, put colloquially, means 'Go, the service is over'! The fear that Protestants have had about this theological approach is that it involves the view that at the eucharist the sacrifice of Christ on Calvary is repeated, that Jesus is actually offered again to God by the hands of the priest. Hence the insistence in Cranmer's service (the Methodist version is *The Lord's Supper*, 1936 service) on 'his one oblation of himself once offered'. Calvary is unrepeatable.

Again, we need not fear too much, though that is not another way of saying that we are all agreed![41] The word 're-presen-

---

[38] MSB, p. B14.
[39] MHB 767, v. 1.
[40] MSB, p. B14.
[41] As A. Raymond George has pointed out in 'The Lord's Supper', in Dow Kirkpatrick (Ed.), *The Doctrine of the Church*, pp. 155–6, the publication of Fr. Francis Clark's *Eucharistic Sacrifice and the Reformation* in 1960 stirred up the whole controversy again.

ted', would find more ready acceptance with Roman Catholic scholars generally than the word 'repeated'. At the same time we have to note that the thought of 're-presentation' is not absent from the theology of the Wesleys. A. Raymond George makes this clear:

> The Wesleys never for a moment doubted that the sacrifice of Calvary, the one oblation once offered, was unique and unrepeatable. But, on their view, in remembering this, we plead it or present it, as what Brevint called a 'commemorative sacrifice'; that is, we spread it before the Father as the only ground of all our hope.[42]

There is a section of Charles Wesley's *Hymns on The Lord's Supper* headed 'The Holy Eucharist as it implies a Sacrifice' and it is full of theology of this kind:

> To Thee his passion we present,
> Who for our ransom dies;
> We reach by this great instrument
> The' eternal sacrifice.
>
> The Lamb as crucified afresh
> Is here held out to men,
> The tokens of His blood and flesh
> Are on this table seen.[43]

5. The eucharist is a foretaste

A foretaste of what?: of the great heavenly banquet when all the redeemed will feast with the Lord and with one another in the fullness of the kingdom.

> Feast after feast thus comes and passes by,
> Yet, passing, points to the glad feast above,
> Giving sweet foretaste of the festal joy,
> The Lamb's great bridal feast of bliss and love.[44]

Such a view is thoroughly biblical for it is in line with all the

[42] 'The Lord's Supper', p. 151.
[43] *The Poetical Works of John and Charles Wesley* (Wesleyan Methodist Conference Office 1869), Vol. III, p. 310.
[44] MHB 772, v. 6.

messianic expectations. At the Passover the Jews looked forward, and still do, to their glorious future. Indeed they expect that when the Messiah comes, he will come at the time of the Passover. The eschatological note is struck too by the words of Jesus as recorded in Luke 22:18:

> For I tell you that from now on I shall not drink of the fruit of the vine until the kingdom of God comes.

A personal illustration may not be intrusive. The last night of my stay in a theological college was marked by a celebration of the eucharist. Men who had worked and played and worshipped together, and in so doing had found a corporate identity, came together for the last time to the Lord's Table. The next day would see them scattered across the country and across the world. Eschatology came into its own when the Principal, the New Testament scholar Wilbert F. Howard, reminded us that we should not eat and drink together again until we sat down in the kingdom of God.

Geoffrey Wainwright, in *Eucharist and Eschatology*, sums the matter up:

> The eucharist is already a meal, and the Bible's favourite picture for the final kingdom is that of feasting. At the eucharist Christ is present to the eyes of faith: at His table in the final kingdom we shall see Him face to face (cf. 1 Cor. 13:12a). The eucharist is a periodic celebration: in the final kingdom the worship and rejoicing, as in the life of heaven, will be perpetual. In the eucharist a part of mankind and a part of the world serve the glory of God: in the final kingdom God will be all in all.[45]

(v) The Church is for ministry
The wording of this title is important because in the minds of many people 'ministry' is something associated only with the ordained ministry. They are *the* ministry, and whatever ministering is done, is done by them. This is not how the New Testament sees the matter at all.

Everything begins with the ministry of Christ himself, the

[45] Epworth 1971, p. 147.

Word of God, without whom there would not be any Christian ministry exercised by anybody. He is the source and pattern of it all. His ministry consisted partly of preaching and teaching and partly of compassionate deeds, and this was the ministry he shared with others. But with whom precisely?

The ministry of Jesus was shared with the whole Church. In the Methodist statement on Ordination of 1960 this is made explicit:

> It is the Church—described both as the People of God and as the Body of Christ—which is the ruling conception. Through this Church Christ Himself, who took 'the form of a servant' and 'came not to be ministered unto, but to minister', continues His ministry in the world.[46]

The ministry of Jesus, then, is continued by his entire body. That is why it is better to begin by saying 'the Church *is for* ministry' rather than 'the Church *has* a ministry'. And that is why Methodists believe in 'the priesthood of all believers', a theological phrase which means not that there is no difference between ordained ministers and lay people, but that both share together in the common ministry of the whole people of God.

From that basic position the next step is taken. In the words of the 1960 statement:

> For the exercise of this ministry the Holy Spirit endows members of the Church with various 'charismata', free gifts springing from God's abundant grace, by which they are empowered to fulfil the[47] ministry's manifold functions of preaching, teaching, healing, administration and pastoral care (1 Cor. 12: 28; Eph. 4: 11–12). Thus within the ministry of the Church there are various 'manifestations of the Spirit' for the building up of the Body of Christ. The Apostles received from the risen Christ the commission to preach the Gospel in all the world, to teach the truth as the truth is in Jesus, and to have the oversight and care of the Churches. Some Christians were called and empowered by

---

[46] 'Ordination in the Methodist Church', *Minutes of the Methodist Conference*, 1960, p. 235.

[47] The definite article is used because this is a Report on Ordination.

345

the Spirit to be 'prophets', inspired preachers of the Word of God; to others was given by the Spirit the authority to superintend, feed and shepherd the flock of God; others, again, were authorized to give instruction in the Christian way of life, others to evangelize far and wide, others to care for the poor and sick.[48]

The ministry of the whole Church then, was not totally diffuse, everybody doing everything. It was ordered by the commission of the risen Christ and by the calling and empowering of the Holy Spirit. Then came a further development:

There is evidence in the New Testament of the appointment by St Paul and others of boards of 'presbyters', who are also called 'Bishops', to exercise leadership and pastoral care in the local Churches (Acts 14:23; Phil. 1:1).[49]

At this point it is true to say both that the Church *is for* ministry, and that the Church *has* a ministry, and there need be no complaint about this provided that, as in the apostolic Church, the latter does not take over the former. As far as this section of the chapter is concerned, however, 'the ministry' will now have to have the attention as that is the way in which traditional theology has usually approached the subject.

(a) The threefold ministry

Out of the situation so far described grew the threefold ministry of bishop, priest and deacon. It is important to recognize that, as far as the New Testament is concerned, there is virtually no difference between a bishop (Greek *episcopos*) and an elder or presbyter (Greek *presbuteros*). C. K. Barrett has established this in his treatment[50] of the five passages where the word *episcopos* occurs and the point is admitted by those churches who set great store by their bishops:

The terms 'bishop' and 'presbyter' could be applied to the same man or to men with identical or very similar functions ... the

48 P. 235.
49 P. 236.
50 'In Opposition to Episcopacy in Methodism', *The London Quarterly and Holborn Review*, April 1956, p. 119.

full emergence of the threefold ministry of bishop, presbyter, and deacon required a longer period than the apostolic age. Thereafter this threefold structure became universal in the Church.[51]

Much theological argument has centred around episcopacy and the subject is a major issue in attempts to unite churches that have bishops with those that do not. It is important always to distinguish between the doctrine of apostolic succession on the one hand and what is generally known as 'the historic episcopate' on the other. The former is the view that there is an unbroken chain of bishops going back to the apostles and that this chain guarantees both the truth of the Church's doctrine and its possession of sacramental grace. Only those ordained by bishops in the succession are true ministers of the Church. Most Methodist scholars, and certainly John Wesley,[52] would approve of C. K. Barrett's words when he described it as 'ridiculous as history, calamitous as theology'.[53] The historic episcopate is the more credible view that bishops have been leaders in the Church since apostolic times, to its considerable advantage. If one takes seriously the promise that the Holy Spirit will guide the Church, then it is reasonable to suppose that episcopacy is a gift to the Church within the providence of God. This the non-episcopal churches have to take seriously.

(b) The Methodist ministry

The Methodist Church believes that its ministry is ordered in harmony with the teaching of the New Testament. There is a single ordained ministry equivalent to that of the 'presbyter-bishops' in the New Testament.[54]

At this point it is necessary to extend the quotation from the Methodist Deed of Union:[55]

[51] *Ministry and Ordination.* A Statement on the Doctrine of the Ministry agreed by the Anglican-Roman Catholic International Commission (Canterbury 1973), p. 5.

[52] In a letter to his brother Charles, dated 19th August 1785, he wrote, 'for the *uninterrupted succession* I know to be a fable, which no man ever did or can prove'.

[53] P. 120.

[54] 1960 Report, p. 237.

[55] See pp. 53, 74.

347

Christ's Ministers in the Church are Stewards in the household of God and Shepherds of His flock. Some are called and ordained to this sole occupation and have a principal and directing part in these great duties but they hold no priesthood differing in kind from that which is common to all the Lord's people and they have no exclusive title to the preaching of the gospel or the care of souls. These ministries are shared with them by others to whom also the Spirit divides His gifts severally as He wills.

It is the universal conviction of the Methodist people that the office of the Christian Ministry depends upon the call of God who bestows the gifts of the Spirit the grace and the fruit which indicate those whom he has chosen.

Those whom The Methodist Church recognizes as called of God and therefore receives into its Ministry shall be ordained by the imposition of hands as expressive of the Church's recognition of the Minister's personal call.

There is more in the same vein, but this is enough to make clear the basic position. The Methodist minister is called by God and ordained by the Church.

Within the pluralism of theology that Methodism affords, two interpretations of this position are current. One can be called the 'functional' view of the ministry. A minister is called and ordained to do certain things ... preaching, celebration of the sacraments, pastoral care ... and as long as he carries out these functions he remains a minister. On this the 1974 Report on Ordination comments:

It would be inadequate to confine the special calling (to the ordained ministry) to a collection of functions. For one thing, they are largely shared with people who are not ordained. ... For another, some ordained ministers are not in a position to carry out all the functions, but their ordination is not questioned on that account.[56]

The other interpretation often goes by the name of 'representative person'. It is concerned with what a minister is as well as with what he does. The 1974 Report describes it:

The whole people of God ... are called, all of them, ordained

[56] Methodist Publishing House, p. 5.

348

and unordained, to be the Body of Christ to men. But as a perpetual reminder of this calling and as a means of being obedient to it the Church sets apart men and women, specially called, in ordination. In their office the calling of the whole Church is focused and represented, and it is their responsibility as representative persons to lead the people to share with them in that calling. In this sense they are the sign of the presence and ministry of Christ in the Church, and through the Church to the world.[57]

The Methodist theological approach to the ministry finds its liturgical expression in the Ordination Service. Ordination has its New Testament antecedents in such actions as the appointment of the Seven (Acts 6:6) and the commissioning of Saul and Barnabas (Acts 13:2-4), and in the service prayer for the Holy Spirit and the laying-on of hands are central.

To have *a* ministry, is not a substitute for, but an encouragement to, the Body of Christ to share in the unceasing ministry of its Lord.

(vi) The Church is for mission

At one time, and it may still be so in some places, mission was something the church engaged in when things were not going well. 'Our membership has declined by 10 per cent in two years. We ought to have a mission.' Flourishing suburban churches, on the other hand, did not need missions.

Such a view of mission would have astonished the early Church. Mission was what it was *for*. The word by derivation means 'sent'. Just as God had sent Jesus (Matt. 10:40), so Jesus sent out his followers (Matt. 10:16), later to be called 'apostles'. (The verb 'to send' is *apostello*.) The apostles had been warned by Jesus to wait quietly at Jerusalem until they received 'the promise of the Father' (Luke 24:49; Acts 1:4), i.e. the Spirit. But once he had come, they first burst out into praise and then nothing could hold them back. That, at any rate, is the clear message of Acts. Whether Luke is over-simplifying and putting into one continuous narrative events and experiences that occurred in other places and in other ways

[57] Pp. 5-6.

at other times, is not a question that can be settled here, thought the student should be aware of the possibility

The only other uncertainty worth mentioning is that of see-ing the precise relationship between the commissions given by the risen Lord (Matt. 28:16–20; Luke 24:46–7; John 20:21; 21:15 f. and to Paul, Gal. 1:16; 1 Cor. 9:1) and the urge to mission resulting from the coming of the Spirit at Pentecost. But is there a need to be so precise?

Under the inspiration of the Holy Spirit, the Church pursued its missionary way. It fanned out from Jerusalem, under the threat of persecution (Acts 8:1). Then came the great decision, inevitable in a Church that was 'sent', to break through the barrier of Judaism. There is no doubting the apostolic charac-ter of a Church that, though rooted in two thousand years and more of Jewish history, could be stunned into silence by hear-ing of Peter's experience in the city of Joppa, and then glorify God and say: 'Then to the Gentiles also God has granted repentance unto life' (Acts 11:18).

Then came Paul, the great missionary, and even if some New Testament scholars will not now allow us to plot his journeys with dotted and broken lines on maps of the Middle East as we used to do and call them 'First Missionary Journey', 'Second Missionary Journey' and so forth, no doubt whatever is cast upon his total commitment to Christ, his energy and his mas-sive intellectual capacity, all at the service of his apostleship.

Obviously not all Christians could engage in the Church's mission to the same extent. Not every tent-maker could take his work around with him as Paul did. The large majority of Christians had to stay where they were, and their mission was to the community in which they lived. There were occasions when, as at Antioch, the Church commissioned one of its members for a special missionary task (Acts 13:1–5), but normally the spread of the Christian faith was through the travel and traffic of everyday life.

There is no space here to record the spread of the Church across the world as the centuries passed by. Christianity has proved itself to be the missionary religion that it is safe to say its founder intended it to be.

Two further points need to be made, one general, the other particular:

(a) The general one is that there should be no tension between the words mission and evangelism[58] and certainly no monopoly of these words by ecclesiastical parties. It can be argued that mission is a wider word than evangelism which seems now to be used of 'offering Christ' in the strict sense of those words. Mission reckons to include all that the Church does in its attempt to set forth in word and deed what God has done, and is doing, in Christ for his world. For example, the healing ministry of the Church, through medicine, caring and prayer, is part of its mission. It is not a question of mission being better than evangelism or vice versa. It is a question of which, in any given culture at any given time, is the right one to be given the pre-eminence, if indeed such a choice has to be made.

(b) The particular point is that in the Methodist Church the transition from a Methodist Missionary Society to an Overseas Division expresses institutionally the precise point that the Church is *for* mission. A Society suggests what the Church does when it can persuade the people and raise the money. A Division alongside other Divisions dealing with such matters as property and finance, suggests that this is what the Church is doing all the time. That is the New Testament view.

(vii) The Church is for unity

Unity is basic to biblical religion. Everything starts from the truth that God is one. It follows that the people of God must also be one. This the Old Testament passes on to the New. There is only one Israel. There can only be one Church. To put the New Testament metaphors into the plural is an absurdity. How can there be brides or bodies of Christ?[59]

If it is asked: what sort of unity is being talked about?, the answer is in John 17:21:

That they may all be one; even as thou, Father art in me, and I in thee, that they also may be in us.

58 See p. 270.
59 A comment I owe to Frederic Greeves.

351

The unity of Christians is of the same nature as the unity of the first two (and, of course, the third) persons of the Trinity. This is why Ephesians 4:4–6 can speak of one body, one Spirit, one hope, one Lord, one faith, one baptism, one God. This kind of statement makes nonsense of the view that all that is asked for is a spiritual unity quite apart from matters like having a mutually recognized ministry and receiving the bread and wine of the eucharist from the same hands. How can one body have only a spiritual unity? The truth is that our religion is incarnational, the Word is made flesh, the spiritual and the physical, the invisible and the visible, are joined together. One cannot reconcile with Ephesians 4 and the theology of the Church that flows from it, a Church which claims an invisible, spiritual unity in Christ and then proceeds to express it in visible, physical divisions. We are dealing here not with 'our unhappy divisions' but with an outrageous denial of God.

It is from this theological base that the Ecumenical Movement begins its work. As one considers the almost infinite variety of churches from Pentecostalists thumping their Bibles in Brazil to Orthodox swinging their incense in Bulgaria one almost despairs of the kind of unity which alone can do justice to the New Testament. Almost, but not quite: for what drives the Ecumenical Movement on is the conviction, not that we manufacture unity by agreements, statements, schemes of union and the rest, but that unity is *already given to us by God*. Our response is to make that unity visible. People talk glibly about the Ecumenical Movement having 'run out of steam'. This is to confuse the failure of one or two particular schemes with a theological conviction from which the New Testament will not allow us to escape.

Two consequences follow from this theology of unity:

(a) It makes sense of mission. This is not to say that if you unite churches they will inevitably grow, for other factors are involved which presently will be considered. But it is to say that if you do not unite them they do not deserve to grow.

(b) The other consequence is that only a church of unity can help to bring about the unity of mankind. If we are to live in what is rapidly becoming one world, we need one Church to show us the way. But this is to anticipate the last section.

352

C. PRESENT CONSIDERATIONS

(1) The Church in decline

That is a rash heading. It is virtually impossible to say whether the Church is in decline or not if by the Church is meant the people of God throughout the world, and by 'decline' is meant a loss of influence and numbers. The situation world-wide is immensely complex, influence is difficult to measure and the methods used to assess membership are a statistician's nightmare. It is safer to be more specific. The churches of the West are at present in decline. Bryan Wilson, the eminent sociologist, began an article in *The Times* in 1973[60] with the words:

> According to recent public opinion polls in both Britain and the United States, the vast majority of people in both countries believe that religion is losing its influence in their way of life. There is a decline, too, in the percentage of those who believe in God and—although the absolute figures for the two countries remain very different—there is a decline in church membership and attendance in each.

It is hard to find evidence to refute that.

Looking at the matter parochially, the Methodist Church in Great Britain demonstrates the truth of what Wilson is saying. As for the figures, the membership of the Methodist Church in 1933 was 838,019. In 1976 it was 528,338. In the early 1960s Methodism had six theological colleges. Four of those buildings have now been sold. We now have two college communities of our own and a share in two others. One of the arguments used to persuade the Methodist Conference in 1933 of the need for 'a Separated Secretary' for Ministerial Training was that in the colleges 'there are about 370 Students in residence'. Today (March 1977) there are 136. In 1933 we had 34,948 fully accredited local preachers. In 1976 we had 16,151. A similar trend, of sure and steady decline, can be found in most areas of Methodism's life—church buildings, Sunday schools, publishing, deaconesses and so forth.

Influence, also mentioned by Wilson, is more difficult to

60 Saturday, 13th October.

353

assess but one would have thought his contention irrefutable. It would be illuminating, though of course impossible, to have some kind of survey on the subject among the young people from Methodist homes, and particularly from the homes of ministers. Some follow in father's (or mother's) footsteps, but one does not need a Gallup poll to establish that a large percentage do not. How large one cannot say, but certainly much larger than forty years ago. And those who might have followed father into the ministry then, become teachers and social workers now. If influence has declined so much at the centre, what is the situation at the circumference?

There is no reason to suppose that the other mainstream churches in Britain are any different. The rate of decline may be slower or faster, but such figures as are published confirm that it is decline. Some of the churches that are not mainstream, such as the Pentecostalist, may not be affected; nor may some sections of the mainstream churches, such as the Conservative Evangelicals. But they do not make Wilson's judgement invalid. An Evangelical swallow does not make a Christian summer.

(2) The Church in the contemporary world

It is tempting to draw up a list of reasons for this state of decline, and to discuss them, but it would be a complex process, for some factors at work seem to be responsible both for a decline in one aspect of the Church's life and for its renewal in another. Fortunately, however, both the space available and the author's competence preclude such an analysis. What I propose to do is to set down ten features of the contemporary world which can be seen alongside the decline of the Church, and indeed related to it, but not to try to assess the precise cause-effect relation as one would have to do in a thorough-going analysis.

(i) Secularization

If, as was contended in chapter 4,[61] the process of secularization makes belief in God difficult, it makes involvement with the

61 Pp. 128–30.

Church even more so. At the superficial level belief in God
is not a demanding exercise. For many of our contemporaries
it would only mean admitting 'I believe in God' and saying the
occasional prayer. But even at that level to be associated with
the Church is more inconvenient. You have at least to give
up your Sunday morning and put your hand in your pocket.
Thus secularization often brings people to a kind of half-way
house in which they have what is sometimes called a 'residual
faith in God', but they give up the Church.

(ii) The effect of two world wars
One can look at this from either the inside or the outside of
the Christian West. From the inside, there were many men
who before the First World War walked dutifully to church
on Sundays, but who, after the horror of the trenches and the
impossibility (for them) of reconciling the death of 'half the
seed of Europe one by one' with a religion of peace and love,
walked to the pub instead. The Second World War seemed to
have a similar effect, though less dramatically so, for the process was not such a surprise. Even so, those who left the
churches to go fighting in the North African desert or in the
skies above Hamburg or in the convoys to Murmansk often
came back, if they did at all, not prepared to give the Church
the place in their lives which it had before they went.

From the outside, the view is of the Christian West at war
within itself, each side calling upon the Christian God to give
it victory over its (presumably Christian) enemies. National
days of prayer filled the churches on the day but they ensured
that they would be empty when it was all over. It is hard to
give credibility to a Church in which half of its members are
busy killing off the other half.

(iii) The growth of Communism
A hundred and forty or so years ago there was only one
Communist, Karl Marx, reading and writing in the British
Museum. Today his work deeply affects the population of half
the world. In relation to the Church, however, a simple analysis
is difficult. An atheist philosophy and a materialistic interpretation of human life and history, such as Marx produced, are

not inclined to favour the Church, a fact borne out, for example, by the persecution in Albania and the severe restrictions imposed in Russia. But in some situations (Poland, Romania) the opposition of Marxism has strengthened the Church. In others, the Church has come to terms with Marxism, even welcomed it, as the following comments from Eastern Germany indicate:

> The social liberation brought about by socialism was bound to cause a crisis in the Protestant Church. . . . Today we are confronted by the urgent task of liberating ourselves from the 'Constantinian era' during which the Church for centuries exercised unquestioned spiritual power and was respected as a spiritual force linked to the power of the state. In the German Democratic Republic the Church is no longer one of those institutions which can exercise power over people. Many of us regard this as a good thing, in the light of the Gospel.[62]

Has Marx done the Church more harm than good or more good than harm?

(iv) The rise of national and anti-colonial movements
Here again the situation is ambiguous. The association of missionary and trader in the past and therefore of the Western Church with the exploitation of colonialist regimes has obviously not put that Church in favour. On the other hand the fact that some of the most prominent nationalist leaders in Africa, for example, are, or have been, ministers, priests or bishops, is an indication that the Church is not under a blanket condemnation. To make matters more difficult, one has to remember that some white imperialists have resigned from churches that have taken a liberal stance.

(v) Racial and cultural alienation
Broadly speaking, the minorities of this world have a rough time. Primitive tribes like the South American and North American Indians and the Aborigines of Australia are subjugated to the dominant culture. Groups following a style of life different from the majority are forced to keep themselves

[62] Michael Knoch, *The Ecumenical Review*, July 1974.

to themselves. Who likes the gypsies parking their caravans at the bottom of the road? The persecution of racial minorities is proverbial. Black Americans, coloured British, Jews in Russia, Asians in Africa, to mention but a few, are the victims of prejudice and the objects of discrimination. Such alienation can even extend to cases where the oppressed outnumber the oppressors, as in South Africa and Taiwan.

What is the performance of the Church in such situations? There is no simple answer. One has to set the immense courage of the Christian Institute in South Africa against the unbelievable theology of the Dutch Reformed Church there or the behaviour of some of the white churches in Texas. If it is further asked whether situations of this kind, and the response to them by the Church, work out to the advance or the decline of the Church, who knows the answer?

(vi) The growth of other faiths
As I look out of my study window I can see, two or three miles away, the trees of Regents Park, and beyond them a sight that would have been impossible only a few years ago. It is the dome of a mosque. If I look through the binoculars on a clear day I can see the crescent and the little balcony from which normally the faithful are called to prayer with those wailings that fall so strangely on Western ears. That is symbolic. The great faiths of the East have come to the West. Now this may be simply because Muslims are here by immigration and, being here, their religious needs have to be catered for. But may it not also be an indication of the expansionist role that other religions are finding for themselves these days? And has this any bearing on the decline of the Church?

Then there are the fringe groups, though they would not thank me for so designating them, Jehovah's Witnesses, Scientology, *Hare Krishna*, occult groups, the cult of Sun Myung Moon and the rest. Is their existence in any way a cause of the Church's decline or are they simply picking up the dissatisfied customers?

(vii) The existence of poverty
This is no new situation for the Church. The poor have always

357

been with us. What is new in the present situation is the global view that can be taken of the poor. As many as 800 million people, from a world population of 4,000 millions, are existing in conditions of malnutrition or starvation, and the world population is expected to double in the next forty years. The rich countries of Europe, North America, Russia and Japan have around 31 per cent of the world's population but consume 85 per cent of the world's resources, and as we are constantly being told the gap between the rich and the poor is not growing narrower but wider. Attempts by poorer countries to improve their lot have often been frustrated by the ability of richer nations to control prices. And when production has increased it has been the foreign investors who have reaped the advantage.

How has the Church performed in this situation? Certainly it does not now administer the bromide that our Lord specially loves the poor. To its credit stand the devotion of those who, like Mother Theresa, have served the poor in the name of Christ, and the magnificent achievements of Christian Aid and all the personal sacrifice that lies behind them. Is it reasonable to ask for more? And if it is, and the Church has not produced it, has it suffered on that account?

(viii) The prevalence of violence
World peace is maintained by the threat of violence. In January 1972 the U.S.A. and the U.S.S.R. possessed enough missiles carrying nuclear warheads to destroy half the population of the world, literally. Furthermore these super-powers, together with Britain and France, supply armaments to much of the rest of the world. In international politics, therefore, saving only where it would prove self-destructive, legalized violence has the last word. 'Unofficial' violence flourishes. Guerrilla warfare, urban and rural, hijackings, kidnappings, muggings, hooliganism and vandalism are all having a long field day.

As for the relation of this to the Church, we have witnessed in our time a vicious civil war in the Lebanon in which one side, in defiance of all theological, moral and political sense, was described as 'Christian'. And in Northern Ireland we have surely reached the depths. How could any person in his right mind be attracted to either Protestantism or Roman Catholicism (and what else is there on offer?) when such appalling deeds are done by their partisans? Religion may not be the whole story, but it is enough of the story to discredit both the faith and the Church in the eyes of all people of sanity and reason. You have to be very discerning and charitable indeed to see this as a case of *corruptio optimi pessima* (the worst is a corruption of the best) and for most people this is asking too much.

(ix) The destruction of nature
Reference has already been made to this subject[63] so two short paragraphs from John V. Taylor's *Enough is Enough*[64] are sufficient to illustrate the point:

> The Cleveland river is so choked with oil and debris it is classified as a 'fire hazard'. In the summer of 1969 40 million fish suddenly died of poisoning in the Rhine. A sportsman trying to swim the length of the Lake of Geneva was forced to give up halfway by the gases rising from the surface.[65]

> The word 'Vietnamization' describes not what President Nixon meant, but something that was happening to human beings that was able to carry them coolly, doggedly, fanatically to the point where there was nothing literally nothing, they would not choose to destroy rather than have their will frustrated.[66]

These facts impinge upon the Church in so far as the Christian doctrines of creation and man are obviously involved, and it rather looks as if the world is taking no notice of them.

(x) Changing social patterns
The Church in Britain, and in other countries for that matter, is organized on the pattern of a community of Christians in a locality focusing upon a building. It is a stable pattern as long

63 See p. 313.
64 S.C.M. 1975.
65 Pp. 31–2.
66 P. 38.

as both building and Christians stay where they are. The parish system of rural England served this country well for centuries. But the way we have to live our lives has changed. Not only have we become more mobile, so that the young executive appointed to be youth club leader one week may have to move 200 miles away the week after, but also in many places, though not all, much of life is lived away from home. Universities, schools, hospitals, offices, sports centres, local government departments, all places of importance in our lives, are often far from where we reside. The Church is, however, sited according to the old residential pattern and only in a few places has adaptation been possible.

The social patterns of the young have changed. Three of my children are in their twenties and unmarried. But they do not live at home. They are in flats and houses with their friends in other parts of London, returning home only when the larder is low or they wish to borrow the vacuum cleaner. If home is too paternalistic (and maternalistic!), then what of Holy Mother Church, to give it its ancient name?

(3) A future for the Church?

It must be said again that the above ten features do not constitute an analysis of why the Church is in decline in our own and in other countries. The presence of so many unanswered, and perhaps unanswerable, questions reinforces the point. What these ten features do is not so much to pass judgement on the Church as to provide guidelines, to lay down the conditions, for the role the Church can and must play. *What sort of Church is it that has a future in a world where these things are happening?* That is the question to be answered before this book closes.

(i) The Church must be open to change in its own life.
The native conservatism of the English in matters of religion (they are not alone in this) makes for suspicion of change and resistance to it. In questions of doctrine some of the mild suggestions that have been made under the 'Present Considerations' sections of this book could be regarded as well-meaning

but misguided. It could, and perhaps will, be said that they try to build a bridge between belief and unbelief but that they succeed only in reducing the glorious mystery of the Christian faith to the level of a humanist in the Lower Sixth. In questions of practice, people who wish to do things differently in the life of the Church are not infrequently regarded as unwelcome disrupters of what has served the people of God so well for so long.

Sometimes, of course, those who react in this way are right. If they are told from their pulpits that God is dead or that virtually nothing can be known about Jesus or that prayer is simply relating oneself to other people (statements that have actually been made in Methodist pulpits), then one has some sympathy with the allegation that those who say such things are boat-rockers who would tip the people of God into the cold, agnostic sea. Again, one can understand that some of the brash changes in worship, made for no good theological or liturgical reason, justify the criticism that their perpetrators have confused change with progress.

Doubtless all parties would agree that what we are looking for is the difference between half-baked and ill-digested ideas on the one hand and the leading of the Holy Spirit on the other; between the 'sell-out' to the latest secular fashion and a proper reinterpretation to our contemporaries of the faith once delivered to the saints. This kind of discrimination cannot be found in a few paragraphs in a text-book for those beginning the study of theology. It will only emerge when those who want change, and those who do not, put their heads down together and pray and think and think and pray until they see the way forward together in the Spirit.

What must be said here is that the Church must be *open* to change, that is to say it must be ready to *consider* whether any given change is in fact the Holy Spirit calling it forward out of its past into its future. It is entirely understandable that when long-accepted beliefs are discarded—as in secularization —or familiar ways of living changed—as in our social patterns and our codes of behaviour—Christians want the Church to be a stable institution in an unstable world, a rock amid the shifting sands. But alas, that is exactly what the Church can

361

never be. Jesus is the same yesterday and today and for ever (Heb. 13:8), but not the Church. We are the pilgrim people of God, moving on from one situation to the next; we are the community under the guidance of the dynamic Spirit; we are the Body of Christ and that body is not in *rigor mortis*.

That is why theology is not simply a matter of soaking up propositions about God, Christ, the Church and so forth, but rather the exciting search for theological treasures *old and new*; that is why the Church has to encourage debates on the practice of baptism in what has become a missionary situation; that is why the movable chair has taken over from the immovable pew; that is why in addition to the preaching of the traditional *Kerygma* there has to be exploration of the pressing questions of the moment; that is why we have decided that Methodist ministers can exercise their ministry in secular situations as well as in circuits; that is why we have to take seriously those who tell us that the Spirit is leading us away from clerically dominated institutions to unstructured cells of fellowship and mission. The Church has to be prepared for any change turning out to be the work of the Spirit.

(ii) The Church has to be totally committed to the deprived. This is not at all the same thing as saying that the deprived are always right, or that they do not abuse what is given to them. Maybe some of the goods supplied by Oxfam find their way into the black market and line the pockets of racketeers; maybe there are those who drive to collect their social security money in their cars and then spend the afternoon in bed; maybe when autonomy is granted to a nation that was colonized the rest of the world has to suffer an Idi Amin; and whatever can be done to ameliorate these abuses must be done. But when that has been said, and all the abuses admitted, it remains true that the Church must always be for the poor, for the homeless, for the hungry, for the oppressed, for the deprived.

Our record in this field is not unsullied, as our detractors never fail to remind us, but we have our successes too. Perhaps the biggest obstacle to further progress is the ability required to move beyond deeds of compassion (not of course giving them up in the process), into the area of political action. This is where we meet controversy and compromise and where our fellowship is tested for its depth. But this is where things happen.

Elsa Tames is a Latin American who has written a modern version of the Apostles' Creed. The style may not be smooth but the meaning is clear. Here is the section on the Church:

I believe in the Church which lives in and for the world,
in the liberation from alienation,
in the equality of men,
in the uprising of the peasants,
in the Prince of Peace
and in the new life which appears.[67]

This is not unlike the *Magnificat* (Luke 1:46–55), in being a manifesto for those 'of low degree'.

(iii) The Church must spend itself in reconciliation

In the light of what has been said about war, violence and alienation, how can the Church avoid seeing its mission in terms of reconciliation between those at odds with one another? But how can it begin to do this with any effectiveness when there is so much of its own life that denies it? Northern Ireland was cited. It could be that by the time this book appears in print the troubles there will be over, or much diminished. One hopes so indeed. But whether they are considered as history or as present reality, they bear witness to the fact that a divided Church cannot speak peace to a divided people. That is not to minimise the efforts of some brave churchmen. It is simply to say that until Roman Catholics and Protestants *actually are* one people in Christ, what they can contribute to the healing of the wounds is not substantial.

If the Church is the *sign* to the world of the kingdom of God, the evidence of that kingdom's reality, the embryo of a renewed, united humanity, then reconciliation within the body of Christ is the inescapable demand. How can it be met? The Ecumenical Movement has its weaknesses, as it has had its bitter disappointments, but it is the agency of our reconciliation and therefore claims our perseverance.

[67] *Risk*, Vol. 1, 1974.

There is endless work for the ministry of reconciliation. In Britain today there is a need to break down the class barriers (a subject on which the Church has been virtually silent), and to pursue conversations with those of other faiths. Moreover the reconciliation of people to people is not confined to what the Church can do corporately. The unceasing ministry of pastoral care, the daily witness of Christians who speak peace by their attitudes, their words and their actions testify to the fact that the Church is engaged in reconciliation in a thousand places every day. The trouble is that we are not doing enough.

In view of what was said about the destruction of nature it is plain that there is a need for the human race to be reconciled to its environment and to the animal kingdom. What we now need is the single-minded ruthlessness that will deal with those who for private gain or personal convenience frustrate that reconciliation. The Church may not be able actually to pass the laws that forbid pumping sewage into the Mediterranean or driving a road through Christ Church meadows or netting migratory birds. But the doctrines of creation and of man made in the image of God can be turned into powerful propaganda, given the will and the imagination.

For the Church, the reconciliation of people to people and people to the rest of creation should be the proper consequence of the reconciliation of people to God. When in 2 Corinthians 5 Paul writes of the ministry of reconciliation that is exactly what he means. The message is that God will not hold things against us (v. 19). In Christ, what is necessary on God's side, has already been done (v. 18). To people so reconciled, the ministry of reconciliation is entrusted (v. 19).

Reconciliation, like justice, is indivisible. Persuading Protestants and Roman Catholics in Northern Ireland, or anywhere else for that matter, to love one another, driving from the high seas men who, for the sake of making money, would kill every living whale, and speaking of what God has done for people in Christ is all one ministry of reconciliation. It is a ministry that the Church cannot evade.

(iv) The Church must witness to Jesus Christ
This is central. And it is not enough for the Church to per-

suade people to 'speak a word for Jesus', however appropriate that may be on some occasions. Martin Luther once used the phrase 'being a Christ to our neighbour'. If something of *that* nature is involved, then the Church has a fair task on hand. For consider again what he was like:

> What confused his critics was that he conformed to no pattern. What were they to make of the wandering teacher who typically carried no purse and who had nowhere to lay his head and yet who appeared to be fond of parties, particularly in disreputable company? How were they to tie him down to a particular breach of the law when his real fault seemed to be a general independence of all the ordinary pressures and claims which both bind and buttress the individual in society? His sense of property was casual and he expected men to lend boat or beast as unhesitatingly as he would have handed over coat and cloak to them. He steadily disobeyed the demands of what we regard as self-interest and self-preservation. He seemed to pass elusive and free as the *ruach* wind through all our interlocking structures of duty and obligation. His whole manner of life and even more the manner of his dying was a challenge to necessity.[68]

The thought of witnessing to a man like that, particularly if witnessing means 'being a Christ', is forbidding. But if the Church is the body of Christ, what else can it mean but that it has to set forth in its corporate actions and in the personal lives of its members the values, the lifestyle and the basic stance of Jesus? And in a Western world dedicated to making money and glorifying possessions what could be more salutary?

It is significant that John Taylor's words about Jesus just quoted follow a passage about the relation of Jesus to God; his prayer-life, his spirituality. Taylor uses the phrase 'his incomparable awareness of God'.[69] To witness to Jesus Christ is to testify, through his body which is the Church, to the reality of God. We may use other words: the transcendental dimension, the Beyond in the midst, the wholly Other, what is of ultimate concern and so forth. If they help people to understand what we mean, very well. But what we, the Church,

[68] John V. Taylor, *The Go-Between God*, p. 98.
[69] P. 93.

have to communicate is that this present world, full as it is of both ruthless struggle and secular joy, is not all, and the values it prizes and pursues are by no means the ones that count in the end. There is at the beginning, and at the end, and always, God.

This means that the Church is not first a fellowship for the religious, nor a service agency for the unfortunate, nor a counselling centre for the disturbed, nor a talking shop for theologians, though these things, and many others, have to follow. The Church is first the community that lives by faith, hope and love, and all for God, because that is how it was with Jesus.

Study Scheme for those using *Groundwork of Theology* for the Methodist Connexional Local Preachers' Examinations

(1) A six-monthly course is envisaged, taking a fortnight over each study. Students working by correspondence course should send the answers to *two* questions every fortnight to the appointed tutor, beginning as soon as possible, and without further notification, after receiving the tutor's name and address. Other students may wish to use the questions for discussion in groups or for examination practice.

(2) The attention of students is drawn to the bibliography.

PART I

Study 1

Chapter 1. *Religion and Theology*

(1) *Religion*
1. Assess the arguments against the descriptive approach to religion.
2. How do you understand myths in religion?
3. 'In religion ritual is the means of getting things done'. Discuss.
4. Write a short essay on 'The place of sacred texts in religion'.

(2) *Theology*
1. What is your understanding of theology?
2. Argue for and against theology being called a science.

3. What is a 'language game'? What should be the characteristics of religious language?

4. What contribution does our present culture have to make to our theology?

Study 2

Chapter 2. *Christian Theology*

1. What some call revelation, others call discovery. Discuss.
2. Explain why you think the Bible is inspired.
3. Discuss the possibilities and limitations of reason in theology.
4. Explain the Methodist doctrinal standards to a Roman Catholic friend.

Study 3

Chapter 3. *Theology and Living*

1. 'Does one start from living and move towards theology or the other way round?' Explain and justify your own practice.
2. Write an essay, with quotations, on 'Faith in the Old Testament'.
3. You have been asked to preach on 'The Christian Hope'. Give a 250-word summary of your sermon.
4. Show how both the Bible and daily living contribute to a Christian understanding of love.

PART II

Study 4

Chapter 4. *God*

1. In what sense is the word 'God' a 'piece of shorthand'?
2. State and then comment upon the supposed dilemma that God cannot be both perfectly good and unlimitedly powerful.

368

3. Summarize in your own words any four of the eleven assertions about God.

4. Write the script of a short discussion between an agnostic and a Christian using the material in *one* of the sections of *Intimations*, i.e. Indicator experiences or Signals of transcendence or Less unhelpful notions of God.

Study 5

Chapter 5. *Jesus Christ*

1. How would you answer someone who said that Jesus was a good man and a great teacher but nothing more?
2. Justify your own view of the Virgin Birth.
3. Do we need the 'Jesus of history' if we have the 'Christ of faith'?
4. Write 300 words of commentary upon:

> Our God contracted to a span,
> Incomprehensibly made man.
>
> (MHB 142, v. 1)

Study 6a

Chapter 6. *The Death of Jesus Christ*

1. 'I love Jesus but I hate God.' Discuss.
2. Which of the traditional theories of the Atonement appeals to you most as a preacher? Why?
3. A. Jesus died on the cross to save you from your sins.
   B. Quite honestly, I do not know what you are talking about.

Continue this dialogue.

Study 6b

Chapter 6. *The Resurrection of Jesus*

1. Give reasons why 'the empty tomb' is, or is not, necessary to your faith.
2. How do you understand the Ascension?

3. How would you try to convince an unbeliever that Jesus is alive?

Study 7a

Chapter 7. *The Holy Spirit*

1. Outline the New Testament doctrine of the Holy Spirit.
2. What is your interpretation of Acts 2:2–4?
3. Give your own assessment of the Charismatic Movement.
4. How can the Church persuade people today to perceive the Holy Spirit at work?

Study 7b

Chapter 7. *The Trinity*

1. Give a full outline of a sermon you might preach on Trinity Sunday.
2. Contrast the Western view of the Trinity with the Eastern, and say which helps you more, and why.

Study 8

Chapter 8. *Man and his Salvation*

1. What is the significance, in the modern world, of man made 'in the image of God'?
2. Discuss the answer of the Senior Catechism to the question 'What is sin?'
3. The Methodist doctrinal emphases include Assurance and Christian Perfection. Give your assessment of both.
4. Discuss the three questions with which this chapter ends.

Study 9

Chapter 9. *The Kingdom of God*

1. Write a commentary on the verses from the Methodist Hymn Book included in the Foundation Documents.

370

2.   What do the parables of Jesus disclose about the nature of the kingdom?
3.   Immortality or resurrection? Discuss.
4.   Argue the case for political sermons.

Study 10

Chapter 10.   *The Church*

1.   'I am a Christian, but I don't go to church.' How would you respond to this statement?
2.   How could the theology of the eucharist be more effectively expressed in its practice?
3.   Along what lines would you like to see the mission of the Church develop?
4.   How can the Church fulfil its role as 'the sign of the kingdom'?

Bibliography

THE books mentioned in the text and the footnotes can be used for further reading. In addition, the following titles of what are, on the whole, slightly easier books, may be found useful. Some may in time go out of print and/or be superseded by others.

Chapter 1. *Religion and Theology*

Eliade, Mircea: *Myths, Dreams and Mysteries* (Fontana)
Holm, Jean: *The Study of Religions* (Sheldon)
Knox, John: *Myth and Truth* (Collins)
Ling, Trevor: *A History of Religion East and West* (Macmillan)
Smart, Ninian: *The Religious Experience of Mankind* (Fontana)
Wilkes, Keith: *Religion and the Sciences* (Religious Education Press)

Chapter 2. *Christian Theology*

Barr, James: *The Bible in the Modern World* (S.C.M.)
Cragg, Kenneth: *The Christian and Other Religions* (Mowbray)
Davies, Rupert E: *What Methodists Believe* (Mowbray)
Klostermaier, Klaus: *Hindu and Christian in Vrindaban* (S.C.M.)
Koyama Kosuke: *Waterbuffalo Theology* (S.C.M.)
Marshall, I. Howard: *Christian Beliefs* (I.V.F.)
Ramsey, Arthur Michael: *Introducing The Christian Faith* (S.C.M.)

Report by The Doctrine Commission of the Church of England: *Christian Believing* (S.P.C.K.)
Stacey, W. David: *Interpreting the Bible* (Sheldon)
Wiles, M. F.: *The Making of Christian Doctrine* (C.U.P.)

Chapter 3. *Theology and Living*

Baelz, Peter: *The Forgotten Dream* (Mowbray)
Bowden, John: *Who is a Christian?* (S.C.M.)
Cox, Harvey: *The Feast of Fools* (Harper)
Gill, Robin: *The Social Context of Theology* (Mowbray)
Guttierez, G: *A Theology of Liberation* (S.C.M.)
Patey, Edward: *Christian Life Style* (Mowbray)
Ward, Keith: *The Christian Way* (S.P.C.K.)
Wiles, M. F.: *What is Theology?* (O.U.P.)

Chapter 4. *God*

Baker, John Austin: *The Foolishness of God* (Fontana)
Davies, J. G.: *Every Day God* (S.C.M.)
Macquarrie, John: *Thinking About God* (S.C.M.)
Schaeffer, Francis: *The God who is There* (Hodder and Stoughton)
Smith, Ronald Gregor: *The Doctrine of God* (Collins)
Ward, Keith: *The Concept of God* (Blackwell)

Chapter 5. *Jesus Christ*

Adams, Karl: *The Christ of Faith* (Burns and Oates)
Dyson, A. O.: *Who is Jesus Christ?* (S.C.M.)
Hunter, A. M.: *Jesus Lord and Saviour* (S.C.M.)
Ramsey, Arthur Michael: *God, Christ and the World* (S.C.M.)
Richards, H. J.: *The First Christmas* (Fontana)
Richards, H. J.: *The Miracles of Jesus* (Fontana)
Richardson, Alan: *The Miracle-Stories of the Gospels* (S.C.M.)
Stacey, W. David: *The Man from Nazareth* (Religious Education Press)

374

Chapter 6

The Death of Christ

Haughton, Rosemary: *The Drama of Salvation* (S.P.C.K.)
Hodgson, Leonard: *The Doctrine of the Atonement* (Nisbet)
O'Collins, Gerald: *The Calvary Christ* (S.C.M.)

The Resurrection of Christ

Fuller, Daniel: *Easter Faith and History* (Tyndale)
Ladd, George Eldon: *I believe in the Resurrection of Jesus* (Hodder and Stoughton)
O'Collins, Gerald: *The Easter Jesus* (Darton, Longman and Todd)
Perrin, Norman: *The Resurrection Narratives* (S.C.M.)
Ramsey, Arthur Michael: *The Resurrection of Christ* (S.C.M.)
Richards, H. J.: *The First Easter* (Fontana)

Chapter 7

The Holy Spirit

Bruner, F. D.: *A Theology of the Holy Spirit* (Hodder and Stoughton)
Davies, J. G.: *The Spirit, The Church and the Sacraments* (S.P.C.K.)
Dewar, Lindsay: *The Holy Spirit and Modern Thought* (Mowbray)
Fison, J. E.: *The Blessing of the Holy Spirit* (Longmans)

The Trinity

Hodgson, Leonard: *The Doctrine of the Trinity* (Nisbet)
Wainwright, A. W.: *The Trinity in the New Testament* (S.P.C.K.)

Chapter 8. *Man and his Salvation*

Cairns, David: *The Image of God in Man* (Fontana)

375

Green, E. M. B.: *The Meaning of Salvation* (Hodder and Stoughton)
Jenkins, David E. *The Glory of Man* (S.C.M.)
Montefiore, Hugh (Ed.) *Man and Nature* (Collins)
Neill, Stephen: *What is Man?* (Lutterworth)
Williams, C. W.: *John Wesley's Theology Today* (Epworth)

Chapter 9. *The Kingdom of God*

Hunter, A. M.: *Interpreting the Parables* (S.C.M.)
Jeremias, J.: *Rediscovering the Parables of Jesus* (S.C.M.)
Ladd, George Eldon: *The Presence of the Future* (S.P.C.K.)
Perrin, Norman: *The Kingdom of God in the Teaching of Jesus* (S.C.M.)
Perry, Michael: *The Resurrection of Man* (Mowbray)
Temple, William: *Christianity and Social Order* (S.P.C.K.)

Chapter 10. *The Church*

Baillie, D. M.: *Theology of the Sacraments* (Faber)
Küng, Hans: *The Church* (Search)
Macquarrie, John: *The Faith of the People of God* (S.C.M.)
Morris, Colin: *The Word and The Words* (Epworth)
Schnackenburg, Rudolf: *The Church in the New Testament* (Burns and Oates)
Slack, Kenneth: *The British Churches Today* (S.C.M.)
Stacey, John: *The New Superstition* (Religious Education Press)
Waal, Victor de: *What is the Church?* (S.C.M.)
Williams, Colin W.: *New Directions in Theology Today, Vol. 4, The Church* (Lutterworth)

Index

Abbott-Smith, G., 105 fn., 288 fn.
Abelard, 185, 191
abortion, 103
Abraham, 54, 90, 93, 94, 96, 131, 167, 277, 323
Achan, 16
Adam, 167, 181, 186, 244, 252, 257, 258, 270, 271
adoption, 266
Adoptionism, 159
Ainu, 21
alienation, 273, 278
Amin, Idi, 362
Anglicans, 76
Anselm, 184
Aphrodite, 24
Apollinarius, 160
Apostles' Creed, 109, 142, 176, 195, 212, 244, 283, 316, 363
Arius, 160, 161
Arminius, Arminianism, 270
Artemis, 23
Arthur, King, 287
Ascension, 196, 202-3
assurance, 60, 69, 267-8, 319
Athanasius, 160
   Creed of, 235, 238-9
Atonement, 61
   doctrine of, 178-85
Attis, 23
Augustine, 123, 239, 241, 256, 258, 259, 260, 261, 323
Aulén, Gustav, 138, 183

Baal, 119
Babel, 18
Baden Powell, 62
Baillie, D. M., 172 fn., 174
Baillie, John, 129, 271
Baker, John, 78

baptism, 225, 259, 317, 319, 320, 332-6, 362
   of Jesus, 156, 219, 305, 333
   in the Spirit, 225, 226, 227
Baptists, 334
Barnabus, 349
Barrett, C. K., 46, 158, 220, 221, 223 fn., 224, 228-30, 265, 303 fn., 330, 346, 347
Barrett, Elizabeth, 102
Barth, Karl, 15, 65, 165
Batey, R., 294 fn.
Beelzebub, 154, 291
Being, 112-13, 140-1, 142, 241
Berger, Peter, 128, 135
Bett, Henry, 86
Bhagavad-Gita, 32
Bible
   See texts, sacred
   See Scripture
   authority of, 57
   inspiration of, 56
   and reason, 62
   biblical scholarship, 55-6
   as word of God, 57
bishop(s), 259, 317, 346-7
Black theology, 84
Blackham, H. J., 272
body, 253
Bonar, Horatius, 106
Bonhoeffer, Dietrich, 129, 161
Brevint, 343
British Israelites, 59
Brown, John Pairman, 208 fn.
Brünner, Emil, 94 fn., 152 fn.
Buber, Martin, 128 fn.
Buddha, Buddhism, Buddhist, 26, 35, 37, 44, 49, 76, 77, 210, 232
Bultmann, Rudolf, 20, 165

Caesar, 287

379

Judgement,
day of Judgement, 95, 97, 285, 299–301, 313
present judgement, 310–11
justification, 60, 196, 247, 265
Justin Martyr, 153

Kaufman, Gordon, 128 fn.
Kee, Alistair, 84, 128
kenosis, 172, 174
kerygma, See preaching
King, Martin Luther, 279
kingdom of God, See Chapter 9, 87, 91, 99, 151, 189, 343, 344, 363
Kirkpatrick, Dow, 224 fn., 232 fn., 241 fn., 333 fn., 342
Knoch, Michael, 356 fn.
Knox, John, 166, 168, 173
Koran, 27, 28
Körner, S., 279 fn.
Küng, Hans, 80, 151 fn.

Lampe, Geoffrey, 211
Lang, Andrew, 24 fn.
language, religious, 40–3, 170, 171, 240
Last Day(s), 293, 299, 304, 309, 333, 334
Last Things, 95–8, 99, 301–2
Lazarus, 56, 200
Leeuw, G. van der, 25 fn., 33
Lenin, 304
Leonardo da Vinci, 271, 272
Léon-Dufour, Xavier, 164–5
Lewis, C. S., 242, 256, 310
Lord, Eric, 157 fn.
Lord's Prayer, 125, 294
love, 100–7, 269
Lubbock, John, 24 fn.
Lucius, 33
Luther, Martin, 82, 124, 183, 197, 229, 261, 265, 365

McArthur, Harvey K., 164 fn.
McKeating, Henry, 96 fn., 295
Macleod, George, 203
Macquarrie, John, 37, 43, 51, 65 fn., 68, 82, 141, 241
magic, 27
Mallory, 233
Man, See Chapter 8 (B)
Mao Tse-tung, 232

Marx, Marxist, 182, 232, 233, 275–6, 279, 355
Mary, 70, 142, 144, 153, 156, 161
Mary Magdalene, 52
Massie, Richard, 197
Maxwell, William D., 205 fn.
Melkart, 119
Mercury, 24
Messiah, Messiahship, 147, 149–51, 155, 179, 215, 219, 235, 290
Methodist(s), Methodist Church, Methodism, 86, 91, 96, 226, 228, 268, 270, 302, 318, 319, 322, 326, 335, 336, 338, 340, 341 fn., 342, 345, 353, 354, 361
and assurance, 267–8
Conference, 76, 335, 353
doctrinal standards of, 53, 60, 74–6
Local Preachers, 330
Methodist ministry, and mission, 347–9, 351, 362
traditions, 60
united Church, 53
Mexican Indians, 23
Meyendorff, John, 241
Mill, John Stuart, 123 fn.
Milton, 172
ministry, 319, 344–9, 362
doctrines of, 60
miracles, 90, 154–6, 291
mission, 74, 320, 349–51, 352
Mithra, 34
Moltmann, Jürgen, 95, 98
Monarchianism, 238
Montgomery, James, 285
moral influence, 185, 191–3
Morison, Frank, 200
Mormon, Mormonism, 28, 45
Mormon, Book of, 28, 29, 51
Morris, Colin, 82
Morris, Leon, 190, 192
Moses, 52, 54, 96, 116, 119, 215, 249, 323
Moule, C. F. D., 182, 204, 205 fn.
Muhammad, Mohammed, 49, 232
Muller's Orphanage, 133, 134
Muslim(s), 27, 47, 77, 233, 357
mystery religions, 157, 204
myth, 17–20, 22, 30, 47, 68

Nanner, 25
Nathan, 51, 118